Japanese Direct
Foreign Investments

JAPANESE DIRECT FOREIGN INVESTMENTS

An Annotated Bibliography

Compiled by KARL BOGER

Bibliographies and Indexes in Economics
and Economic History, Number 8

GREENWOOD PRESS
New York • Westport, Connecticut • London

Library of Congress Cataloging-in-Publication Data

Boger, Karl.
   Japanese direct foreign investments : an annotated bibliography /
compiled by Karl Boger.
     p. cm.—(Bibliographies and indexes in economics and
economic history, ISSN 0749-1786 ; no. 8)
   Includes indexes.
   ISBN 0-313-26318-3 (lib. bdg. : alk. paper)
   1. Investments, Japanese—Bibliography.   I. Title.   II. Series.
Z7164.F5B722 1989
[HG4538]
016.3326'7352—dc20   89-7488

British Library Cataloguing in Publication Data is available.

Library of Congress Catalog Card Number: 89-7488
ISBN: 0-313-26318-3
ISSN: 0749-1786

First published in 1989

Greenwood Press, Inc.
88 Post Road West, Westport, Connecticut 06881

Printed in the United States of America

The paper used in this book complies with the
Permanent Paper Standard issued by the National
Information Standards Organization (Z39.48-1984).

10 9 8 7 6 5 4 3 2 1

CONTENTS

INTRODUCTION

This annotated bibliography is concerned with the postwar era, especially the last few decades when the literature on this topic makes its appearance. By this time, the Japanese economy became large and powerful enough to extend investments internationally. The great number of articles in this field, and the relatively few books, indicated the need for greater research, especially in the United States, which receives the bulk of Japanese investments.

From Maine to California, Americans are feeling the impact of Japanese direct investments in their area. Sometimes these investments, and the Japanese "know-how," are sought after and welcomed, while in other cases they are considered a threat and resentments develop. The Japanese often invest in American industries to gain access to American developing technology, and therefore some Americans feel their country is turning into a Third World nation. Whether we like it or not, Japanese firms are with us not only as competitive importers, but also as producers and financiers within our borders.

Just as this is happening in the United States, it is happening around the world. The mixture of concerns and blessings are the same, but the faces and places change. This annotated bibliography is arranged according to geographical distribution of Japan's overseas investments. The chapters include North and South America, Europe, Africa, Asia, and the Pacific Ocean Region. As the length of the sections indicate, the United States and Southeast Asia have received the heaviest attention on account of the volume of Japanese investments concentrated in these areas. Africa and South America account for less material, but this is likely to change with the developing pattern of investments.

A number of reasons account for Japan's phenomenal appearance on the international scene as a major foreign

investor. Since World War II, the Japanese economy has
concentrated on developing a highly sophisticated and
advanced technology, coupled with a highly productive form
of production management. This has lead to the Japanese
success in dominating the international markets in a number
of product lines, including automobiles, high-tech business,
and consumer products. Japan's international balance of
payments ran high, the yen soared, and Japan's largest
producers turned into multinational corporations.

The fear of rising protectionism, especially in the
United States and Europe, most likely spurred the flow of
investments into these countries. Having already penetrated
the markets of these countries, Japanese firms also found an
economic incentive in manufacturing closer to their already
established markets. The path to accomplishing this has not
always been easy; there has been opposition from domestic
competitors, labor unions, and politicians.

The development of the Japanese economy can be
characterized in the following stages: first, the rebuilding
of the economy after World War II with the assistance of a
national industrial policy; second, Japan's emergence as a
major force in the international markets with its success in
technological domination of key areas; third, the move into
overseas acquisitions and the establishment of manufacturing
facilities; and fourth, the internationalization of its
banking and financial services industry. In this bibliography, there is theoretical and statistical material
covering each of these areas.

The material covered is limited to the English
language, and largely addresses the question of Japan's
investments from a U.S. perspective. Books, short
monographs, U.S. government documents, Japanese government
reports, and articles make up the bibliography's contents.
Only articles that have a direct bearing on Japan's overseas
investments or its multinationals have been selected. More
latitude was given to books, since they cover a subject
matter in greater depth, relating it to a wider range of
social and economic relations. Articles from newspapers,
news magazines, and the like have been excluded.

To aid the use of this bibliography, an Author and
Editor Index, a Title Index, and a Subject Index have been
created. An attempt has been made to place material under
the most appropriate heading, but this is often ambiguous.
To correct this, the Subject Index allows access to
information beyond geography to industries, products,
companies, and related topics.

I

GENERAL WORKS ON JAPAN'S OVERSEAS INVESTMENTS

This chapter covers works concerned with general treatments of Japanese foreign investments. It includes three subdivisions: multinationals and general trading companies, foreign aid, and specific industry studies. See the subject index for additional works on these topics in other chapters.

1. Abegglen, James C. <u>The Strategy of Japanese Business</u>. Cambridge, Mass.: Ballinger, 1984.

This collection of essays and speeches by the author covers four aspects of Japanese business and economy: foreign trade, management, direct foreign investment, and research and development. In less than three decades, Japan has undergone a period of rapid industrialization now producing 10% of world output. This is a point of departure for modern history dominated by Western countries. The Japanese have created their own economic system distinct from the Soviet-type planned economy and the American-type free economy. It is economically sound and rational. The Japanese firm is a communal organization that has successfully separated ownership from control and management, dissolving the conflict between management and labor. Their management system has its limits, but it flourishes in an environment of high savings, capital abundance, a motivated labor force, and good government-business relations. Japan's industrial policy must be understood in its own context and does not fit into a Western paradigm. The government is neither the origin of command nor an adversary of private business. It is small, efficient, and development orientated with a wide consensus between government and business on national, international, and industry issues. Japan is becoming more involved in direct foreign investment and the internationalization of its economy. Japan's R&D efforts are striving to catch up in biogenetics, aerospace, atomic energy, and ocean-resource development.

2. Aoki, Tomoichiro. "Increasing Japan's Direct Overseas Investment." LTCB (Long-Term Credit Bank of Japan) Research. (Sept./Oct. 1986): 1-8.

   The findings of a July 1986 survey showing increasing numbers of Japanese companies moving production offshore or expanding their overseas production. It compares the Japan's direct foreign investment before and after the Group of Five meeting in New York on Sept. 1985. The effects of a strong yen on Japan's international expansion are examined.

3. Araki, Motoaki. "Trends in Japan's Direct Investment Abroad for FY 1983." EXIM Review. 5.2 (1984): 37-68.

   Japanese direct foreign investments are delineated by type of investment: equity or loan; by region and country; and by sector: manufacturing, natural resources, commerce and services.

4. Armstrong, Larry. "Japan's Latest Triumph: Hurdling the High Yen." Business Week (Industrial/Technology Edition). 3034 (Jan. 18, 1988): 36-40.

   This article discusses the strength of the Japanese yen, as a major factor in present Japanese policy. There are government officials, union leaders, bankers and others concerned with a national policy to respond to the present situation. In April of 1986, the Maekawa report stated that the nation could no longer operate as an export-driven economy. Instead, Japan must move its manufacturing overseas. Credit will be available for the new policy, because of government-induced cuts in the rate of interest. At the same time there has been an increase in the investment in technology. Hitachi has, for instance, achieved new heights of automation with its videocassette recorder plant. Other positive factors, such as the drop in the price of oil and the low price of the dollar, have helped to secure the direct foreign investments.

5. Arndt, H. W. "Professor Kojima on the Macroeconomics of Foreign Direct Investment." Hitotsubashi Journal of Economics. 15.1 (June 1974): 26-35.

   Professor Kojima's macroeconomic theory of direct foreign investment is discussed.

6. Ballon, Robert J. "Japan's Investment Overseas." Aussenwirtschaft. 28.3/4 (Sept./Dec. 1973): 128-153.

   An overview of Japan's direct foreign investments for the 1950-1970 period is provided with prospects for future growth. The article delineates sub-periods, types of investments, geographical and industrial distribution. It also focuses on Japanese national

policies, as well as corporate policies, and the
influence they have had on overseas investments.

7. Ballon, Robert J., and Eugene H. Lee, eds. Foreign
   Investment and Japan. Tokyo: Sophia University, in
   cooperation with Kodansha International, Tokyo, Palo
   Alto, California, 1972.

   The Japanese legal background for international
   investment is considered in this study, both in terms
   of corporate law and anti-monopoly law in Japan.
   Investment in Japan is considered, as well as Japanese
   investment abroad. The papers on direct foreign
   investment reveal some of the problems involved in
   doing business. Most of the papers in the collection
   come from International Management Development Seminars
   sponsored by the Sophia Univesrsity Socio-Economic
   Institute. Presenters come from an international
   field, and the results of interchanges at the seminars
   appear in the text.

8. Behrmann, Neil. "Japan Abroad: Moving from Bonds to
   Buildings." Financial World. 156.6 (March 24, 1987):
   16-17.

   The rising yen, overpriced Japanese stock prices, and
   the worldwide move toward protectionism have seen
   the emergence of the Japanese multinational
   corporation. While net external assets reached an
   estimated $130 billion in 1985 and investment in
   equipment and plants has surpassed $10 billion per
   year, the Japanese government is encouraging overseas
   investment to sustain trade and stem the adverse impact
   on the economy. Less expensive equities on Wall Street
   and in London have attracted Japan's fund managers, who
   feel confident in their country's long-term growth
   potential, despite crash warnings. Banking and
   insurance firms, high-tech companies and automobile
   makers have been the most aggressive in current foreign
   markets.

9. Bellanger, Serge. "Discipline and Diffusion Ahead for
   Japan's U.S. Payments Surplus." Financier. 10.4
   (April 1986): 36-40.

   Japan's balance of payments surplus is growing at a
   rapid rate. This appears to be a long-term trend
   because of economic and demographic forces at work,
   including the age of the Japanese population and their
   high propensity to save. On the other hand, Japan is
   exporting capital in several ways: 1. foreign real
   estate investments, 2. direct investments in industrial
   facilities, and 3. portfolio investments. By so doing,
   Japan hopes to prevent the spread of protectionism.
   With these surplus funds, Japan is becoming
   increasingly involved in international financial
   markets. The U.S. will receive the majority of these
   investments, owing to its large domestic market and
   access.

10. Bellanger, Serge. "Understanding Japanese Capital
    Flows." Bankers Magazine. 169.5 (Sept./Oct. 1986): 7-
    12.

    Japan's coordinated economic efforts, referred to as
    Japan, Inc., are now surging ahead in financial areas,
    just as they previously gained dominance in the
    industrial world. This has produced considerable
    surplus funds; its 1985 capital outflow was $82.5
    billion and Japanese investors own majority interests
    in over 520 U.S. plants. Both European and U.S.
    institutions are seeking the expected $100 billion
    capital outflow in 1986. Despite problems of cultural
    differences, Japan is expected to invest in real
    estate, production facilities, and debt capitalization
    worldwide. The Japanese financial service industry is
    beginning to internationalize its operations. But for
    real continued success, Japan must develop new products
    and ideas while opening its doors to imports.

11. Bronte, Stephen. "The Japanese Revel in Their Freedom
    to Invest Abroad." Euromoney. (March 1981): 83-96.

    A new Japanese foreign exchange law took effect on
    December 1, 1980. For the first time there are no
    restrictions on how Japanese citizens can transfer
    savings abroad. The desired effects of the law are to
    revolutionize Japanese saving habits, speed
    liberalization of yen trade deposits, open Japanese
    markets to foreign investors, begin new funding
    opportunities for corporate treasurers, and stimulate
    Tokyo's foreign exchange market. On the negative side,
    the law will affect some businesses unpleasantly, by
    squeezing the money sources of Japan's cash-hungry,
    long-term credit banks, allowing the securities
    industry to bypass the costly foreign exchange bank
    commissions, and forcing the foreign exchange brokers
    to go international sooner than desired. Despite
    uncertainty and confusion surrounding the law, it
    represents a great change in policy.

12. Buckley, Peter J. "Macroeconomic Versus International
    Business Approach to Direct Foreign Investment: A
    Comment on Professor Kojima's Interpretation."
    Hitotsubashi Journal of Economics. 24.1 (June 1983):
    95-100.

    Buckley criticizes the explanation of "Japanese type"
    direct foreign investment put forward by Kiyoshi Kojima
    and clarifies his criticism of the "international
    business approach".

13. Buell, Barbara. "Will Japan Face Up to Its Global
    Responsibilities?" Business Week
    (Industrial/Technology Edition). 3034 (Jan. 18,
    1988): 40-41.

    Japan is increasingly called upon to exercise a
    leadership role for stabilizing the world economy. The
    role it plays in Asia, for instance, is beginning to

overshadow that of the U.S. While in the past it has
been thought that Japan uses capital-intensive and
mercantilist style business approaches when investing
abroad, it now has a proposal to recycle $20 billion of
its current-account surplus to the Third World. This
should help change that image. Yet there is a serious
shortage of trained personnel to manage such a foreign
investment drive. Many executives do not receive
adequate appreciation for working abroad, and the key
aid bureaucracies are suffering from serious shortages
of staff.

14. "A Business in Billions, a Profit in Thousands."
    Forbes. 122.1 (July 10, 1978): 89-92.

    Japan's balance-of-payments surplus is creating an
    economic and political problem for the Japanese
    government. In trying to hold this trade surplus down,
    Japanese businesses are encouraged to invest in U.S.
    companies. This helps U.S. businesses as well, by
    increasing their products' share in the international
    market. Some large Japanese trading firms have begun
    investing in America: C. Itoh & Co. owns 50% of General
    Knits of California, the Mitsubishi Corp. holds 10% of
    the U.S. assets of Nissan Foods Co., and Mitsui & Co.
    invested $135 million in Alumax, Inc. of San Francisco,
    CA.

15. Caplan, Basil. "No Easy Solution to the Japan Trade
    Problem." Banker. 135.715 (Sept. 1985): 46-57.

    Japan's sizable trade surplus, a result of modest
    imports and a vast quantity of exports, has created
    notable tensions between the country and its trading
    partners. A short-term solution to this problem seems
    unlikely for 2 reasons: 1. Japan will not become an
    open marketplace for foreigners if they continue with
    their piecemeal trade concessions and, 2. their trade
    surpluses are the result of the greater efficiency with
    which Japan produces high quality goods. There is a
    positive trend taking the form of interconnections
    between U.S. and Japanese companies and Japan's growing
    amount of foreign investment. But financial market
    developments, particularly the price of the yen, will
    have the final effect on trade tensions. Further
    liberalization of Japan's financial institutions and
    the diversion of Japan's vast savings into domestic
    growth could help the situation also.

16. Carson-Parker, John, and Norman Peagam. "Capital
    Floods In and Pours Out." Euromoney; Japan Supplement.
    (Aug. 1986): 14-15.

    Capital has now joined the list of items the Japanese
    export. Now the world's largest exporter of capital,
    Japan is accumulating foreign assets in such amounts
    that their investment decisions have the power to
    strongly affect markets. These vast overseas holdings,
    the result of Japan's manufacturing and trading success
    as well as low world prices for some commodities, have

created Japanese trade surpluses that overflow into
foreign investment. U.S. dollar bonds have shown an
overwhelming attraction, although, as the worldwide
financial community begins courting the Japanese
investor, there will be added Japanese interest in
foreign equities, real estate, and non-U.S. dollar
debt. The Japanese can maintain their competitive edge
by shifting production offshore and acquiring foreign
companies.

17. "Changes in the Pattern of FDI: An Update." CTC
     (Centre Transnational Corps) Reporter. (Spring 1987):
     3-7.

     Based on a report prepared for the thirteenth session
     the the Commission of Transnational Corporations, this
     article gives a detailed analysis of foreign direct
     investment flows between nations, the major countries
     which were involved, and regional analysis during
     the years 1980 through 1985. Subjects discussed
     include the U.S. as a host country, the emergence of
     Japan as a major new home country, and flows of foreign
     direct investment to developing countries.

18. Chowdhury, Amitabha. "Japan: A Move Towards
     Deindustrialisation?" Asian Finance. 13.2 (Feb. 15,
     1987): 33-56.

     The skyrocketing value of the yen has hurt company
     profits in Japan, with average recurring corporate
     profits dropping some 19.3% in fiscal 1986. Export-
     oriented manufacturing companies are the hardest hit.
     The precision industries are now focusing on research
     and development and there seems to be a trend away from
     the processes, technologies, and production lines of
     the 1960's and 1970's. This movement, the deindust-
     rialization of Japan, may bring about radical redevel-
     opment and economic restructuring. The Nakasone
     government, which requires a balanced budget, has
     received criticism from the business and financial
     sectors. The high yen has opened up Asia's finished
     and semifinished goods industry exports, while Japanese
     multinationals look for Asian opportunities for factory
     sites, joint venture partners and merger possibilities.

19. Chowdhury, Amitabha, and Masaki Hideno. Masaki.
     "Japan Sees Early Pick-Up After a Modest Recession."
     Asian Finance. 12.2 (Feb. 15, 1986): 41-68.

     Japan's yen revaluation had a strong effect on its
     corporate and export prospects, but analysts expect
     signs of a slight recovery by the last quarter of 1986.
     80% to 100% of Japan's auto export contracts are
     denominated in dollars, which means smaller income in
     yen, a problem manufacturers are trying to handle by
     cutting production costs. If the yen rose in value
     17%, there could be an approximate 10% rise in prices
     of Japan's exports. To increase imports and decrease
     its trade surplus, Japan must have as its goal a
     minimum economic growth rate of about 4%. This will

require a concentrated effort to accelerate domestic
consumption. Insurance companies, pushed by the yield
differential between domestic and foreign investment
and perennial predictions of a major Japanese
earthquake, have invested about 9% of their assets
abroad. However, business observers believe a steady
recovery in Japanese corporate performance will occur
in 1986.

20. Cohen, Jerome B., ed. Pacific Partnership: United
    States-Japan Trade, Prospects and Recommendations for
    the Seventies. Lexington, Mass.: Lexington Books, D.C.
    Heath, 1972.

    The background of the U.S. balance of payments deficits
    is explored, especially in relation to Japan. The
    historical perspective and the impact of Japan's recent
    growth is offered. Price and cost comparisons for
    Japanese and American industries are outlined. The
    foreign trade pattern of Japan is examined, with its
    history and its future prospects. Direct foreign
    investments are discussed, and a treatment is given of
    the textile and auto industries. Conclusions are
    offered as to the competitiveness of Japan and the
    trade balance that might be achieved in the future. A
    reduction in Japan's reliance on the U.S. as a trade
    partner is likely, but it will be difficult for Japan
    to stand alone in the face of problems of international
    currency, balance of payments deficits and emergence of
    developing economies.

21. "Country Risk Check of 104 Major Companies Shows
    Enterprises Are More Wary in Investing in Non Oil-
    Producing Developing Nations." Japan Economic Journal.
    18.911 (July 8, 1980): 11.

    This piece analyzes the relative risks for Japanese
    enterprises in overseas investments and exports, with
    an emphasis on those deals which will have long-term
    results. Contained in the article are the results of a
    survey conducted by the top 104 Japanese firms, ranking
    countries by risk. The U.S. appears at the bottom of
    the list with the least risks. The Netherlands is in
    fifth place. The Japanese firms considered such risks
    as fluctuation, stability, non-payment troubles,
    countermeasures and nationalization problematics.

22. "Direct Foreign Investment." Fuji Bank Bulletin. 30.4
    (April 1979): 59-65.

    This article provides an overview of Japanese direct
    foreign investments in 1977. It analyzes changes in
    investment conditions and forecasts the investment
    outlook for the coming year.

23. "Direct Investments Abroad Rose Sharply in FY 1978;
    Reached an Estimated U.S. $4.5 billion." Japan
    Economic Journal. 17.853 (May 22, 1979): 1-2.

    An overview is presented of Japanese direct foreign

investments for 1978, showing their geographical
distribution. International comparisons are made with
other industrial countries' international investments.
Japanese overseas investments rose rapidly in 1978. A
look is taken at the impact this will have on jobs in
Japan and the trade union reactions.

24. "Dollar's Slide Lifts Japanese Business." Chemical &
    Engineering News. 56.34 (Aug. 21, 1978): 14.

    The appreciation of the yen against the dollar is
    producing windfall profits to Japanese industry
    estimated to reach 2.5 trillion yen. The rise of the
    yen may help reduce Japan's foreign trade surplus by
    stimulating imports into the country. It will also add
    greater impetus for increased Japanese direct foreign
    investments in manufacturing facilities and investments
    are sure to increase over the next decade. Little of
    the windfall profits are passed on the Japanese
    consumer. Highly regulated industries like airlines
    and utilities are benefitting the most.

25. Dunning, John H. "Explaining Changing Patterns of
    International Production: In Defense of the Eclectic
    Theory." Oxford Bulletin of Economics and Statistics.
    41.4 (Nov. 1979): 269-295.

    There have been changes in the geographic spread of
    international investment in productive activities.
    These are outlined, and a review of the theories which
    are attempting to explain the changes is offered. An
    eclectic theory of international production is the best
    way to explain the facts. With this theory, it is
    possible to offer suggestions as to the reasons for the
    differences in the industrial pattern of the direct
    foreign investment of the U.S., the U.K., West Germany,
    Japan, and Sweden, in 1975.

26. Frank, Isaiah, ed. The Japanese Economy in
    International Perspective. Baltimore: Johns Hopkins
    University Press, 1975.

    This collection of essays was written against the
    background of Japan's phenomenal rate of economic
    growth, low rate of inflation, and growing balance-of-
    payment surpluses during the late 1960's to 1972. At
    the same time, Japan experienced severe strains in its
    economic relations with other countries, especially the
    United States. These problems stemmed from a
    combination of three factors: 1. sharp increase in
    Japan's international competitiveness, 2. a set of
    foreign economic policies out of phase with Japan's
    economic strength, and 3. an international framework of
    institutions and rules incapable of adjusting to
    changes in the world economic community. Topics
    covered include: Japanese industrial policy, foreign
    trade, Japan's fiscal incentives for exports, Japanese
    foreign direct investment, and the international
    corporations.

27. Franko, Lawrence B.   "The Pattern of Japanese
    Multinational Investment." Multinational Business.
    1 (1984): 1-11.

    A key factor in the success of Japanese industrial
    processes has been the degree to which Japan
    understands the international division of labor.
    Rather than exporting its most advanced industrial
    activities to overseas locations, the Japanese have
    tended to move out the more standardized and less
    skilled labor processes which bring with them lower
    wages and lower production costs. This technique of
    selective industrial exporting has not been appreciated
    in the West. Other important trends in Japanese
    foreign investment include multinationalization of
    domestic activities, use of international trading
    company groups, taking small business abroad, expansion
    of larger firms' investments independently, moving
    weaker industries, not stronger ones abroad,
    concentrating production in third world countries,
    investing adjunct activities in Europe, and finally
    expansion in North America.

28. Furuta, Hideyuki. "Current Status and Outlook of
    Japan's Direct Overseas Investment: Report on 1987
    Survey." LTCB (Long-Term Credit Bank of Japan)
    Research. (Dec, 1987): 1-20.

    The Long Term Credit Bank of Japan conducted a survey
    of 737 companies, and this report covers various
    topics: overseas footholds for production; trends in
    production by area; share of foreign production;
    markets for products from foreign production; impact of
    advancement of foreign production on domestic
    employment; counteracting negative impact of foreign
    production on domestic employment; imports of parts and
    commodities.

29. Gall, Norman. "It's Mighty Cold Out There." Forbes.
    131.4 (Feb. 14, 1983): 38-40.

    This work concentrates on the flow of capital from
    Japan to the rest of the world, giving attention to the
    reasons and the effects of this movement. In the past
    2 years, the outflow of capital has more than doubled.
    The background to this situation includes many factors:
    the tightly regulated financial system had been opened
    up in the 1970s, and banks in Japan had received
    significant protection from shocks, with provision of
    artificially low domestic interest rates. The oil
    crisis began to set Japanese banks on edge, and exposed
    significant problems for Japanese financial
    institutions.

30. Givant, Marlene and David Kilburn. "Choices After
    October; Explosive Japan Looking Overseas." Pensions &
    Investment Age. 16.6 (March 21, 1988): 17, 24.

    This is an account of the various modes of investment
    available to Japan. Several courses of action are

possible, with Japan's large surplus of capital. They
can raise their foreign equity investments, carry out
more foreign bond purchases, and increase direct
foreign investment at a faster rate than securities
purchases. Japanese firms are expected to be the
leaders in terms of the range of their investments.
The investment of surplus corporate assets which have
gone into tokkin and related fund trust accounts may be
growing somewhat more slowly. There are more
investments in capital projects, instead.

31. "The Global Position of Japanese Industry and Its
    Transformation." Survey of Japanese Finance and
    Industry. 26.1/2 (April/June 1974): 1-30.

    This work discusses the market shares of various
    Japanese industries in the world economy. Japanese
    activities in production, and constraints which impinge
    on production are traced. There is a treatment of the
    deployment of Japanese industries throughout the
    foreign arena, and projections of the foreign
    investment in the 1980s are offered.

32. Higashi, Chikara and G. Peter Lauter. The
    Internationalization of the Japanese Economy. Boston:
    Kluwer Academic Publishers, 1987.

    This book begins with a serious historical treatment of
    the economic status of Japan. The evolution of the
    economy is outlined, and the key economic conflicts
    between the U.S. and Japan are traced. The myths and
    realities of the trading relationship are described.
    Some political factors are examined, with the
    leadership style and policy formulation process in
    focus. There is a detailed analysis of the Maekawa
    Commission Report and the potential constraints on
    internationalization. Domestic attitudes and
    sociocultural and political constraints are revealed.

33. Higashi, Kiyoshi. "Economic Growth in Developing
    Nations and the Role of Direct Investment and Plant
    Exports." EXIM Review. 4 (March 1984): 20- 42.

    This article primarily focuses on Japanese and American
    investment in developing countries and the effects that
    these investments have on economic development.

34. Hiraoka, Leslie S. "Japan's Increasing Investments
    Abroad." Futures. 17.5 (Oct. 1985): 495-508.

    A review is given explaining the reasons for Japan's
    dynamic program of foreign direct investment in the
    changing international environment. The increased
    purchasing power of the yen combined with trade
    surpluses formed the basis for a strong financial
    incentive for overseas acquisitions. After World War
    II, political and economic factors influenced the
    distribution of Japanese investment, developing a
    multinationalism distinct from Western industrial
    countries'. Japanese firms concentrated on profit-

optimizing investments in various countries, attempting
to avoid problems encountered by U.S. and European
multinational companies. Automobile manufacturers'
moves overseas signaled a major policy shift, and
investments by steelmakers and high-technology
industries followed. The future shows Japan continuing
to benefit from overseas investments.

35. Hughes, Helen, and You Poh Seng. Foreign Investment and
    Industrialization in Singapore. Madison, Wisc.: The
    University of Wisconsin Press, 1969.

    This study was organized jointly by the Economic
    Research. Centre of the University of Singapore and the
    Department of Economics of the Research School of
    Pacific Studies, the Australian National University.
    The research involved a series of questionnaires and
    interviews with manufacturing firms having Japanese and
    Australian investment. Firms having investment from
    the U.K., Hong Kong, Taiwan, and the U.S. are also
    reviewed. The course and effects of foreign investment
    were examined. In the section detailing Japanese
    investment, data is presented about the amount of
    capital involved, the types of industry represented,
    and the management practices.

36. Ikeda, J. "Japan's Direct Investment Abroad."
    Management Japan; The Magazine of Multinational
    Businessmen. 12.2 (Autumn 1979): 14-17.

    A general description is presented of the rise of
    Japanese overseas investments since 1978. Reasons for
    the rise of these investments include wages, natural
    resources, environmental pollution, and growing
    protectionism abroad. The changing pattern of
    investment trade is traced for the 1951-1978 period.
    Recent developments are also reported.

37. Ishimine, Tomotaka. "Fiscal Incentives for Japan's
    Export and Direct Foreign Investment." Bulletin for
    International Fiscal Documentation. 32.4 (April 1978):
    173-177.

    This article discusses the Japanese government's
    corporate income tax incentives for exports and
    investments. In addition, incentives for market
    development, technical transactions and foreign
    investments of Japanese companies are described. Some
    export and investment statistics are provided. The
    article concludes that fiscal export incentives are
    unlikely since none have been given since 1964,
    although some fiscal foreign investment incentives are
    forthcoming.

38. "Japan; Reaching Out; A Survey." Economist. 297.7423
    (Dec. 7, 1985): I-XVII.

    This investigation demonstrates how intertwined the
    Japanese economy has become with that of other
    countries, especially with the U.S. economy. Politics

in Japan tends to be "inward" and the bureaucracy does
not encourage overseas policy. Defense, and the
relations with the U.S.S.R. and China influence this.
Direct investment also plays a part in the economic
picture. The challenge remains, through the period of
1958-1985, for Japan to reconcile its domestic and
foreign investment patterns, to smooth the way for
balanced trade in the international scene.

39. Japan Economic Research Center. Japan's Economy in
    1980 in the Global Context: The Nation's Role in a
    Polycentric World. Tokyo: Japan Economic Research
    Center, 1972.

    The projection of the nature of the Japanese economy
    requires an analysis of the world economic environment.
    Problems for such a projection include foreseeing the
    future of the lingering world monetary system, and
    trends in international politics which are not amenable
    to quantitative analysis. But this work attempts to
    posit the changes that can be expected for Japan and
    the world system, as the world becomes polycentric in
    the coming years. The global context is sketched, and
    topics are analyzed in turn: world trade, international
    monetary system, direct investments, Japanese resource
    problems, industrialization of the developing nations,
    and trade systems and policy.

40. Japan External Trade Organization. Potential Investors
    from Japan. Tokyo: JETRO, 1987.

    This is a directory of Japanese companies interested in
    foreign investments. It is arranged in alphabetical
    order, by planned area to be advanced, and by sector.
    For each company, an address, telephone and telex
    numbers, CEO, number of employees, year of
    establishment, capital, annual sales, line of business,
    planned projects, and planned areas to be advanced are
    given.

41. "Japan Feels the Heat in the Industrial Kitchen."
    World Business Weekly. 3.13 (April 7, 1980): 22-23.

    The problems of Japanese industry are outlined, and the
    role of overseas investment as a solution to some of
    those problems is explained. There is a rise in
    inflation, and an increase in protectionist moves from
    many trading partners. Lower growth rates and social
    problems are also impacting on industry. There have
    been increases in unemployment and questions raised
    about the lifetime employment schemes in Japan. At the
    same time, industry is concerned to hold on to the
    labor force and keep its domestic workforce interested
    in industry. Foreign investment is distributed about
    25% in Asia and 25% in the U.S. Plans by trading
    companies for increasing foreign investment are active,
    and the MITI has endorsed this policy.

42. "Japan - Pressures to Invest More Money Abroad."
    Business Week. 2509 (Nov. 14, 1977): 63.

This studies the trend for Japanese companies to invest abroad, in the context of the need to put the Japanese currency on a strong footing and strengthen foreign currency reserves. Inducements and incentives to movement of investment are treated. Among these are the attempt to avoid foreign import quotas, and the availability of cheap labor. Limitations on investment abroad include the tendency for companies to carry high levels of debt for previous expansions.

43. "Japan - Tactics to Outwit U.S. Protectionists - West Germany - Preemptive Jawboning Astonishes Business." Business Week. 2476 (March 28, 1977): 36-37.

Plans for Japanese firms to increase their investments abroad are discussed in terms of the need to skirt protectionist import tariffs and restrictions which effectively close markets to the Japanese. In the U.S., where 50% of the Japanese TVs are sold, several Japanese manufacturers already have established plants. There are other TV makers who are planning to move to the U.S. For automobiles, however, the size of Japanese share of the U.S. market has not yet warranted large scale production plants in the U.S. West German car makers' pricing is also discussed.

44. "Japan Trims Overseas Investment Plans." Chemical & Engineering News. 54.4 (Jan. 26, 1976): 12-13.

The MITI of Japan has lowered its expectations for direct foreign investment over the next ten years, even though expansion of overseas investment was originally a hallmark of the plan before the mid-1970's. The reasons for slowing expansion of direct foreign investment include industry objections and doubts about the maintenance of profitability and financing for the overseas expansion. Nonetheless, the plan still shows a need for significant reductions in Japanese energy consumption over the ten-year period.

45. "Japanese Corporations in World Arena." Oriental Economist. 43.780 (Oct. 1975): 6-11.

This is a survey of the current situation of Japanese investments. The amount spent overseas is expected to grow twice as large during the period between 1980 and 1985. Mitsui is the leader. A discussion of home electric machines and automobiles is offered. There is data presented for investments, the volume of production, and sales by corporation.

46. "Japanese Direct Foreign Investments. Past and Future." Business Asia. 6.14 (April 4, 1975): 107-109.

Japan is the largest foreign investor after the U.S. The forecast calls for a growth in these investments, and a portrait of the future is offered industry by industry, through 1985. Data is also offered for each major industry and by geographic area through early 1974.

47. "Japanese Direct Investments Overseas Still Need to
    Recover from Past Sharp Decrease." Japan Economic
    Journal. 14.715 (Sept. 7, 1976): 11.

    This is a study of the short-term changes in Japanese
    direct foreign investment. While overall investment
    figures rose, the number of sites for investment
    actually declined over 16%. There is a consideration
    of geographic areas and various industrial types.

48. "Japanese Foreign Direct Investment: Moving to the
    Markets." Economist. 306.7538 (Feb. 20, 1988):
    75-76.

    This article offers a description of the size and
    import of Japanese foreign direct investment. The
    increase from April to September 1987 was $15.8
    billion, or 70% more than in the same period a year
    before. Finance, insurance and real estate accounted
    for half the investments, with the U.S. the most
    popular destination. Manufacturing made up only 17% of
    the investments. The major concern for the host
    countries is the fact that there is no reciprocity in
    the direct investments. Japan does not have foreign
    investors on its soil in any significant amount. It is
    felt that this policy will have to change, in order to
    allow continuing foreign direct investment by Japan.

49. "Japanese Foreign Investment; What Next?" Business
    International; Weekly Report to Managers of Worldwide
    Operations. 33.46 (Nov. 17, 1986): 361-364.

    As the yen's value rises on international markets,
    there are negative ramifications in terms of the
    relative strength of Japanese exports. At the same
    time competition from direct Japanese investment in
    other countries is on the rise. The trends for
    increased foreign investment by Japan will develop
    different patterns in various regions of the world.
    Data is offered for various industrial sectors and
    covers the years 1981-1985.

50. "Japan's CPI Is Exporting Capital as Well as Goods."
    Chemical Week. 124.23 (June 6, 1979): 16-17.

    This analysis of Japanese trade compares the trading
    surplus and the outflow of capital from Japan. While
    the Japanese accumulated a large surplus in 1978, its
    capital exports amounted to $2.36 billion, an increase
    of 45.5%. In 1979, that investment should reach $4
    billion. Chemical process industry and other
    manufactures will be among those Japan will be sending
    abroad. The U.S. will be a focal point for the
    Japanese foreign investment due to the currency
    exchange rate changes, the natural resources available
    in the U.S. and the need to skirt U.S. tariffs.

51. "Japan's Direct Investment Abroad." Tokyo Financial
    Review. 4.8 (Aug. 1979): 1-3.

This is a study of the Japanese direct foreign
investments. Their pattern and trends are examined for
the period 1951-1978. Attention is given to the value
of the investments, and the expansion of production and
distribution networks to support the investments. The
use of raw materials and resources from abroad is
investigated. The climate for Japanese investment is
compared, with consideration given to the developing
nations and to the advanced industrial countries.

52. "Japan's Direct Investment Overseas Expands." Fuji
Bank Bulletin. 36.1 (Jan./Feb. 1985): 4-11.

The expansion of Japanese direct investment has
increased rapidly since 1980. The expectation is that
the investment will continue to proceed, because
companies will be seeking to escape trade barriers and
counter a domestic savings surplus. The availability
of cheap labor overseas is also likely to be a factor.
An overview of the operations of Japanese direct
foreign investments is offered, with a consideration of
the impact on the Japanese economy as a whole.

53. "Japan's Direct Outward Investment." Fuji Bank
Bulletin. 24.10 (Oct. 1973): 199-205.

The impact of Japan's direct foreign investment is
examined. Currently 23% of the total long-term private
foreign assets fit into this category. The study
identifies factors leading to the growth of the direct
investment, and motivations of firms engaging in the
investment. Prospects for future change and increased
growth are examined.

54. "Japan's Direct Overseas Investment." Tokyo Financial
Review. 10.11 (Nov. 1985): 2-7.

This work offers some historical perspective on the
current status of Japanese direct foreign investment.
The postwar activities of a number of trading houses
led the way. Sales through subsidiaries in the U.S.
were later to develop into more genuine foreign
investment with a lasting impact. In 1984, investment
had amounted to over $10 billion, accounting for 8% of
GNP. The pattern of growth in investments in the
advanced countries, as against slower growth in the
developing world is examined. The oil crisis was
responsible for this shift in geographic emphasis. The
future is expected to bring a reduced trade surplus,
thanks to even more shifts of production to foreign
soil.

55. "Japan's Direct Overseas Investments." Focus Japan.
7.8 (Aug. 1980): JS-C-D.

This is an outline of the investment by Japanese
corporations in countries overseas. The data analyzed
comes from the period 1970-1977. The impact of direct
investment on employment, profits and other economic
indications is explored. The role of small companies

and their prospects for engaging in direct foreign
investment is treated.

56. "Japan's Economy in Transition - Overseas Moves - The
    Industry Exodus to Foreign Locales." Business Week.
    2388 (July 7, 1975): 50.

    The increase in foreign investment by Japanese firms
    can be traced to several factors. One is the lack of
    expansion opportunities in the domestic market, and
    another is the need to supply raw materials and
    semifinished products to the industry located in Japan.
    A larger segment of the direct foreign investment is
    expected to take place following markets. For
    example, the Japanese are manufacturing TV sets in
    Taiwan for a U.S. market, and there will be more
    activity in fields like hotels, restaurants, banks and
    real estate.

57. "Japan's Foreign Investment Pattern Is Changing."
    Japan. 69 (July 1979): 11-14.

    This is a treatment of the foreign investments of Japan
    in the year 1978. Special note is given to the
    manufacturing operations overseas, and the relationship
    of loans to capital export. The investment structure
    by industry is outlined for 1971 and 1977, with a
    review of the changes that took place during the
    period. Chemicals, machinery and manufacturing are
    examined with sales data by region. Consideration is
    also given to the trade conflicts and their impact, as
    well as the influence of competition.

58. "Japan's Foreign Investment Reduces Economic, Political
    Risk in 1981." Business Asia; Weekly Report to
    Managers of Asia/Pacific Operations. 14.35 (Aug. 27,
    1982): 278-279.

    This treatment of the general conditions for Japanese
    direct foreign investment outlines the regions which
    receive the bulk of the investment attention.
    Indonesia is dominant among Asian nations, with an
    emphasis on non-manufacturing industries. There are
    statistics offered for the period 1951-1981, and an
    analysis of the trends is offered.

59. "Japan's Foreign Investments." Business International.
    25.5+6 (Feb. 3 & 10, 1978): 33-34 & 44-45.

    This is an examination of the reasons why Japan has
    been increasing its direct foreign investments so
    rapidly. Some factors include the developing of
    resources needed in Japan and cheaper labor costs.
    There is a treatment of investments by industry and by
    geography. Some reasons for the pattern seen in
    European and North American foreign investments in 1985
    are given special note.

60. "Japan's Legal Security for Overseas Investment."
    Management Japan; The Magazine of Multinational

Businessmen. 14.1 (Spring 1981): 15-28.

A summary of legal measures against foreign investment-
risks is offered, including investment promotion and
protection agreements. Overseas investment insurance
programs are described. In addition, reserve for
losses, protection of life and individual property, and
Japanese legal measures are discussed. Figures are
present for 1964-1980.

61. "Japan's Licensed Overseas Investment in F.Y. 1977."
    News from MITI. 176 (Aug. 28, 1978): 1-7.

    Japan's licensed investments by categories, regions and
    industries in 1977 are presented. Main countries are
    the U.S., Indonesia, and Brazil. Shares and loans are
    given for 1951-1977 along with overseas direct
    investments outstanding of major countries for 1971-
    1976.

62. "Japan's Overseas Ventures." Oriental Economist.
    41.755 (Sept. 1973): 16-21.

    In a general treatment of the status of Japanese direct
    foreign investment, this offers an assessment of the
    role Japan occupies in relation to the rest of the
    world. As number 4 in overseas production in 1972,
    Japan shows a distinct pattern of sales and production
    emerges. The structure of capital and types of
    employment are also discussed.

63. "Japan's Overseas Ventures." Oriental Economist.
    42.769 (Nov. 1974): 17-22.

    This is a treatment of Japanese direct foreign
    investment in the year 1973. The largest investors are
    identified, and a consideration of overseas production
    volumes be each is provided. Textiles, electric
    machinery and manufacturing corporations are discussed.
    Sales rankings of 1973 overseas operations are given.

64. "Japan's Overseas Direct Investments and International
    Payments." Bank of Tokyo. Semi-annual Report.
    (April/Sept. 1974): 15-34.

    An account of Japan's expansion of overseas direct
    investments is given for 1960-1973 with distribution by
    industry and area. Comparisons are made with West
    Germany, Great Britain, and the U.S. The effects of
    overseas direct investments on the balance of payments
    are drawn with an assessment of the role of external
    assets and liabilities.

65. Kaletsky, Anatole. "Holding the Restless Yen."
    Financial Planning. 14.1 (Jan. 1985): 54-58.

    The more than $30 billion which is invested abroad by
    the Japanese each year comes from a variety of sources
    and factors. There is a high savings rate in Japan, a
    limited consumer credit market, and rather low interest

rate domestically. To absorb the high level of
savings, the Japanese government must increase its
deficit or encourage the outflow of capital. After
debt grew from 10% to 40% of the GNP, Japan turned
toward the direction of its savings to overseas
investments. The outcome has been a reduction of
deficits in Japan, lighter restrictions on foreign
investment by Japanese financial firms, and low
interest rates. Fluctuations in the yen are also
taking place.

66. Karger, Delmar W., and Tsune Fujita. "R&D in Japan
    Revisited -- The 1970 Decade." Management
    International Review (Germany). 14.4-5 (1974): 31-38.

    A review of the trends in Japanese economic growth,
    technology, exports, and management is offered. The
    1960s give the statistical basis for this study.
    Predictions are for an investment shift away from
    excessive concentration on private industrial
    facilities and toward areas like pollution control and
    foreign investments. R & D will be shifting toward
    certain sectors as a complement to these changes.

67. Kashiwagi, Yusuke. "Japan's Expanding Role:
    Responsibilities as a Capital Exporter." Vital
    Speeches. 54.3 (Nov. 15, 1987): 79-83.

    The speaker here offers views on the role Japan should
    play in helping to even out the economic imbalances in
    the free world while still protecting the Japanese
    national interest. Measures such as the shift of the
    economy to a structure led by domestic demand, and the
    adjustment of its production to harmonize with world
    trends are discussed. The establishment of methods to
    recycle the current account surplus is advocated.
    Suggestions for the U.S. to follow are also offered.

68. Kawahara, Isao. "Trends in Japan's Direct Investment
    Abroad for FY 1979." EXIM Review. 2.1 (1981): 2-19.

    An overview of Japanese direct foreign investments is
    presented for FY 1979. Information is provided on type
    of investment, country and region, and sector.
    Prospects and problems are discussed.

69. Kitamura, Hiroshi. Choices for the Japanese Economy.
    London: Royal Institute of International Affairs
    (Distributed by Humanities), 1976.

    The author views the present Japanese position as
    standing on the edge of a turning point, with many
    vital problems of social and economic importance
    developing. On the domestic side, there are topics
    such as growth and development patterns, planning for
    social welfare of the population, inflation, and
    restructuring needed at the end of the "economic
    miracle" period. For the international aspect of
    Japan's position, the author considers factors such as
    international payments, differing growth rates and

balancing of trade. Trade adjustments are discussed,
in terms of the discriminatory policies of Japan,
protectionism, and prospects for trade expansion.
Financial issues are also treated, including the
capital flows, foreign economic aid, and foreign
investment trends.

70. Kojima, Kiyoshi. "A Macroeconomic Approach to Foreign
     Direct Investment." Hitotsubashi Journal of Economics.
     14.1 (June 1973): 1-21.

     A macroeconomic theory of foreign investment is given,
     drawing from currency-premium, development stages, and
     dynamic comparative-advantages approaches. This method
     opposes the monopolistic theory of overseas investments
     based on microeconomics of the firm. Two methods of
     foreign investments are seen: American-type (growth of
     the firm) and Japanese-type (comparative-advantage).

71. Kojima, Kiyoshi. "Transfer of Technology to Developing
     Countries - Japanese Type Versus American Type."
     Hitotsubashi Journal of Economics. 17.2 (Feb. 1977):
     1-14.

     A study of the transfer of technology to developing
     countries is made comparing the Japanese and American
     methods. Direct foreign investment is analyzed in its
     role as a potent agent of economic transformation and
     development. Japanese transfer of technology is seen
     to take place in an orderly fashion, where as American
     technology is viewed as occurring in the reversed
     order. The comparative advantages of improving
     productivity is examined. Japanese-type technology
     transfer functions primarily through direct investment.

72. Kojima, Kiyoshi, and Terutomo Ozawa. "Micro- and
     Macro- Economic Models of Direct Foreign Investment;
     Toward a Synthesis." Hitotsubashi Journal of
     Economics. 25.1 (June 1984): 1-20.

     A model of direct foreign investment is developed to
     synthesize the macroeconomic and microeconomic theories
     usually called upon. While the multinationals are
     generally explained in terms of the microeconomic view,
     there are also theories such as the currency-premium,
     the development-stage, and the dynamic comparative-
     advantage theory, which take a macroeconomic approach.
     The present view uses a consideration of the compat-
     ibility of the social and private interests in direct
     foreign investment. The Heckscher-Ohlin factor
     endowment model and the E model are used, developing a
     special case of the factor endowment theory. The
     nature of competition between the U.S. and Japan is
     discussed.

73. Krause, Lawrence B. and Sueo Sekiguchi, eds. Economic
     Interaction in the Pacific Basin. Washington, D.C.:
     Brookings Institution, 1980.

     This study investigates the transmission of economic

impulses among six countries chosen as representative
of the Pacific basin: Australia, Japan, the Republic of
Korea, the Philippines, Thailand, and the U.S. It
compares the economic performance of the countries
during the 1970s and examines the domestic and international effects of the economic policies they have
pursued. Monetary, fiscal, and financial exchange
policies are reflected in many of the studies as an
emphasis. The emergence of Japan's dominance during
the period is documented, and the end of U.S. hegemony
is traced. The changes in relative strength among the
other countries are examined.

74. Lake, David. "Japan Survey: Cash-Rich Giants Ready for
    Corporate Raids." Asian Finance. 12.8 (Aug. 15,
    1986): 14-20,43.

    Cash-rich Japanese export firms are ready to take over
    nonexport businesses and use their cash flow to finance
    future investments. Previously, these exporters invest-
    ed their reserves in domestic government bonds and
    Japanese equities. Declining revenues have pressured
    them to maintain non-operating profits. Unfriendly
    takeovers do exist in Japan, and mergers and acquisit-
    ions are accepted as part of corporate strategy. Rescue
    -type takeovers are considered ethical. Japanese
    financial companies have been active in international
    mergers and acquisitions. Sanwa Bank has entered the
    U.S. market, specializing in smaller businesses.
    Industrial Bank of Japan uses U.S., state and local
    bonds to finance construction of U.S. plants.

75. Lee, Chung H. "On Japanese Macroeconomic Theories of
    Direct Foreign Investment." Economic Development &
    Cultural Change. 32.4 (July 1984): 713-723.

    Since it has been noted that Japanese direct foreign
    investment has some unique properties, the "mono-
    polistic theory" of international investment seems to
    be inadequate to explain the Japanese investment in
    manufacturing. Another viewpoint is developed here,
    which will address this question from a macroeconomic
    starting point. The intangible-capital hypothesis as
    normally used in microeconomics is shown not to apply
    to macroeconomic conditions. Incorporation of the
    intangible-capital hypothesis can be brought into play,
    however, to explain the investment in manufacturing
    industries. An opinion is developed that the Japanese
    macroeconomic theories are based on Japanese past
    experience and outlooks.

76. Lincoln, Edward J. Japan: Facing Economic Maturity.
    Washington, D.C.: Brookings Institution, 1987.

    This volume is primarily a treatment of the history and
    future of the Japanese economy, and includes treatment
    of the role of Japan's international activities. The
    background to the book is the belief that Japan has
    been experiencing enormous current account surpluses in
    the 1980's because of the slowdown in economic growth

that occurred in the 1970's. Pressure toward international investment has resulted. There are considerations of U.S.-Japan bilateral relations, with
conclusions and policy recommendations provided.

77. "Long-Term Capital Deficit on a Sharp Upcurve."
    Mitsubishi Bank Review. 14.11 (Nov. 1983): 775-777.

    Japan's balance of payments on current account recorded
    a surplus of about $13.2 billion during the first half
    of fiscal 1983. The capital balance however registered
    a deficit in Japan's long-term capital account in the
    first half reaching an annualized rate of $19.3
    billion. The deficit arose from rapidly increasing
    foreign securities investment and the growing foreign
    direct investment by Japanese companies stepping up
    foreign operations. The inflow of foreign capital into
    Japan has been on a downtrend, caused partly by the
    weakness of the yen relative to the dollar and the gap
    between domestic and foreign interest rates. The
    largest factor, however, has been the retreat from the
    Japanese market by oil-producing countries.

78. Marsh, Felicity. "Future Trends in Japanese Overseas
    Investment." Multinational Business. 2 (1984): 1-11.

    Japanese investment overseas is modest compared to
    other advanced industrialized nations, but significant
    growth has occurred over the last decade with 87% of
    total Japanese overseas investment outstanding
    occurring then and over 30% of the total occurring in
    the past 2 years. Trends in Japan's future overseas
    investment include: 1. reducing dependency on overseas
    supplies of many commodities; natural resource
    development aimed more toward securing supply than
    toward increasing volume; 2. exporting manufacturing of
    both labor intensive and natural- resource-related
    heavy industries and manufacturing overseas products
    threatened by anti-Japanese protectionism; and 3.
    offerings of tax concessions and the lack of
    restrictions on exports.

79. Marsh, Felicity. Japan's Next Export Success: The
    Financial Services Industry. Crawford's Special
    Reports 1066. New York: The Economist Publications
    Limited.

    This report provides an overview of the Japanese
    regulatory environment for banking, in order to explain
    the international activities of Japanese financial
    institutions. Japan's position in 1986 involves a
    large trade surplus, a strong currency, low interest
    rates, corporate cash surpluses, and a savings rate
    that is still relatively high. These indicators point
    to a readiness for Japanese financial institutions to
    break into the world markets which are undergoing
    considerable upheaval. Japan stands poised to take
    advantage of some unique opportunities. Some of the
    key topics discussed are the government's influence,
    liberalization, changing patterns of overseas

investment and trade, securities investment, current
trends, long term credit, regional banks, profitability, and securities houses. International fund
management, insurance companies, sogo shosha, and
promising markets are also discussed.

80. Mason, R. H. "A Comment on Professor Kojima's
    'Japanese Type Versus American Type of Technology
    Transfer'." Hitotsubashi Journal of Economics. 20.2
    (Feb. 1980): 42-52.

    This article comments on Professor Kojima's conclusion
    that Japanese technology transfers are more beneficial
    than are U.S. technology transfers. Institutional
    arrangements and methods of transferring technology are
    discussed along with the relation between technology
    transfer and operating characteristics of firms.

81. Matsumoto, Katsuo. "More Enterprises Are Starting to
    Advance Overseas with the Appreciation of Yen. Prodded
    also by Threat of Import Restrictions." Japan Economic
    Journal. 16.828 (Nov. 21, 1978): 11-12.

    The appreciation of the yen and the threat of protect-
    ionistic measures against Japanese exports are causing
    Japanese manufacturers to consider more closely
    overseas investments. Japanese wage levels are
    discussed for 1978 along with the growing need for
    foreign investments. The U.S. is an attractive
    location for overseas purchases.

82. Montagnon, Peter. "It Still Has to Be the Dollar."
    Banker. 136.719 (Jan. 1986): 57-61.

    This is an assessment of the nature and extent of
    Japanese foreign investment. While the net amounts are
    large, and grow larger as a result of the surplus in
    the Japanese balance of payments, there are certain
    limitations on the growth of investments abroad. On
    the one hand, capital exports can lead to a weakening
    of the yen. Currency fluctuations can also be a
    problem. Foreign bonds judged on the basis of yield
    and not on credit quality can have concealed risks.
    The dollar is still the currency most referred to, and
    U.S. bond markets are popular. The attainment of quota
    limits for institutional investors and lower corporate
    profits will tend to bring about a reduction in the
    foreign investment, however.

83. "Multiplicity of Global Investments Creates Need for
    Following Guidelines." Trade and Industry of Japan.
    23.1 (Jan. 1974): 25-28.

    This article reviews the problems facing Japan while
    investing in developing countries (47% of total foreign
    investments) and in the U.S. and advanced European
    countries (44%.) Investment guidelines are offered to
    overcome these problems. There follows an overview of
    Japanese investments by area and by category as of mid
    1973.

84. Murakami, Yasusuke, and Yutaka Kosai, eds. <u>Japan in the Global Community: Its Role and Contribution on the Eve of the 21st Century</u>. Round Table Discussions on Japan in the Global Community. Tokyo: Dist. by University of Tokyo Press, 1986.

The basic purpose of this report is to propose an ideal future direction for Japan in the global community and to point out a general path toward achieving that goal. While its underlying tone is theoretical, it attempts to bridge the gap between theory and reality. Part I places Japan in the 21st century in an historical perspective and tries to assess its economic, political-al, and cultural roles in the context of world trends. Part II then explores the basic conceptual framework that should inform Japan as it enters the next century. Concrete suggestions are made to realize these basic concepts. Part III sums up the discussion by focusing on the Japanese people.

85. Nakatani, Keiji. "Trends in Japan's Direct Investment Abroad for FY 1985." <u>EXIM Review</u>. 7.2 (1987): 2-31.

Japan's trends in direct foreign investments are discussed by type of investment, region, and sector. Opinions are given on prospects and problems for the future.

86. "New Formula to Recycle Japan's Surplus for LDCs." <u>Asian Finance</u>. 12.9 (Sept. 15, 1986): 81-84.

Japan's trade surplus is expected to grow at even a faster rate. A study by the World Institute for Development Economics Research concluded that Japan's growth would decrease and unemployment increase because of policies placing greater emphasis on its domestic market. The Institute recommends international initiatives that would channel Japan's surplus to less developed countries (LDC.) A mechanism for recycling Japanese capital to LDC's should incorporate investment guarantees of an international institution and a fair return on investments. Government incentives could further accelerate the process. The study recommends the creation of an international fund to promote private capital flows from developed economies to LDC's.

87. Okawa, Kazushi, and Nobukiyo Takamatsu. <u>Capital Formation, Productivity and Employment, Japan's Historical Experience and Its Possible Relevance to LDCs</u>. Tokyo: International Development Center of Japan, 1983.

This work analyzes the experience of Japan in industrializing as a dual economy, particularly as this experience sheds light on the future for the less developed nations today. The problem of development analysis is examined by the use of the total product-ivity concept, which relates capital formation, productivity and employment. Empirical studies on

Japan's historical experience follows in the framework
of dualistic growth, comprising the industrial and
agricultural sectors. Japan's experience is then
related to contemporary LDC's from various viewpoints,
focusing on the problem of development plan formulation
and making long-term perspectives. An appendix covers
statistical material.

88. Okimoto, Daniel I., ed. Japan's Economy: Coping with
    Change in the International Environment. Boulder, Co.:
    Westview Press, 1982.

    This book treats the question of Japan's direction in
    the changing international economy of today. It
    considers Japan's need to adjust its policies in
    reaction to the energy crisis, problems of the nation's
    expanded military role, and changes in its financial
    system. Conflicts that have arisen in U.S.-Japan
    relations are also given an examination. Cyclical
    problems and macrostructural issues in U.S.-Japan
    economic relations are treated, and the prospects for
    the U.S.-Japan alliance are considered.

89. Organization for Economic Cooperation and Development.
    Committee for Invisible Transactions. Liberalization
    of International Capital Movements: Japan. Paris:
    Organization for Economic Co-Operation and Development,
    1968.

    This work defines the term "direct investment" and
    proceeds to offer considerations of the promotion,
    volume, distribution, and earnings of direct investment
    in foreign countries by Japan. A treatment of foreign
    investment in Japan is also given. Regulations of the
    foreign investment in both forms are then described in
    detail. Portfolio investment, issue of securities, and
    credits and loans are then treated as separate topics,
    with the regulations spelled out for each. The main
    provisions are then reviewed and summarized. The
    history, law, and administration of foreign investment
    are outlined. Export and import of capital, as well as
    balance of payments are considered.

90. "Overseas Advances of Japanese Firms." Oriental
    Economist. 45.805 (Nov. 1977): 6-10.

    This article provides detail on the overseas
    investments by major Japanese corporations, giving the
    results of two research studies. First, the history of
    Japanese overseas investments is covered for the 1967-
    1976 period. Then investments are delineated as of
    March 1977 with investment plans projected for 1977-
    1979. This latter report divides investments by
    corporation and by part of the world. Overseas
    production values is given for 1976.

91. "Overseas Business Activities of Japanese Enterprises
    in 1979 - Eighth Survey." News from MITI. 217 (Oct.
    22, 1979): 1-26.

This survey reports trends in direct investments by
Japanese enterprises in overseas markets in FY 1978, as
well as the results of the survey on trends in overseas
business activities of Japanese enterprises in FY 1977.
It further discusses trends in management and
developments in subsidiary companies.

92. Ozawa, Terutomo. "International Investment and
Industrial Structure: New Theoretical Implications from
the Japanese Experience." Oxford Economic Papers.
31.1 (March 1979): 72-92.

The distinctive features of Japan's recent overseas
investment are analyzed in the context of the
monopolistic theory of direct foreign investment. This
is viewed as an extension of the Kojima model of
foreign investment and knowledge transfer. The
compatibility of international investment with a
relatively competitive market structure is discussed.

93. Ozawa, Terutomo. "Japan's Largest Financier of
Multinationalism: The EXIM Bank." Journal of World
Trade Law. 20.6 (Nov./Dec. 1986): 599-614.

Since World War II Japan has rebuilt its trade-based
economy and now dominates the world market as an
exporter and importer of raw materials. The Export-
Import Bank of Japan has linked Japan's trade to its
foreign investment activities in a mutually augmenting
manner. The Bank's involvement as a trade-cum-invest-
ment institution is examined. The Bank takes a neoclassical view of trade and investment in that international engagements are considered beneficial to both
Japan and the foreign nations involved. The Bank
places emphasis on: 1. plant exports, 2. the development and import of energy and other natural resources,
and 3. overseas investment in manufacturing and other
sectors. As a trading economy, Japan benefits more
from wider trade flows than capital ownership abroad.

94. Porter, Michael E. "Changing Patterns of International
Competition." California Management Review. 28.2
(Winter 1986): 9-40.

This article is based on a lecture. It is concerned
with the strategies that various countries are pursuing
in the international markets. The experience of
Japanese companies is observed. Much of the success of
Japan is due to the structure and position of its
firms, geared as they are toward introduction of new
technology, high productivity, and national
coordination. Many of the other Western countries have
difficulty with these areas.

95. "Quarterly Review of the Japanese Economy." Mitsubishi
Bank Review. 14.4 (April 1983): 733-735.

This economic assessment portrays Japan in recession.
Stagnation of export and capital expenditures, as well
as consumer spending is noted. A growth rate of 3% in

1982 has occurred, making it the lowest since 1975's
rate at 2.4%. Projections are offered. The effect of
reduced crude oil prices, and expectations for the
surplus in 1983 trade are considered. Japanese government expenditures are assessed, and the deficit's
effect on future spending is examined. The demand for
lending and the stock and bond situation is described.
Union-management relations are outlined. The probab-
ility is for increased foreign investments in natural
resources development and more movement of plants to
the U.S. and other advanced countries.

96. Reed, Karl. "Japan Plays Win-Win Game by Increasing
    Foreign Investments." Computerworld. 20.48 (Dec. 1,
    1986): 110.

    The Japanese economic success formula is analyzed, with
    the acceleration of direct foreign investments seen as
    the key to future success. While the U.S. has operated
    on a free trade philosophy, Japan has pursued its "plan
    rational" approach. A close relationship between the
    Japanese government and industry has allowed them to
    develop new industries and coordinate existing ones,
    for a smooth growth pattern. Restrictions in imports
    to Japan, through they may decrease in the future, have
    also played a role in the success pattern.

97. "Reinvestment of Profits on the Local Level by Japanese
    Industries Abroad." Management Japan. 12.1 (Spring
    1979): 24-30.

    This article deals with the sensitive question of the
    profits obtained from Japanese direct foreign
    investment, and their recycling. Where and how the
    reinvestment occurs can be of concern to the host
    countries. Certain problems are discussed.

98. "The Report of the Advisory Group on Economic
    Structural Adjustment for International Harmony:
    Submitted to Prime Minister Yasuhiro Nakasone on April
    7, 1986." Business Japan. 31 (May 1986): 24-27.

    This high level study group offers its policy
    recommendations. There is advocacy of expansion of
    Japan's domestic demand levels. Various means are
    suggested. Also considered is the need for the further
    promotion of direct foreign investment. Reasons are
    outlined. It is also recommended that Japan attempt to
    improve market access in various different markets.
    Finally, the determination to stabilize exchange rates
    is discussed.

99. Robins, Brian, Gary Evans, Vickie Smiles, et al.
    "Unstoppable Japan." Euromoney; Japan Supplement.
    (April 1987): 6-9.

    This assessment of Japan's position in the inter-
    national money market presents a picture of Japan as
    extremely powerful. The possibility for Japan to
    reach $1 trillion in foreign investments by 2000 is

interpreted as a sign of this strong position. The
large trade surplus, the capital surplus, and the need
for places to invest all contribute to Japan's growth
in financial power. The service sector is beginning to
supplant the heavy industry dominance of the past.
Japan's currency is also growing in acceptance worldwide. Issues for the Japanese government include
overseeing the move from exports to the domestic
market.

100. Roemer, John E. "Japanese Direct Foreign Investment in
     Manufactures - Some Comparisons with the U.S. Pattern."
     Quarterly Review of Economics & Business. 16.2 (Summer
     1976): 91-111.

     There are various types of influence upon the
     investment pattern of Japan in foreign countries.
     Domestic politics, wage and regulation patterns, and
     economics play a role. Some observations are offered
     about the manufacturing that Japan does overseas; it
     is not labor intensive, but high technology oriented.
     In less developed countries Japan uses government loans
     in return for a share of production, rather than direct
     investments. Japan's move to establish manufacturing
     in the more advanced nations will increase as the wages
     in Japan begin to reach those of these other countries.

101. Roemer, John E. U.S.-Japanese Competition in
     International Markets: A Study of the Trade-Investment
     Cycle in Modern Capitalism. University of California.
     Institute of International Studies. Research Series
     Berkeley: Institute of International Studies,
     University of California, 1975.

     Using a case study type approach, this work
     investigates specific economic variables in
     international trade and foreign investment in
     manufactures. Competition is examined to determine
     what structural changes in trade accompanied the U.S.
     decline and the role of Japan in the decline. Four
     stages are outlined in the life of an international
     competitor, demarcated in terms of the strength of its
     trade and foreign investment. With the four stage
     scheme, the competition of the U.S., Great Britain,
     Germany, and Japan during the 1960's is examined. The
     usual characterization of the Japanese investment
     approach, which claims that Japan has solved the
     problem of the product cycle by exporting capital only
     in its labor intensive sectors, is challenged. A new
     form of international capital penetration is foreseen,
     because of the cyclical nature of hegemony.

102. Sagara, Junji. "Private Investments Overseas Appear
     Due to Slacken Temporarily in Fiscal 1979." Japan
     Economic Journal. 17.847 (April 10, 1979): 11-12.

     This is a survey of 361 Japanese companies, giving the
     findings as pertaining to investment this year as
     compared to last year. The overall result shows a
     decline of investment. Geographic location of the

foreign investments, distributed among the U.S. and
other countries, is given. Uranium is mentioned as an
investment interest.

103. Saunders, Christopher T., ed. The Political Economy of
New and Old Industrial Countries. Butterworths Studies
in International Political Economy Series. Boston:
Butterworths, 1981.

This volume is a treatment of the rising "new
industrial countries," in Southern Europe, Latin
America, and East Asia: Greece, Portugal, Spain,
Yugoslavia, Brazil, Mexico, Hong Kong, South Korea,
Singapore, and Taiwan. The way these countries fit
into the economic system is described, along with an
outline of the development strategies they have used.
Policies that are appropriate for coping with the
emergence of new relationships are offered. The status
of the "NICs" is compared with that of the older
industrialized nations, in Europe, North America, and
Japan.

104. Sekiguchi, Sueo. Japanese Direct Foreign Investment.
Montclair, N.J.: Allanheld, Osmun & Co., 1979.

This book studies the impact of Japanese direct foreign
investments on the interdependence of national economies. Both points of view, the Japanese and the host
countries,' are examined. There is a survey of
theoretical hypotheses about direct foreign investment.
Primary commodities and pricing are examined. The
controversy surrounding the side-effects of investment
in developing countries is scrutinized, including the
real income effects and the technology transfer
effects. The performance of Japanese investments is
assessed, and an evaluation of the activities of
general trading companies is offered. Comments about
the conventional business management practices of Japan
are also made.

105. "Sharp Gains in Overseas Investment & Loan Income."
Mitsubishi Bank Review. 13.9 (Sept. 1982): 691-693.

The outflow of capital from Japan is one of the major
reasons for a fall in the foreign exchange rate of the
yen. A number of factors contributed to this capital
outflow: 1. the lifting of restrictions on overseas
investments, 2. declining demand for funds in the
domestic market, and 3. the wide interest rates
differential between yen and dollar funds. Japanese
direct foreign investments increased more than 6-fold
from $32.8 billion in 1971 to $209.3 billion in 1981.
The last decade has shown a marked advance in the
investment-and-loan profit ratio, moving from 5% in
1972 to 10.7% in the first half of 1982. This
improvement arose from a sizable increase in stock and
bond investments, direct investments in joint ventures,
production operations, sales bases, and high interest
rates in overseas financial markets.

106. Simonis, Heide, and Udo Enrest Simonis, eds. Japan;
     Economic and Social Studies in Development. Wiesbaden:
     Otto Harrassowitz, 1974.

     This is a collection of essays with varied topics and
     points of view. For example, some consideration of how
     well the national welfare is represented by the gross
     national product concept is offered. There are
     presentations on the small and medium industries,
     collective bargaining, Japanese investment in foreign
     countries, trading companies, technology, the Pacific
     region, economic planning, and other diverse issues.
     There is also some examination of the impact of Japan's
     rapid economic growth and its causes.

107. Sinha, R. P. "Japanese Foreign Investment." World
     Today. 4 (April 1975): 141-152.

     An overview of Japanese direct foreign investments is
     outlined since 1951 with their geographical distrib-
     ution given for 1969, 1973, and 1980 (estimated.) In
     addition, the type of investment is given with
     geographical and sectoral distribution of portfolios.
     Profitability is examined and the future of Japanese
     foreign investments is depicted.

108. "Some Features of the Recent Outflow of Japanese
     Capital." Mitsubishi Bank Review. 13.8 (Aug. 1982):
     685-687.

     In fiscal 1981, Japan had a net outflow of capital
     amounting to $25.7 billion, leaving a deficit of $14.8
     billion in the long-term capital account. Even though
     there was a favorable current balance, Japan's total
     international balance of payments was $7.9 billion in
     deficit. Three reasons contributed to this outflow of
     Japanese capital: 1. differences in interest rates
     between Japanese and foreign bonds widened; 2. the
     inflow of foreign capital consisted mostly of invest-
     ments in Japanese securities and the flotation of
     foreign-currency bonds on foreign capital markets by
     Japanese firms;and 3. surplus funds increased in the
     domestic financial markets. Consequently, the exchange
     rate of the yen has declined, creating the possibility
     of renewed inflation by increasing the price of raw
     materials.

109. Stokes, Henry. The Japanese Competitor. New York: FT
     Publications Limited, 1976.

     This is a general treatment of Japanese economics, and
     chapter four is devoted to the subject of direct
     investment. This part focuses on Japan as it relates
     to Asia, then moves to consider the investment in the
     West. Steel, electronics, and textiles receive special
     treatments. The countries of Thailand, Malaysia, and
     Singapore are also singled out for more detailed
     review. Statistical data that reflect the size and the
     future impact of Japanese direct investment include
     analysis of marketing and a review of the chief

predictions of Japanese financial analysts. Conclusions are offered.

110. "Strong Yen and Protectionism Spur Marked Acceleration
of Japan's Foreign Investment." Business
International; Weekly Report to Managers of Worldwide
Operations. 30 (July 27, 1987): 233-236.

Japan's Ministry of Finance released data showing that
Japanese direct foreign investment is primarily
concentrated in finance, insurance, services, and real
estate. The data also showed a strong increase in
offshore manufacturing and a growing tendency to prefer
acquisitions and mergers. The geographical distribution of Japan's investments reveal the following
pattern: North America 46%; Asia/Pacific 25.5%; Latin
America 19.2%; Europe 13.7%; Africa 3.5%; and the
Middle East 2.8%. Japan's overseas investment by
sectors is given for fiscal year 1986.

111. "Surge in Investment Spurs Japanese Firms in Key
Overseas Markets." Business Asia; Weekly Report to
Managers of Asia/Pacific Operations. 17.41 (Oct. 11,
1985): 322-323.

During the 1984/85 fiscal year, Japanese direct foreign
investments reached a record level of $10.16 billion.
Generally investment activity was reduced in the Asian
region with a surge in investments to the Peoples'
Republic of China, India, and Hong Kong. Japanese
firms appear reluctant to invest in high-tech
electronics ventures in Asia. In Indonesia, Australia,
and the Middle East, Japanese investments are moving
away from resources operations. A strong shift is
being made toward the U.S. and Europe in automotive,
electronics, steel, and service industries. Japanese
firms are now concentrating on finance, insurance,
commerce, and transportation services. Statistics are
given for 1983/84.

112. "A Survey on Japanese Private Investment Overseas."
Management Japan. 9.2 (Summer 1976): 32-34.

A survey is provided for 1975 on the opinions of
Japanese industries on foreign investments. The
outlook for foreign investment is described along with
projections of the direction Japanese corporation will
take with their overseas investments. The level of
confidence in foreign projects is discussed with more
influence expected by host countries on investments.

113. Take, Kazuteru. "Trends in Japan's Direct Investment
Abroad for FY 1980." EXIM Review. 2.2 (1981): 21-38.

Japanese overseas investments are outlined for FY 1980.
Investments are are organized by type, by country and
region, and by sector. Opportunities and possible
obstacles are discussed.

114. Take, Kazuteru. "Trends in Japan's Direct Investment

Abroad for FY 1981." EXIM Review. 3 (Dec. 1982): 32-
52.

Trends in Japanese direct foreign investments are
discussed for FY 1981 with investments classified by
type, by country and region, and by sector. Prospects
and future problems are reviewed.

115. Take, Kazuteru. "Trends in Japan's Direct Investment
Abroad for FY 1982." EXIM Review. 4 (March 1984): 2-
19.

Japan's overseas investments are discussed for FY 1982.
Information is provided on investments by type, by
country and region, and by sector. Prospects for
future investments are considered.

116. "Trends in Japan's Direct Investment Abroad for FY
1978." EXIM Review. 1.1 (1980): 4-17.

Japanese overseas investments are delineated for FY
1978. Investments are grouped by type, by country and
region, and by sector. Future trends are discussed.

117. Tsukazaki, Seiichi, Hayato Ishii, and Tsukasa Fukuma.
"Japanese direct investment abroad." Journal of
Japanese Trade & Industry. 6.4 (July/Aug. 1987): 10-
17.

The amount and pattern of Japanese direct foreign
investment is described, showing that for 1986 $22
million in investment abroad was held. The sectors of
investment are broken down, giving figures for each.
Manufacturing, resource development, and commercial and
services categories are identified. Growth in foreign
investment is expected, because of the strength of the
yen and the inevitable trading restrictions. More
experience on the part of Japanese executives in how to
understand foreign investment opportunities leads to
better investments as well.

118. Turner, Louis. "Industrial collaboration with Japan."
Euro-Asia Business Review. 6.3 (July 1987): 11-15.

Japanese direct foreign investment has placed emphasis
on industrial collaboration. The official Japanese
policy since the early 1980's has been to encourage it.
However, a perception gap has occurred between Japan
and the targeted countries for investment by counting
100% controlled direct investment as a collaboration.
The Japanese consider industrial collaboration more of
a guide for continued Japanese investments than for
foreign firms investing in Japan.

119. Turner, Louis. Industrial Collaboration with Japan.
Chatham House Papers. Routledge, 1987.

This study is the product of an international team of
economists, in light of the increasing internationalization of investment. After some general consider-

ations, there is a treatment of European and American perceptions of Japanese business. These sectors are then analyzed: consumer electronics, automotive, information technology, and aerospace. Issues for corporate strategists and governments to consider are then explained.

120. Uri, Pierre, ed. Trade and Investment Policies for the Seventies: New Challenges for the Atlantic Area and Japan. New York: Praeger Publishers, 1971.

While there appears to have been progress made in the establishment of world trade, disappointment is evident as to the lack of success in removing the final barriers that remain after the Kennedy Round. High tariffs, quota restrictions, and nontariff barriers remain. The relations between Japan and other countries have not been fully normalized, and the developing countries' pressure for industrialization has not been handled satisfactorily. Other obstacles also plague the nations engaged in setting up such agreements. This book explores the future of inter-national trade, its worldwide options, and the role of Japan. Japan's role regarding the other industrialized countries, its general trading companies, and its trade and investment policies are examined.

121. Vogel, Ezra F. "Pax Nipponica?" Foreign Affairs. 64.4 (Spring 1986): 752-767.

By the mid-1980's, Japan may reach world economic dominance over the U.S. Japan has increased exports to the U.S. far in excess of its imports, $50 billion annual trade surplus versus a $150 billion annual trade deficit. In addition, Japan has become the world's largest creditor, while the U.S. has become its largest debtor. Japan's economic development is the outcome of policies emphasizing production technology, R & D, and growth of the service sector. The U.S. will have to adapt to Japanese dominance of international trade, characterized by neomercantilist policies - emphasis on exporting and cartel arrangements to maintain competitive balance between powerful older industries and newly emerging ones.

122. Walton, Jack. "Japan Surges Ahead with a New Export: Money." ICC Business World. 3.4 (Oct.-Dec. 1985): 32-34.

Japan has now become a leading exporter of money as well as goods. With net external assets of $75 billion, Japan is just behind U.K. in foreign invest-ments. Increased overseas Japanese investments are resulting from Japan's balance of payment surplus, liberalization of banking laws, and the fear of protectionistic legislation in other countries. In the U.S., for example, approximately 440 Japanese manu-facturers have started operations. In addition, the Japanese continue to save 20% of their disposable income. The low interest rates offered by Japanese

banks are making Japan a major force in international
banking markets. Other analysts believe the massive
outflow of capital is a sign that investors have lost
confidence in their own economy and politics.

123. Watanabe, Soitsu. "Trends in Japan's Direct Investment
Abroad for FY 1984." EXIM Review. 6.2 (1985): 21-55.

An overview is presented of Japanese foreign
investments for FY 1984. Investment trends are
organized by type of investment, by region, and by
sector. Prospects and problems for the future are
discussed.

124. Wilson, Dick. "Foreign Investments Breaking Records?"
Banker. 129.637 (March 1979): 69-71.

Japanese direct foreign investments may break all
records when released this month, as well as Japanese
acquisition of foreign securities. This increase in
foreign investments resulted from higher interest rates
overseas, the availability of surplus funds for Japan's
corporations and institutional investors, and the
belief the appreciation of the yen has peaked. Japan
is still far behind other industrial countries in terms
of the total value of foreign investments; the
government only started to encourage overseas investments five years ago. The U.S. is of particular
interest to Japanese investors, where they have
established manufacturing facilities. The Japanese
have also begun to buy into American and European
firms, and to make joint ventures with local partners.
Japan's domestic situation still favors foreign
investments.

125. Wilson, Dick, R. Pringle, M. Hayami, et al. "Japan,
a Survey." Banker. 129.637 (March 1979): 45-67.

This collection of contributions covers the political
climate in Japan, foreign policy, economic adjustment,
the yen's international reserve role, changes in the
financial and banking system, the Samurai bond market,
and Japanese direct foreign investments.

126. Woronoff, Jon. Japan's Commercial Empire. Armonk,
N.Y.: M.E. Sharpe, 1984.

This book deals with the impact of Japanese direct
foreign investment in terms of the exaggerations
offered by the opposing viewpoints. Where the Japanese
investor may portray himself in a thoroughly positive
light, bringing employment and benefit to the host
nation, often there is a spirited reaction character-
izing the Japanese as imperialists. The present volume
offers a presentation of the biases of both views, so
that both sides may be seen as disproving each other.
By piecing the parts together, it becomes clear that
neither side is correct. Topics such as neocolonial-
ism, the enrolling of foreign labor, and the possibilities of a new order are treated.

127. Yoshino, M. Y. "The Multinational Spread of Japanese
     Manufacturing Investment since World War II." Business
     History Review. 48.3 (Autumn 1974): 357-381.

     Responding to a variety of pressures, Japanese firms
     have developed significant amounts of direct foreign
     investment. The magnitude, evolution and general
     characteristics of the investment in manufacturing are
     explored. MITI survey data are used to elucidate the
     relations between parent and subsidiary entities
     abroad. The diversity and size of the investments are
     growing. For the future, it can be predicted that more
     sizable, capital-intensive industries may be located
     overseas.

MULTINATIONALS AND GENERAL TRADING COMPANIES

128. Abegglen, James C. "Japan's Kaisha Go Multinational
     and Learn to Innovate." International Management
     (Europe Edition). 40.12 (Dec. 1985): 94-104.

     Kaisha (Japanese companies) are become more involved in
     multinational operations. The multinationalization of
     Japanese businesses will mean increased international
     competition in markets they already dominate as well as
     new ones. The Japanese economy's high rate of growth
     in real terms demands a constant shifting of Japan's
     industrial mix, forcing the kaisha to be innovative and
     flexible.   Microelectronics is an industry where the
     kaisha have responded successfully with new technology.
     Although kaisha may have difficulty withdrawing from
     dying industries, they are likely to be innovators in
     product design and new product development. The
     evolution of the kaisha into the multinational sphere
     will create special problems for them including
     homogeneity and integration.

129. Abegglen, James C., and George Stalk. Kaisha, the
     Japanese Corporation: The New Competitors in World
     Business. New York: Basic Books, 1985.

     This book offers a detailed study of the internal
     workings and structure of the Japanese corporation.
     The role of the government, the banks, and management
     is reconstructed, and the part played by employee-
     management relations, the external environment, and
     foreign influences is described. The behavior and
     decision-making patterns that the kaisha have followed
     in regenerating the economy are uncovered. The
     successful strategies that have led to the expansion of
     the Japanese market share in so many industries are
     analyzed. The technological drive that motored much of
     the development is discussed, with the role of the
     government. Financial conditions and multinational
     ventures are reviewed, and the future prospects are
     outlined.

130. Cho, Dong Sung. The General Trading Company: Concept
     and Strategy. Lexington, Ct.: Lexington Books, 1987.

The growth of the Japanese economy and its changing
role in the world economy is causing the general
trading companies to modify their international
strategy. The historical background of the trading
companies is described, reviewing the network of
trading relations they have established, their role as
third country intermediataries, and their role in
increasing imports and exports. As providers of
capital for Japan's industrial growth, they are
becoming outdated and, subsequently, are moving into
global finance, joint ventures, and mergers and
acquisitions. Survival strategies entail greater
market orientation, better organizational management,
and greater coodination of interunit and interfirm
relations.

131. Coulbeck, Neil. <u>The Multinational Banking Industry</u>.
     New York University Press, 1984.

     This treatment of multinational banking offers a review
     of the banking structure of U.S., Japanese, British,
     French, West German, Canadian and Swiss institutions.
     First there is an overview which treats the banks'
     services, their universal and international inter-
     mediation aspects, as well as their markets, and
     regulatory structures. A useful note for the study of
     Japanese direct foreign investment is the case study of
     the Mitsubishi Bank, and the general treatment of the
     strategic development of Japanese multinational banks.
     Their function and foreign investment mechanism is made
     apparent. A projection of activity in the near future
     is also provided.

132. Enderwick, Peter. "Between Markets and Hierarchies:
     The Multinational Operations of Japanese General
     Trading Companies." <u>Managerial & Decision Economics</u>.
     9.1 (March 1988): 35-40.

     The Japanese trading companies are examined. The
     framework of markets and hierarchies is used, and the
     Japanese type theories of multinational business come
     into question. While the multinational investments fit
     into a microeconomic framework, if there is enough
     attention given to the economic incentives for
     federated businesses, there are also instances where
     they do not fit. The Kojima-Ozawa treatment depends
     too heavily on a theoretic base and relies on selective
     treatment of the features of trading companies. This
     critique offers questions about the welfare effects of
     the multinational investments, as well.

133. Frank, Isaiah. <u>Foreign Enterprise in Developing
     Countries</u>. Committee for Economic Development.
     Supplementary Paper. Baltimore: Johns Hopkins
     University Press, 1980.

     This study is based on interviews with top management
     personnel of 90 transnational companies based in the
     United States, Japan, Australia and Western Europe. Its
     aim is to promote an understanding of innovative

company decision making and improved public policies.
The issues treated include the scope and trends in
investment in developing countries, and a general
overview of the means by which the process of foreign
direct investment can be evaluated. The divergence
between corporate and national goals is described.
Types of arrangements for the investments are examined.
Transfer of technology is analyzed, and host-country
policies are detailed. Home-country policies and their
influence are explained. International programs and
arrangements are then considered. Conclusions are
offered.

134. Franko, Lawrence. The Threat of Japanese
      Multinationals; How the West Can Respond. New York:
      John Wiley & Sons, 1984.

      This book examines the reasons why the Japanese
      companies have been so successful in international
      markets. Contrary to the view that Japanese compet-
      itiveness resulted from the government's industrial
      policy, it is argued that success originated from the
      fierce competition within the Japanese market. The
      market forced research and development efforts toward
      commercial goals. The utilization of existing
      technology for marketable commodities was channelled
      through mass distribution systems. The twice yearly
      bonus system creates an important source of incentive
      for workers. The Japanese export their weaker
      industries and attempt to keep only those which are
      competitively stronger. The key to their success is
      strategic pragmatism, producing what the market wants,
      upgrading quality, and selling goods as cheaply as
      possible. These domestic market forces and strategies
      have produced Japan's international success. Case
      studies are given of how American companies that
      resemble Japanese companies have responded to the
      Japanese and won. The author advocates closer
      cooperation between American companies.

135. Franko, Lawrence. "Multinationals: The End of U.S.
      Dominance." Harvard Business Review. 56.6
      (Nov./Dec. 1978): 93-101.

      Though there were predictions of a U.S. domination of
      the multinational corporations, the U.S. positions has
      actually declined in world economics relative to
      Japanese and European companies. The U.S. lost its
      lead in the field of international exporting and
      foreign manufacturing. At the same time, the degree of
      management effectiveness among the companies of Europe
      and Japan excelled. Then changes in market conditions
      arose, especially as regards the need for energy
      conserving products during the oil crisis. These
      conditions intervened to give the advantage to Japanese
      and European firms which were already operating under
      more stringent needs for energy conservation.

136. Goldsbrough, David J. "The Role of Foreign Direct
      Investment in the External Adjustment Process."

International Monetary Fund Staff Papers. 26.4 (Dec. 1979): 725-754.

This paper develops a model to explain how a multinational firm locates its production facilities among different countries. The aim of the investigation is to explain the role of direct foreign investment in the external adjustment process. The model is used within a neoclassical investment function, to explain the plant and equipment expenditures by multinationals around the world. The factors which influence the distribution of financing for the expenditures are described. The results show that flows of foreign direct investment are influenced by changes in both real levels of demand and by countries' relative competitiveness.

137. Gregory, Gene. "Japan's New Multinationalism - The Canon Giessen Experience." Columbia Journal of World Business. 11.1 (Spring 1976): 122-129.

Canon's experience at Giessen provides possible solutions for problems which have inhibited Japanese direct investments abroad. Four valuable lessons were learned: 1. changing technologies produce major changes in Japanese overseas investment strategies; 2. these changes offer Japanese multinationals opportunities to develop new management formulae; 3. competent, highly motivated European managers respond well to the Japanese management system; 4. this positive European response to Japanese management philosophy shows that it can survive in a foreign environment.

138. "The Growing Multinationality of Japanese Industry; Lessons of the Textile Industry." Multinational Business. 2 (June 1974): 11-21.

Although Japanese foreign investments are still modest, there are signs of changing policies. Japan' s diffidence in investing overseas is being overcome. MITI has developed a policy of expansion of direct overseas investment. A description of Japan's pattern of investment is given by size of investor, as well as providing overseas investments by business and region. Currently, Japan's textile multinationals are leading changes in overseas investment. Projections are made for how the new Japanese multinationals will develop in the future.

139. Helou, A. "Sogo Shoshas and Japan's Foreign Economic Relations." Journal of World Trade Law. 13.13 (May/June 1979): 257-263.

This article describes the activities and influence of the leading general trading firms in Japan. Their role in the coordination of Japan's policies for imports, exports and overseas investments is examined.

140. Japan External Trade Organization. Japan into the Multinationalization Era. Tokyo: Japan External Trade

Organization, 1973.

This work begins by noting that the Japanese have been
forced into internationalizing, because the export
oriented philosophy has lost much of its luster.
Reduced profitability of exports and the rise of
barriers have made significant changes, encouraging the
move into direct investment. Developing countries are
demanding a share in the world's wealth, and Japan is
feeling this pressure. Some of the problems of
international investment are outlined, and the impact
of Japanese enterprises in Southeast Asia is described.
Standards for Japanese conduct overseas are reviewed,
along with government promotional and regulatory
policies.

141. "Japan on the Road to Multinationalization." Journal
     of American Chamber of Commerce in Japan. 10.9 (Sept.
     5, 1973): 13-27.

     This offers an outline of the general characteristics
     of Japanese direct foreign investments. Thirty-two
     different enterprises are examined, and the reasons why
     each is advanced overseas are traced. There is also a
     comparison of these industries with their American
     counterparts. A discussion of future possibilities for
     overseas investments is then offered, with some
     attention to the upcoming problems that will need to be
     overcome.

142. "Japanese Multinationals-Covering the World with
     Investment." Business Week (Industrial Edition).
     2641 (June 16, 1980): 92-102.

     Japanese firms are accelerating their direct invest-
     ments in overseas factories and resources, following up
     on the export success of production facilities. Their
     investments are primarily aimed at the industrial West.
     Japan's major trading companies are leading this
     investment drive with the U.S. the location for the
     multinationals with heavy involvement in manufacturing
     and resource extraction. U.S. offers cheaper petro-
     leum, feedstocks, and lumber. Japanese investments in
     Europe have not matched that of the U.S., where they
     are running into hostile opposition of European
     businessmen. Japan's activities should lessen trade
     tensions and hasten Third World industrialization, and
     cross investment and cooperation with the U.S. should
     increase.

143. Johansson, Johny K. and Israel D. Nebenzahl.
     "Multinational Production: Effect on Brand Value."
     Journal of International Business Studies. 17.3
     (Fall 1986): 101-26.

     One of the results of direct foreign investment for the
     firm is the changing perception of the firm's brand in
     the marketplace. Consequences can be considerable when
     the brand is closely associated with the country of
     origin. Changes in perception can be assessed before

the investment decision and the consequences of a particular location can be estimated. An example is given,
using the case of an automobile company's entry into
the U.S.

144. Kobayashi, Noritake. "The Present and Future of
     Japanese Multinational Enterprises: A Comparative
     Analysis of Japanese and U.S.-European Multinational
     Management." International Studies of Management &
     Organization. 12.1 (Spring 1982): 38-58.

     The management practices of Japanese corporations doing
     overseas business were compared to those of U.S. and
     European multinationals. Studied were the factors
     influencing differences in corporate international-
     ization. Areas of comparison included: 1. planning
     and decision making, 2. organization and control, 3.
     personnel administration, 4. purchasing and production,
     5. marketing, 6. research and development, and 7.
     finance. Japanese firms lagged in multinational
     development because of their reliance on export
     opportunities and their reluctance to modify Japanese
     management techniques for other cultures. The high
     demand for import substitution industries will force
     Japanese firms to become more involved in overseas
     investment and production to remain internationally
     competitive.

145. Kojima, Kiyoshi. Direct Foreign Investment; A
     Japanese Model of Multinational Business Operations.
     London: Croom Helm, 1978.

     Direct foreign investment and multinational
     corporations are examined in the framework of two types
     of direct foreign investment. "American-type" or
     "anti-trade-oriented" emphasizes the growth of firms to
     justify oligopolistic direct foreign investment and
     the domination of world production by giant
     multinationals. The "Japanese-type" or "trade-
     oriented" direct foreign investment proceeds along the
     lines of comparative advantage, contributing to steady
     industrialization and economic development of the host
     country. This book seeks to identify, theoretically
     and practically, these two types of direct foreign
     investment. As a result, this dichotomy will shed
     light on policy implications and recommendations about:
     1. direct foreign investments for developing countries;
     2. investments by an advanced industrialized country in
     another advanced country; 3. investments in resource
     security; and 4. the code of conduct of
     multinational corporations. A macro-economic approach
     is employed, using the theory of the international
     division of labor.

146. Kojima, Kiyoshi. "Giant Multinational Corporations:
     Merits and Defects." Hitotsubashi Journal of
     Economics. 18.2 (Feb. 1978): 1-17.

     An examination is made of real and pseudo economics of
     scale (pseudo such as utilization of tax incentives,

tax havens and other world market imperfections) with
regard to multinational corporation operations. A
comparison is made of the efficiency of multinational
corporations and market integration by independent
trading firms. The role of Japanese trading companies
is studied as an agent tying together Japanese foreign
investments, making Japanese industries multinational-
ized as a group. Suggestions are offered for a code of
conduct for multinational corporation.

147. Kojima, Kiyoshi. "Japanese-Style Direct Foreign
      Investment." Japanese Economic Studies. 14.3
      (Spring 1986): 52-82.

      There is a consideration of the definitions of
      multinational and direct foreign investment, as a
      preliminary approach to the clarification of Japanese-
      style direct foreign investment. Some world trends are
      outlined. Problems in Japan's investment are
      identified. The statistics that are used to track
      direct foreign investment by the Ministry of Finance
      are discussed. There are ties to national interest for
      the Japanese foreign investment, unlike the direct
      investments performed by multinational corporations in
      the U.S. style. Transfer of technology is considered,
      and new forms of foreign investment are discussed.

148. Kojima, Kiyoshi, and Terutomo Ozawa. Japan's General
      Trading Companies; Merchants of Economic Development.
      Development Centre Studies. Paris: Development Centre
      of the Organization for Economic Co-Operation and
      Development, 1984.

      This study examines the overseas investment activities
      of Japan's general trading companies, particularly
      those of the "Top Nine," and pinpoints their major
      characteristics. The goal is to assess the signif-
      icance of the companies on their host countries.
      Investment activities are divided into four major
      areas: trading networks, manufacturing, resource
      development and non-trade service ventures. A
      historical background is also provided, to outline the
      birth and growth of the general trading companies, and
      to characterize their functions. The motive for
      internationalization is uncovered. Included in the
      study are the overseas ventures of the Top Nine trading
      companies and those business activities that are
      closely linked to their overseas investment, such as
      third country intermediation, overseas direct loans and
      plant exports on a turnkey or product-in-hand basis.

149. Kotabe, Masaaki. "Changing Roles of the Sogo Shoshas,
      the Manufacturing Firms, and the MITI in the Context of
      the Japanese 'Trade or Die' Mentality." Columbia
      Journal of World Business. 19.3 (Fall 1984): 33-42.

      The changes and development of Japan's economy in the
      recent period have focused around the relationship
      between the government, the general trading companies,
      and the manufacturing companies. Direct foreign

investment has been either trade oriented or anti-trade oriented, and new trends are the product of many influences. The MITI and the business community worked together harmoniously during the postwar era, until the oil crises came about. Multinationals, protectionism, and the changes in the role of the MITI are explored.

150. Lake, David. "Japan Corporate Finance: The Trading Giants Begin to Compete in Global Finance." Asian Finance. 13.1 (Jan. 15, 1987): 69-72.

Japan's general trading companies (sogo shosha)are emerging as new powers in global finance. They have suffered losses since the 1973 "oil crisis" and their role as providers of capital for Japan's industrial growth is outdated. The sogo shosha now must rely on zaiteku techniques to rebuild profitability. Shosha money managers deal in options and warrants using complicated asset swap techniques to capture good spreads. The risk assumed by zaiteku practices is less than that involved in the trading houses' financing of Third World development. To supplement their financial techniques and their zaiteku market plays, trading houses are turning to joint ventures and mergers and acquisitions. The sogo shosha recognize their role in improving the Japanese economy and help remove worldwide protectionist barriers.

151. Matsumura, Shigeya. "The Sogoshosha; A Challenge for International Trade." LTCB Research; Quarterly Review of Japanese Industry. 53 (May/June 1982): 1-8.

The sogo shosha have an important role in the Japanese economy, with a significant part to play in the import and export departments. The trend toward increasing business overseas is documented. The framework in general in which the sogo shosha operate overseas is outlined. The prospect for increased foreign activity is described. Statistics are offered from 1960-1980.

152. McAbee, Michael K. "Japanese Firms Shun Multinational Approach." Chemical & Engineering News. 51.29 (July 16, 1973): 8-9.

The Japanese removed the restrictions on exporting capital in the early 1970's, and the results were a dramatic increase in foreign investment. In 1970 the amount was $913 million. Tax and finance advantages accrue to those promoting exports. The use of multinationals however, should be reduced, according to this Japanese study released by Sanwa Bank. The corporate structure of the multinational is said to be growing obsolete, and the joint venture approach is preferred. The reasons are discussed.

153. Misawa, Mitsuru. "A Japanese Perspective - Is Worldwide Unitary Taxation Fair?" Sloan Management Review. 26.2 (Winter 1985): 51-55.

Approaches to the taxation of multinationals are

discussed. The proposal of many U.S. states for
worldwide unitary taxes would allow the earnings of the
corporation to be considered in total, no matter where
that income was generated. This would drastically
alter the tax base and increase tax owed by Japanese
firms' operations in the U.S. There are problems with
jurisdiction, and conflicts in the principles of
taxation, as well as procedural difficulties with this
proposal. The water's-edge approach, which is proposed
by the U.S. Treasury Department task force, would give
another taxation concept. In this one, the income
earned in other locations would only become taxable by
a particular locality under special conditions. This
alternative is supported, with refinements, as a fair
way of dealing with many of the multinationals.

154. Momigliano, Franco; Balcet, Giovanni. "Patterns of
     Multinational Enterprise and Old and New Forms of
     Foreign Involvement of the Firm." Economic Notes.
     3 (1983): 42-68.

     This is a study of the patterns of international
     organization taking place within Japanese and German
     firms. These are shown to differ from the model which
     U.S. multinationals follow. Theories of the
     multinational are assessed, and shown to miss some of
     the Japanese and German features. The various new
     forms of foreign investment, as alternatives to export
     and majority-owned investment are explored. There is
     also consideration of the need of a model which can
     cope with the changes now underway. A need for
     critique of the Japanese school and the Reading school
     theories is expressed.

155. Negandhi, Anant R. "Management Strategies and Policies
     of American, German and Japanese Multinational
     Corporations." Management Japan. 18.1 (Spring
     1985): 12-20.

     The U.S. multinational corporation (MNC) has evolved
     from a simple export department to a transnational
     enterprise structure. Similar developments are
     expected for European and Japanese MNCs. Important
     aspects of global rationalization and its impact on
     organizational relationships are examined. Subsid-
     iaries of 158 manufacturing MNCs and their respective
     39 headquarters were studied. In addition, interviews
     were conducted with the chief executive officers and
     other managers from all participating companies. The
     levels of formalization in the MNCs were analyzed by
     assessing subsidiary dependence on their headquarters.
     Organizational control processes were studied through
     ownership policies, technological transfer policies,
     intracompany sales and purchases, and other items. The
     results show a tension between centralization and a
     strategy of global rationalization.

156. Negandhi, Anant R., Golpira S. Eshghi, and Edith
     C. Yuen. "The Management Practices of Japanese
     Subsidiaries Overseas." California Management Review.

27.4 (Summer 1985): 93-105.

This study of Japanese management problems with
overseas subsidiaries is based on empirical studies
undertaken from 1968-1984. The major management
problems of Japanese subsidiaries include 1. highly
centralized decision making, 2. low levels of
confidence in subordinate abilities and a lack of trust
in local managers, 3. limited promotion of local
managers, 4. lack of a clear human resource policy, and
5. difficulty dealing with unions and complying with
equal employment rules, particularly in industrial
countries. Japanese subsidiaries have developed
effective production operations and good relations with
host government. Findings also indicate that Japanese
management methods may be of questionable value in
other societies.

157. Negandhi, Anant R., and Martin Welge. Beyond Theory
     Z: Global Rationalization Strategies of American,
     German and Japanese Multinational Companies. Advances
     in International Comparative Management. Supplement.
     Greenwich, Conn.: Jai Press, 1984.

This study examines the organizational strategies,
structures, control processes, and decision-making
aspects in American, German, and Japanese multinational
companies. The means with which these strategies are
accepted and responded to in each country are outlined.
Various environmental demands from both home and host
countries are also described. The early promise of
multinational business as the harbinger of a better
world has given way to new realities: stagnation,
decline, stabilization,and lowering of expectations in
most of the countries around the world. The impact of
global rationalization processes is observed in the
relations between headquarters and subsidiaries within
multinational firms, as well as the relations between
companies and nations. Implications and possible
policy alternatives are offered.

158. Ozawa, Terutomo. "The Emergence of Japan's
     Multinationalism: Patterns and Competitiveness."
     Asian Survey. 15.12 (Dec. 1975): 1036-1053.

An overview of Japan's direct foreign investments is
presented for 1951/61 and 1962-74 with distribution
given by industrial sector and region. Sectoral
distribution within different regions is also outlined.
Competitiveness, profitability, and major characteristics of Japanese multinationals are discussed.

159. Ozawa, Terutomo. Multinationalism, Japanese Style;
     The Political Economy of Outward Dependency.
     Princeton, N.J.: Princeton University Press, 1979.

This book undertakes to explore some of the common
hypotheses about multinational business. Issues
include the American experience as a precursor to the
multinational phase of economics, and the roles of

government and market forces in shaping decisions to
invest abroad. There are also observations as to how
heavily the attitudes of host countries are affected by
political, cultural, and other local attributes of
multinational businesses. The analysis is related to
existing theories of direct foreign investment.

160. Ozawa, Terutomo. "Peculiarities of Japan's
     Multinationalism: Facts and Theories." Banca
     Nazionale del Lavoro. Quarterly Review. 115 (Dec.
     1975): 404-426.

     Patterns and competitiveness of Japan's multinationals,
     by region and industry are covered in this article. It
     presents the distribution of Japanese direct foreign
     investment by sector and by region, giving rate of
     return on sales of overseas ventures. The relevance of
     Western theories as applied to the Japanese case are
     analyzed with attention paid to the industrial organ-
     ization and product cycle approaches. In addition,
     monetary aspect of the phenomenon of direct foreign
     investment are examined.

161. Prindl, Andreas R. "The Coming Japanese Multinational
     Borrower." Euromoney. (Sept. 1977): 65+.

     Foreign direct investment by Japanese firms may grow $8
     billion a year between now and 1985. Most of that will
     be financed by borrowing on international markets. The
     effect may be the creation of multinational Japanese
     corporations, in the true sense. One of the chief
     characteristics of Japanese firms has been their
     reliance on outside banks, with high debt to equity
     ratios. This trend seems to be reversing, and it could
     bring significant changes in the savings/investment
     conditions in Japan. These patterns are examined and
     analyzed.

162. Reich, Robert B. "The Threat of the Global
     Corporation." Canadian Business. 56.8 (Aug. 1983):
     57-58+.

     The growing number of multinational corporations is a
     major factor in the developing of national industrial
     policies. Two types of multinational corporations are
     discussed. An explanation of methods used by Japanese
     companies to penetrate growing markets in developing
     countries is provided, as well as their marketing
     systems in Europe and the U.S. The operations of some
     American multinationals are analyzed with a prediction
     of long-range results. By 1988, 300 international
     firms will produce 50% of all goods and services, with
     component parts manufactured in various countries. The
     U.S. must face this reality directly, or suffer further
     economic decline.

163. Saso, Mary. "The Roots of Japanese Manufacturing's
     Competitive Edge (Aspects of Japanese Direct Foreign
     Investment)." Multinational Business. 3 (1984): 1-
     13.

This is an analysis of the competitive position of
Japan's multinational manufacturing firms. It is noted
that some industries do not seem as successful as
others. Thus the Japanese competitive edge is not
something that comes about automatically. It is also
clear that the phenomenon of Japanese success cannot be
explained simply in terms of the fluctuations of the
currency. There are genuine differentials in the areas
of quality and productivity. There is a consideration
of the Japanese expenditure for R & D, as well.

164. Sethi, S. Prakash, and Carl Swanson. "How Japanese
Multinationals Skirt Our Civil Rights Laws." Business
& Society Review. 44 (Winter 1983): 46-51.

Direct foreign investment is increasing in the U.S. by
foreign multinational corporations (MNC). The
establishment of manufacturing and other related
operations means greater competition for U.S. firms and
changes in traditions and values, the social structure,
and worker and consumer expectations. These MNC's are
required by the U.S. Treaties of Friendship, Commerce,
and Navigation to follow laws governing employment and
operations. In particular, the Japanese MNC's have
stretched the interpretation of these laws to suit
their needs. This presents a challenge to U.S. courts,
who seek to set rulings promoting long-term equity,
harmony, and productivity in the workplace.

165. Sherwood, Stanley G., Yuji Gomi, and Dean Yoost.
"Japan's New Intercompany Pricing Rules in Light of
Section 482." Tax Management International Journal.
15.10 (Oct. 10, 1986): 373-385.

In March 1986, Japan enacted specific intercompany
pricing rules that apply to Japanese corporations with
foreign affiliates as well as to U.S. and foreign-based
multinationals with Japanese subsidiaries. A review of
the Japanese tax system and the legislative history of
the intercompany pricing legislation illustrates the
problems at which the law is directed. In examining
the new legislation, attention is focused on: 1. its
applicability, 2. the types of transactions covered,
and 3. the method of arm's length price determination.
Japan's National Tax Administration (NTA) will
introduce a confirmation system providing for the
preapproval of a firm's intercompany pricing policies.
The new pricing legislation gives the NTA the authority
to request foreign-based information related to
foreign-affiliated transactions in connection with an
audit. The legislation includes an annual reporting
requirement for companies with foreign-affiliated
transactions.

166. Shinohara, Miyohei. "MITI'S Industrial Policy and
Japanese Industrial Organization: A Retrospective
Evaluation." The Developing Economies. 14.4
(December 1976): 366-380.

Diverging views of the MITI in Japan have been offered,

in which the agency is decried as the monolithic source
of big business conglomeration. This view is
considered in terms of the actual structure of business
groups in Japan. General trading companies and large-
scale mergers are delineated. Policies which tend to
favor the development of "infant" industries are
examined. While the MITI policies are almost
universally considered to run counter to the nation's
anti-monopoly laws, this article advocates their
assessment in a larger perspective, since the MITI
policies are so important for the success of the
present economy.

167. Shoda, Nagahide. "The 'Sogoshosa' and its Functions in
     Direct Foreign Investment." The Developing
     Economies. 14.4 (December 1976): 402-418.

     Characteristics peculiar to the large trading companies
     are delineated. Their foreign trade activities are
     examined. A profile of the overseas investments of the
     trading companies is given, in which it is shown that
     actions differ in various regions of the world.
     Problems they have encountered include changing trends
     in heavy industries, decline of their share of foreign
     trade, failures in the consumer goods markets,
     limitation of the indirect financing function, and the
     developing countries' criticism of
     multinationalization.

168. Takamiya, Susumu, and Keith Thurley, eds. Japan's
     Emerging Multinationals; An International Comparison of
     Policies and Practices. Tokyo: University of Tokyo
     Press, 1985.

     This book aims to elucidate the organizational
     consequences of Japanese overseas investment in full
     context. In part I, there are essays which detail the
     current position of multinational research, with all
     its cultural influences. Then follows a section on the
     European study which Takamiya initiated to test his
     ideas about the effect of Japanese investment on labor
     and personnel policy in the host countries. In part
     III, the authors are concerned with future trends in
     industrial relations. In the U.S., the collaboration
     of American and Japanese labor unions is producing
     interesting results. The changing style of Japanese
     management is also described.

169. Tang, Roger Y. W. Transfer Pricing Practices in the
     United States and Japan. Praeger Special Studies
     Praeger, 1979.

     This book deals with the multinational and domestic
     dimension of transfer pricing. The importance of
     transfer pricing is keen, as it is vital to company
     profits and the evaluation of divisional performances.
     This work offers heavy statistical information on
     Japanese transfer pricing activities, to correlate with
     the many theoretical efforts to elucidate the subject.
     The ultimate goal of the book is to provide a

comparison of the transfer pricing practices of large
firms in Japan and the U.S., in order to offer some
indications of the merits of the different philosophies
used in the making of these decisions.

170. Trevor, Malcolm. Japan's Reluctant Multinationals:
Japanese Management at Home and Abroad. New York: St.
Martin's Press, 1983.

This is a review of Japanese management practices both
domestically and abroad. Different approaches to
Japanese management and a concept of multinationalization are identified. A contrast with Western
management practices is offered. Key areas of
management activity, such as decision-making, are then
outlined. The application of Japanese management in
Britain is described. The data examined were gathered
in interview processes.

171. Tsurumi, Yoshihara. The Japanese Are Coming; A
Multinational Interaction of Firms and Politics.
Cambridge, Mass.: Ballinger Publishing Co., 1976.

This work begins with the belief that the rapid
increase in multinationalism for Japanese firms has
indicated Japan's success in adapting to changing
conditions, and the conditions of today imply still
further need for change. Topics are considered, such
as the rise in Japanese investments, the need for
natural resources, the position of manufacturing firms
abroad, the penetration of the U.S., and the role of
the large trading companies. The possibility of the
rise in Japanese multinational banks is also treated.
Transfer of technology and the quest for majority
ownership are investigated. The Japanese corporate
culture and attitudes toward the Japanese overseas are
also described. General conclusions are offered.

172. Tsurumi, Yoshihara. Multinational Management:
Business Strategy and Government Policy. 2nd. ed.
Cambridge, Mass.: Ballinger, 1984.

A complete revision and update of the 1977 work, this
textbook offers a comparative treatment of Japanese and
American business practices in managing international
firms. It is built around a dynamic theory of
international trade and investment often referred to as
the product life cycle theory, as this has proved
useful in the author's teaching and research. Key
concepts treated include an evolutionary pattern of
activity for any given firm, which includes trading
activities, management of manufacturing and service
investments in foreign countries, and divestiture of
given foreign operations.

173. Tsurumi, Yoshihara, and Rebecca Tsurumi. Sogoshosha;
Engines of Export-Based Growth. Montreal: Institute
for Research on Public Policy (Distributed by
Renouf/USA), 1980.

This is a description of the large trading companies of
Japan which includes a history and a profile of their
current operations. The internal workings, current
problems and survival strategies are examined. The
potential for them to contribute to U.S. and Canadian
development and trade is assessed, and models for
"sogososha" for U.S. and Canadian firms are outlined.
The ability of the large trading companies to use
specialized market knowledge, an ability to make deals
which interlock, and the introduction of small and
medium sized firms to foreign trade are described.

174. Tung, Rosalie L. "Human Resource Planning in Japanese
     Multinationals: A Model for U.S. Firms?" Journal of
     International Business Studies. 15.2 (Fall 1984):
     139-149.

     The role of human resources in the efficient operation
     of a multinational corporation is a major component of
     its success, along with technology, capital, and
     knowledge. Human resources makes possible the effect-
     ive utilization or transference of other resources from
     corporate headquarters to worldwide subsidiaries. The
     author sees a need to devote more effort to human
     resource planning as part of the firm's planning and
     control process. A contrast is made between U.S. and
     Japanese multinationals human resource development
     programs. The Japanese tend to give overseas transfers
     to managers, who adjust well to their new environments,
     while U.S. corporations tend to believe that successful
     domestic managers will be successful in a foreign
     country. U.S. failure rates are high, and the
     implications for U.S. multinationals are discussed.

175. Tung, Rosalie L. "Selection and Training Procedures of
     U.S., European, and Japanese Multinationals."
     California Management Review. 25.1 (Fall 1982): 57-
     71.

     A survey was recently made of U.S., West European, and
     Japanese multinationals to study their respective
     policies and practices in selecting and training
     personnel for overseas assignments. Among the areas
     questioned were: 1. the extent to which affiliates are
     staffed by parent country nationals, 2. the criteria
     used for choosing personnel for various overseas
     assignments, 3. training programs used for candidates,
     and 4. the failure rate and the underlying reasons for
     failure. Generally, the more rigorous the selection
     and training procedures used, the better the
     performance of the expatriate tended to be in a foreign
     setting. In the U.S. sample, the family situation and
     relational abilities were found to be significantly
     related to good performance abroad. The high rate of
     failure of U.S. managers abroad indicates that
     multinationals need to use more host-country nationals.
     The U.S. and West European data tend to support the use
     of a contingency model for a training paradigm. This
     study contends that no one selection criterion or
     training program should be used.

176. Vargas, Allen H. "The Role of Trading Companies in
     Stimulating Exports." South Dakota Business Review.
     42.4 (June 1984): 1-2, 4-7.

     The early history of the trading company is reviewed,
     tracing Japanese trading companies to the mid-19th
     century. Japan's modern trading companies are the
     world's largest and most successful and are essential
     to Japan's survival. They are highly diversified
     multinational businesses, capable of stimulating
     exports. Their close ties to financial institutions
     give them access to capital needed for expansion and
     the ability to direct investments with their suppliers,
     helping them to grow and creating a strong business
     relationship. Japanese trading companies stress the
     long-term, are market oriented, and are beneficial to
     industrial nations at their various stages of
     development.

177. Wiegner, Kathleen K. "Outward Bound." Forbes.
     132.1 (July 4, 1983): 96-99.

     Japan's leading trading companies are having lower
     profits resulting from the world's challenge to
     Japanese exports. Nine trading companies account for
     30% of Japan's GNP. Mitsubishi Corp. and C. Itoh & Co.
     Ltd are among these firms and are quite adaptable.
     Foreign investments are now being made directly by
     Japanese manufacturers, and less so by trading
     companies. In addition, exports like steel and
     petrochemicals, once handled by traders, are being
     eliminated from export plans. The cost of skilled
     manpower keeps rising, while profits have not. To
     counter this trend, the trading companies are
     attempting to become Japan's first multinationals.
     They have increased direct foreign investments, have
     become major equity partners in production and natural
     resource development, and are increasing third-country
     deals not involving Japan. Trading companies are
     highly skilled and particularly suited for the
     increasing role of services and flexibility in the
     world economy.

178. Yonekawa, Shinichi, and Hideki Yoshihara. Business
     History of General Trading Companies. The
     International Conference on Business History 13.
     Tokyo: University of Tokyo Press, 1987.

     These are essays which deal with management of the
     British, French, German, and Japanese merchant firms
     which specialize in international trade. In Japan the
     general trading companies have a long history. They
     were established under governmental initiative. The
     course of events for various companies is traced.

179. Yoshihara, Kunio. Sogo Shosha; The Vanguard of the
     Japanese Economy. Oxford: Oxford University Press,
     1982.

     In the need to link small and medium-sized companies to

the export market, sogo shosha organization has been of
great interest to industrial countries. Developing
nations also see the structure as useful, as it helps
to bring foreign trade which has been dominated by
foreign companies under their own control. This unique
phenomenon, which is quintessentially Japanese, is here
studied in detail. The size, influence and rationale
for sogo shosha are analyzed. The need for them in the
Japanese context is explored. The role they played in
industrialization is examined. Their importance as
intermediaries is outlined. Their human relations
impact is detailed, and their political ramifications
explored.

180. Yoshino, Michael Y. Japan's Multinational
     Enterprises. Cambridge, Mass.: Harvard University
     Press, 1976.

     This book presents the Japanese version of the
     multinationalizing trend in business evolution.
     Elements particular to the Japanese process are
     isolated and analyzed in their historical setting. The
     evolution of Japan's oil industry is reviewed with its
     overseas ventures and government involvement. The
     spread of manufacturing into developing and advanced
     countries is discussed as well as investments in the
     U.S., Japanese trading companies, and Japan's
     strategies toward foreign direct investment. The
     manufacturing firm is analyzed in terms of its
     international divisions, its changing strategies, and
     ownership policies, and is seen to be converging with
     its American counterpart. In the area of management,
     the Japanese and American methods and practices are
     distinctly different.

181. Yoshino, Michael Y., and Thomas B. Lifson. The
     Invisible Link; Japan's Sogo Shosha and the
     Organization of Trade. Cambridge, Mass.: M.I.T.
     Press, 1986.

     This book studies the sogo shosha (trading companies)
     as a Japanese business institution. Topics discussed
     include the historical evolution of sogo shosha, their
     distinctive capabilities and economic function, and the
     types and dynamics of competitions they face. The
     internal workings of these trading companies are also
     explored. A number of organizational managerial
     aspects and practices are covered: organizational
     structures, administrative processes, human resource
     systems, career patterns, the use of interpersonal
     networks as a primary channel and tool of management,
     interunit coordination, and interfirm coordination. A
     look is taken at the challenges facing the sogo shosha
     in the modern Japanese economy and society.

182. Yoshitomi, M., I. Ozaki, M. Shinohara, et al. "Major
     Aspects of Japanese Economy in the Mid-Seventies."
     The Developing Economies. 14.4 (Dec. 1976): 319-486.

     This issue contains essays on major aspects of the

Japanese economy. Included are papers by M. Yoshitomi on the oil crises and the Japanese transition to medium growth path; I. Ozaki on industrial structure and employment, 1955-68; M. Shinohara on industrial policy and industrial organization; Y. Miyazaki on big corporations and business groups; N. Shioda on the ten leading trading companies of Japan (sogo shosha) and its functions in direct foreign investment; T. Ogura on the declining food self-sufficiency; S. Jinushi on life cycle planning for social welfare;. and S. Tanaka on anti-pollution measures.

183. Young, Alexander K. The Sogo Shosha: Japan's Multinational Trading Companies. Boulder, Co.: Westview Press, 1979.

Japan's multinational trading companies are analyzed. Their business methods, sales and profit trends, strategies, national influence, and future prospects are described. The structural characteristics of these multinationals are outlined, in contrast to the prewar structures and to Western multinationals. The role of these multinationals in Japan is explained as importers of food, raw materials, and equipment, and as exporters of Japan's goods. They are important as a force behind Japan's economic system, because they are influencing the distribution of goods domestically and they make investments in international natural resource development programs.

FOREIGN AID

184. "The 1975 White Paper on the Current State and Problems of Japan's Economic Cooperation." News from MITI. 83 (Jan. 16, 1976): 1-45.

An overview of Japanese foreign aid is presented, detailing the significance of economic cooperation for Japan. It explores the problems Japan faces and the hurdles to be overcome to move closer to ideal economic cooperation. Developments in the area of technical cooperation are discussed. A survey is given of the flow of financial resources to developing countries and multilateral agencies.

185. Akira, Kubota. "Foreign Aid: Giving with One Hand?" Japan Quarterly. 32.2 (April/June 1985): 140-144.

This article considers the political and strategic aspects of Japan's Official Development Aid program. Some instances of discontent among ASEAN recipient countries are described. Recommendations for Japan to correct the situation include opening its markets to foreign primary goods, transferring the production of some of the industrial goods needed in Japan to the developing nations, and refraining from blocking the rapidly increasing imports from these nations.

186. Clause, A. W., S. Shahid Husain, J. Pramar, et al.

"World Bank '82." <u>Far Eastern Economic Review</u>. 117
(Sept. 3, 1982): 49-63.

This article sheds light on the World Bank's activities
in the fiscal year 1982. Subjects covered include
loans, credits, co-financing, and borrowing. There is
a detailed accounting of the developmental aid that
Japan has been transferring to its Asian neighbors.
This branches out into a discussion of the World Bank's
role in Asia. The operations of the I.F.C. during 1982
are summarized. There is a survey of the effect of
foreign aid on such countries as Thailand, Indonesia,
and Korea.

187. "Development Aid: Another Year of Disappointing
Results." <u>OECD (Organization for Economic Cooperation
and Development) Observer</u>. 93 (July 1978): 19-22.

Most of the nations offering development aid are
showing lower ODA/GNP ratios. These declining rates of
aid are a disappointment. The article analyzes the
participation of various countries, with emphasis on
aid from western Europe, Canada, the United States and
Japan. The view is presented that the broad human
needs objectives which the developing nations are
pursuing cannot be met unless the aid levels are
increased dramatically.

188. "Economic Cooperation." <u>Technocrat</u>. 12.2 (Feb. 1979):
3-6.

This article provides an overview of Japanese economic
cooperation for the 1973-1977 period. It describes
official development assistance in the context of trade
between Japan and developing countries. Japan's
assistance is ranked internationally.

189. "Flow of Japanese Funds into Developing Countries
during 1976." <u>News from MITI</u>. 135 (July 13, 1977):
1-6.

Data is presented on net payments made by Japan to
developing countries for official development
assistance during 1976. Also provided are other
official and private flows such as direct investments.
The terms and conditions for this assistance are
described.

190. "Flow of Resources from Japan to Developing Countries
during 1977." <u>News from MITI</u>. 172 (July 19, 1978):
1-6.

An account of Japan's net flow of resources to
developing countries for official development
assistance is given for 1977. In addition, other
official and private flows, such as direct investments,
are provided. Terms and conditions of this assistance
is described.

191. "Foreign Aid at a Turning Point." <u>Oriental Economist</u>.

42.761 (March 1974): 8-11.

This article summarizes Japan's "Economic Aid White
Paper." This paper outlines the course to be followed
in providing economic aid to less-developed countries
on account of changes in the world situation. The
policy is in line with the modification of the position
taken by all the industrial countries.

192. A Guide to Japan's Aid. Tokyo: Association for
Promotion of International Cooperation, 1982.

This guide was prepared under the direction of the
Japanese Ministry of Foreign Affairs. It aims at
making known the actual status of Japan's economic
cooperation, especially Official Development
Assistance, and presenting an accurate explanation of
its significance and mechanism. Detailed material is
presented for grant aid, technical cooperation, and
loan assistance. Additional coverage is provided for
economic aid on a non-governmental basis.

193. Holbik, K. "Economic Growth and Foreign Aid." Inter
Economics. 10 (Oct. 1973): 307-310.

Economic growth and foreign aid are placed in the
context of industrial production, GNP, exports,
imports, and international reserves. An overview of
the commodity composition and the geographic
composition of foreign trade is present. In
particular, recent trends in Japan's Far East trade is
discussed with a look at the flow of resources to less
developed countries in the form of development aid.

194. Holtham, G. "A Rising Sum, Japanese Resource Flows to
LDCs." Overseas Development Institute Review. 1
(March/April, 1974): 38-55.

Japan is the second most important national supplier of
financial resources, behind the U.S. Japan's aid
programs are discussed and official development
assistance is covered for the 1966-1972 period. Terms
of aid are described with geographical and sectoral
distribution of aid provided. In addition,
multilateral aid, private foreign investment, and
Japan's generalized system of preferences are
discussed.

195. International Bank for Reconstruction and Development.
The World Bank Group and Japan. Washington, D.C.:
IBRD, 1967.

Japan has been expanding rapidly its role as a major
supplier of aid to developing countries. This pamphlet
explores Japan's current position as a leader among the
Bank member nations which provide the bulk of financial
and technical assistance to less developed nations and
whose cooperation the Bank must draw as an international development agency. A second part is
concerned with Japan's recent position as a substantial

user of development assistance channeled through the
World Bank into key sectors of the Japanese economy.

196. Japan. Ministry of Foreign Affairs. Japan's Economic
     Cooperation. Tokyo: Ministry of Foreign Affairs,
     Japan, 1975.

     This pamphlet provides a statement of Japan's
     commitment to international economic assistance and
     brief history of it. It primarily focuses on Japan's
     performance for 1973. Grants, loans, export credit,
     and direct investments are discussed under three
     separate headings: official development assistance,
     other official flows, and private flows. This is
     followed by characteristics and trends, which examines
     the rapid growth of volume, technical cooperation,
     geographical distribution, multilateral assistance and
     other factors. The executing agencies and mechanisms
     involved in economic cooperation are described. The
     recent changes in the international economic situation
     - oil crisis, commodity problems, and food shortages -
     require the exploration of a new system of inter-
     national cooperation and promotion of assistance to the
     developing countries.

197. "Japan; In Aid of Developing Countries." Pakistan and
     Gulf Economist. 2.18 (April 30, 1983): 48-54.

     An outline is presented of the forms, amount and
     expansion of the Japanese economic and technical
     cooperation to contribute to the assistance to
     developing countries. Special attention is given to
     the Official Development Assistance, particularly
     grants, loans, other capital flows. Forms of technical
     cooperation include dispatch of experts, provision of
     machinery and equipment, and involvement in projects.
     The functioning of agencies and other organizations
     involved are described. Prospects and policy for
     expansion are discussed. Statistics given for 1967-
     1980.

198. Japan's Economic Co-operation with Developing Nations.
     1967.

     This pamphlet is concerned problems of the North-South
     issue and the economic relations and cooperation
     between advanced and developing countries. Japan's
     economic cooperation is the focus. Japanese economic
     cooperation with the developing nations can be broadly
     classified into bilateral and multilateral relations.
     Bilateral aid consists of grants, which include
     technical assistance, governmental loans, private
     overseas investments, export credits, and the develop-
     ment of foreign resources by a product-sharing formula.
     Multilateral economic assistance is administered
     through international financial institutions (World
     Bank,) U.N. organizations, or country groups estab-
     lished to assist developing countries.

199. Kinoshita, Masaaki. "Japan's Program to Aid Water

Supply Development in the Third World." <u>Business
Japan</u>. 32.10 (Oct. 1987): 85-89.

The years 1981-1990 were declared the International
Drinking Water Supply and Sanitation Decade by the U.N.
Japan's Ministry of Health and Welfare has supported
technical and financial aid to upgrade water supplies
in various countries. Japan subsidized 14 projects to
begin water supply systems and to develop urban
cleansing services in the Peoples' Republic of China,
Bangladesh, the Philippines, Sudan, Togo, and Somalia.
By June 1, 1987, Japan had 14 specialists overseas in
Asia and Africa also receives foreign trainees. Large-
scale training centers in developing nations are
expected to occur with substantial technology transfer.
Around 5% of Japan's Official Development Assistance
(ODA) goes to water supply projects, but due to the
language barrier and other reasons, ODA has not been
handled appropriately.

200. Mino, Hokaji. "Japan's Aid to Developing Countries."
<u>Business Japan</u>. 28 (Nov. 1983): 38-39.

Japanese aid to developing countries is discussed for
1981-1982 in its various form: technological,
financial, and research and development cooperation.

201. Shinsuke, Samejima. "Can Japan Steer Its Foreign Aid
Policy Clear of Militarism?" <u>Japan Quarterly</u>. 29.1
(January 1982): 30-38.

While Japan's foreign aid policy has been aimed at non-
military purposes, there are pressures which tend to
steer it toward such considerations. Some of the
issues are explored. There is no statutory regulation
for aid in Japan, but the Prime Minister has said that
its principle is the stabilization of livelihood and
welfare of the people of the recipient countries.
Ambiguity in the government's pronouncements remains
the rule. U.S. diplomacy favors non-military use of
Japanese aid. Some Japanese critics argue that
Japanese aid is being used as a tool of the U.S. in its
foreign policy. Two cases are presented in a detailed
form, Thailand and South Korea.

202. Suzuki, Shigeru. "Japan Contributes to World Health
Through Waterworks Aid." <u>Business Japan</u>. 30.7 (July
1985): 89-107.

Since the U.N. declared International Drinking Water
Supply and Sanitation Decade in 1981, Japan has
steadily increased its number of cooperative waterworks
projects in underdeveloped countries. In the first
four years, Japan has sent short- and long-term
specialists to work on these projects, as well as
training personnel in waterworks. The Japanese have so
far given 21.7 billion yen for 32 cases, primarily
providing assistance to the least developed countries.
Examples are given for Burmese cities and Lima, Peru.
Continued aid needs to be provided by Japan to secure

daily water supplies for household use and self-
dependency in waterworks management.

203. White, John. <u>Japanese Aid</u>. London: Overseas
     Development Institute Ltd., 1964.

     This is a description of the Japanese aid program. It
     investigates the origins and motives, and gives an
     account of the government mechanisms involved in
     administering aid. Some details are offered of the
     Economic Planning Agency, and the Ministry of
     International Trade and Industry, as well as the
     Overseas Economic Co-operation Fund and others. The
     conclusion is that Japan's program has considerable
     merit, and while other donor nations have offered
     criticisms, it stands on its own. Some possibilities
     for improvement of the program could be seen, however.

204. Woronoff, Jon. "Japan's Money Starts to Talk." <u>Asian
     Business</u>. 23.7 (July 1987): 44, 46.

     Japan is now the second largest contributor to the
     World Bank, and shortly to become the bank's second
     largest shareholder with 6.5% of total shares. U.S.
     shareholding will be reduced, but bank members have
     agreed that the U.S. should retain its veto power.
     Japan has opened its capital market to the bank and has
     interceded in the International Development Assoc-
     iation's 8th replenishment of funds. The World Bank in
     return is recruiting and promoting more Japanese
     personnel. Japan is using its influence to promote the
     interest of other Asian countries. These are signs
     that Japan is becoming more deeply committed to inter-
     national cooperation, even though its Overseas Economic
     Co-operation Fund competes with the International
     Development Association.

205. Yasutomo, Dennis T. <u>The Manner of Giving; Strategic
     Aid and Japanese Foreign Policy</u>. Columbia University
     East Asian Institute Studies. Lexington, Mass.:
     Lexington Books, 1986.

     This volume treats the use of strategic aid as a
     component of economic policy alongside direct foreign
     investment. It is discussed in terms of overall
     Japanese foreign policy, then as concept. The policy
     implications of strategic aid are examined. There
     follows a discussion of the limitations of strategic
     aid, particularly in terms of the ambiguity it creates.
     The tendencies toward globalism and regionalism are
     outlined, and a review of the "legacy" of strategic aid
     complete the volume.

INDUSTRY STUDIES

206. Ajima, Yukuo. "Electronic Makers Move Offshore."
     <u>Economic Eye</u>. 7 (Dec. 1986): 21-24.

     This article discusses problems related to Japanese

investment in overseas electric machinery and
electronics industry facilities. A table provides
information on the distribution of overseas
subsidiaries of electrical manufacturers by area and
type.

207. Aoki, R. "Overseas Investment of Japanese Paper
Companies." LTCB Research; Quarterly Review of
Japanese Industry. 44 (Jan./Feb. 1981): 6-8.

This article examines the factors influencing Japan's
international competitiveness in the paper and pulp
industry. It looks at the overseas investment
activities of Japan's paper companies and the impact
overseas production will have on the domestic supply
system.

208. Celarier, Michelle. "The New Japanese Imperialism."
United States Banker. 98.10 (Oct. 1987): 12-19.

The ever-strengthening Japanese yen and the
deregulation of the country's capital markets has
caused an increase in "Zaitech," a hybrid Japanese and
English word meaning financial speculation. Japan's
extreme wealth, which carries its own peculiar
problems, has caused a decline in industrial
corporations and a gain in currency speculation and
stock market activity. The country's interest in
global capital markets is exemplified by its $180-
billion-per-year Eurobond market lead. With $12
billion invested in U.S. junk bonds, Japanese banks are
now the world's largest lenders, but their returns are
low. Some observers fear that the most vulnerable part
of Japan's financial system is the stock market,
dominated by 4 securities firms. Charts and graphs
illustrate these points, and that in 1986, Japan had a
net capital outflow of $100 billion, mostly into U.S.
government securities.

209. Chowdhury, Amitabha. "Tokyo Races Towards Yet Another
Big-League Trophy; Banks Emerge Fitter from
Rationalization." Asian Finance. 12.5 (May 15,
1986): 19-24.

Tokyo seems to be advancing to the position of world's
third largest financial center, behind New York and
London. Japan's $56.9 billion in total capital
exports, $15 billion in net capital inflows through
issuance of securities abroad, $17 billion in net
outflows via loans and trade credit, and $5.9 billion
in direct investment abroad support this. Government
financial liberalization and the possibilities of a
global role for the yen have inspired money managers.
Japan has maintained sound stock market standing,
profits and growth, which has dispelled the 1983 scare
of Japanese City Banks from the effects of interest
rate deregulation and shrinking corporate loan demand.
They, plus regional and sogo (rural) banks have
successfully changed their cost structure and reduced
the ratio of operating costs to deposits quite well.

210. Curtin, Donal. "Japanese International Finance; A
     Better Lubricant than Oil." Euromoney. (March
     1984): 159-173.

     Japanese banks will take a dominant share of new
     international lending with Japan's continuing trade
     surplus. Two events in 1983 indicate this direct: 1.
     Fuji Bank outbid Security Pacific National Bank for two
     commercial finance subsidiaries of Walter E. Heller
     International Corp. and 2. Mitsubishi Bank held off
     Wells Fargo in the bidding, and succeeded in taking
     over BanCal TriState Corp., parent of Bank of Califor-
     nia. In addition, Japanese banks are strengthening
     their involvement in syndicated loan operations.
     Japanese banks are internationalizing on account of the
     slow growth of the domestic banking marketing and
     greater competition from other financial institutions.
     The leading Japanese banks are setting up operations to
     enter the Eurobond business; banks and brokerages will
     gain from new rules liberalizing overseas bond issues
     by Japanese entities from April 1984.

211. Dirks, H. "Japan Ups Investment Overseas to Diversify
     Food Sources." Foreign Agriculture. 12.36
     (Sept. 9, 1974): 7-11.

     Japan's strategy for diversifying food import sources
     and gaining access to new food supplies is discussed.
     This will entail greater emphasis on technical aid and
     capital investment abroad.

212. "Future Plans for Petrochemicals." Focus Japan. 2.7
     (July 1975): 12-14.

     This is a study of Japan's most important foreign
     products in the petrochemical industry. The country of
     origin, the role of Japanese participants, and an
     itemization of particular products are discussed. The
     costs and status of each is also analyzed.

213. Hagura, N., A. R. Prindl, S. Sakata, et al. "Japan - A
     Survey on International Banking." Euromoney. (March
     1978): i-xxiv.

     Contributions are presented on Japanese international
     banking. Included are articles on the involvement of
     Japanese banks in dollar markets, inflation, corporate
     structure, corporate finance practices, international-
     izing of the yen, overseas fund raising by Japanese
     corporations, direct investments abroad, and the yen
     rate.

214. Hashimoto, Sadao. "International Financial Market
     Makes Way for Japanese Banks and Securities Firms."
     Business Japan. 31.5 (May 1986): 31-33.

     The liberalization of international financial
     transactions in Japan is causing Japanese banks and
     securities companies to accelerate their overseas
     markets operations. In addition, it has led to the

promotion of the internationalization of the domestic
market and promotion of a new Euroyen market. The
total amount of foreign bonds issued by the overseas
subsidiaries of Japanese banks and long-term credit
banks reached 4,200 billion yen during 1985, and the
number of cross-border overseas loans by Japanese banks
is on the rise. The increase in overseas securities
investments by the Japanese led to an expansion of the
bond-dealing operations of securities firms in Japan.
The integration of financial markets, the operational
areas of banks and securities firms, and the
internationalization of the Tokyo market are major
factors to consider for shaping future developments.

215. Holden, Ted, and Amy Dunkin. "Japan Is Getting Too
     Small for Dentsu." Business Week
     (Industrial/Technology Edition). 3023 (Oct. 26, 1987):
     62, 66.

     Dentsu Inc., Japan large advertising agency, is being
     forced to seek business overseas. Japanese exporters
     have cut domestic ad spending to reduce cost because of
     the effects of the strong yen. Ad revenue growth in
     Japan has greatly slowed. Dentsu had a previous
     venture with Young & Rubicam Inc, which increased its
     overseas billings from 1% to 7% of its total billings
     over a six-year period. A new venture will include
     Dentsu, Young & Rubicam, and Eurocom (Paris.) The
     venture, called HDM Worldwide, will link 39 cities on
     the 3 continents. Dentsu is behind U.S. agencies that
     have already gained a global foothold. McCann-Erickson
     Worldwide has a network that is triple the size of
     HDM's. In addition, many Japanese exporters have
     relationships with U.S. and European agencies.
     Cultural affiliations may however attract Japanese
     exporters to move their business to Dentsu.

216. "Internationalization of Japan's Consumer Electronics
     Industry." EXIM Review. 1.2 (1980): 3-25.

     The Japanese consumer electronics industry is expanding
     overseas. This article explores the reasons behind
     this expansion and the problems encountered in making
     direct investments for overseas production.

217. "Japan: The Sun Rises Again." InterMarket. 4.7
     (July 1987): 33-48.

     For the fiscal year ending in March 1987, Japanese
     holdings in foreign securities of all types totaled
     $257 billion, up from $145 billion in 1986. On April
     23, 1987, Japan's Ministry of Finance announced
     permission to trade foreign financial futures and
     options. Initially, only securities firms, life
     insurance companies, and banks may trade for their own
     accounts, leaving the issue of brokerage unclear. The
     Long-Term Credit Bank of Japan says it is not planning
     to use futures too actively because it must pay
     margins. Asahi Mutual Life Insurance Co. says that the
     liberalization measure provides another investment

opportunity but the learning process is going to be
slow.

218. "Japan Electronic Industry; Overseas Production Plants
Expected to Account for a Greater Share of Equipment
and Components." Asia Research Bulletin; Monthly
Economic Reports with Political Supplement. 10.5
(Oct. 31, 1980): II 732-3.

The Japanese electronics industry is expected to expand
its overseas investments and production of equipment
and components, relatively increasing its share in
total production. Domestic and foreign production
statistics of consumer electronics are given for 1979
and 1982.

219. "Japan Looks Abroad for Growth." Chemical Week.
129.15 (Oct. 7, 1981): 50-52.

In this discussion of the chemical manufacturers of
Japan, an assessment of the profitability of the
industry is offered. The domestic production of
chemicals has been discouraged by flat profits and
government opposition to increased imports of oil and
oil products used for feed production. These factors
have stimulated greater interest in foreign investment.
Several installations, located in Iran, Canada, and
Malaysia are outlined. The interference of the Iran-
Iraq war with the $4 billion petrochemical complex has
not prevented Japan from exploring other possibilities
in the area. Future trends are discussed.

220. King, Paul. "Japanese Securities Companies: Hot on the
Heels of the Big Four." Euromoney; Japanese
Securities Companies Supplement. (Sept. 1987): 5-7,
14-17.

The top four securities houses of Japan, Nomura, Daiwa,
Nikko, and Yamaichi, are investigated in terms of their
impact on international finance. They emerged during
the late 1980s and each underwent a series of growth
changes. Some of that history is recounted through the
beginning of 1987. The U.S. Treasury market is
dominated by Japanese securities firms, and the firms
have also created other foreign branches. One of the
keys to their influence is their ability to manage
distribution networks, and their protective regulation
advantages. Gains as shown through pre-tax profits
were as high as 86% in 1985-86.

221. Kolenda, T. E. "Japan's Develop-for-Import Policy."
Resources Policy. 11 (Dec. 1985): 257-266.

An examination is made of Japan's overseas investments
in metal and mining production, aimed at filling its
need for imported minerals.

222. Lee, Peter and Gary Evans. "Mergers & Acquisitions:
More Power to the Japanese; Japanese May Nibble, Not
Devour." Euromoney. (Feb. 1988): 76-78.

Facts about the status of Japanese banks and securities firms are offered. By the end of 1987, the top 21 financial institutions were all Japanese. Sumitomo Bank, the largest, has a market value of $58.85 billion. Its earnings are rising and leading European and U.S. firms' market values have decreased. The largest U.S. firms are American Express, J. P. Morgan, and Citicorp, with Salomon Brothers and Merrill Lynch taking lower places in the ranking than they held previously. While the Japanese insist they are not thinking of buying any large institutions, they may consider acquiring small firms which have special niches, such as real estate, leasing, or arbitrage.

223. Lim, Quek Peck. "The Year of the Samurai." Euromoney. (Feb. 1978): 10-15.

This offers an account of the lending activities of major Japanese banks during 1978. The Japanese banking regulations, and the exchange rate changes for the yen are also given consideration. More data is offered for the years 1972-1977.

224. Mendelsohn, M. S. "Japanese Banking's Global Challenge." Banker. 136.722 (April 1986): 46-47.

This analysis shows the role of Japan as an international lender. The Japanese are leading the currency lending based in London, and at the end of September 1985, Japan had outstanding claims of $125 billion as compared with $24 billion on the part of U.S. banks. In certain areas the dollar is used by Japanese securities firms and in others, the main currency is the yen. This flexibility has been significant as a factor in Japanese international investment success.

225. Monroe, Wilbur F. Japan: Financial Markets and the World Economy. New York: Praeger Publishers, Inc., 1973.

This book investigates important topics in the area of the Japanese financial system. The effects of the 1971 international monetary crisis and the exchange market crisis are explored. The role of the Tokyo Foreign Exchange Market is examined. The various financial instruments and their internationalization are studied, including the short-term money markets, bonds, stocks, and government securities. Foreign banks and direct investments in Japan are outlined. Implications of Japanese financial power for the world economy and for the future stability of international relations are assessed.

226. "Nissan Shifts Gear." Economist. 290.7313 (Oct. 29, 1983): 88-89.

This article presents an overview of the development of the Japanese car manufacturer Nissan. It covers production, sales, exports, net profits, and foreign

investments. In addition, Nissan's overseas plants are
discussed with an analysis of Nissan's strategy for the
1980's. Statistics are given for 1962-1982.

227. Ohira, Yasuo, Shigeru Negishi, Teruhisa Yuasa, and
     Shoji Tojo. "Storage Batteries Keep Pace with Widening
     Applications; Battery Maker Shifts Production to Meet
     New-Product Demand; Start Internationalizing Early,
     Says Yuasa Battery President; Demand for Smaller
     Batteries Increasing." Business Japan. 31.10 (Oct.
     1986): 81-87.

     The demand for storage batteries has increased
     dramatically in recent years. Sanyo Electric Co. Ltd
     produces batteries diverse in size with high operating
     temperature reliability and increased energy density.
     Japan Storage Battery has won world recognition for its
     batteries, predominately with lead storage batteries.
     Yuasa Battery Co. Ltd has become the biggest firm in
     world storage battery sector. In 1965, the firm
     created the Great Prosperity 13-Year Plan stressing
     internationalization. Currently, it has 14 factories
     in 13 countries, enabling Yuasa to make a flexible
     response to the critical international situation
     accentuated by the yen's appreciation. The Furukawa
     Battery Co. Ltd. is seeking the market for smaller
     batteries.

228. Oka, S. "A Trend of Japanese Textile Industry 1973-74;
     Overseas Advances." Japan Textile News. 230 (Jan.
     1974): 20, 73-79.

     This is a detailed report with data on all sectors of
     the textile industry. It discusses the industry's
     recovery and rapid improvement, but now sees indications
     of a slowdown. The year 1973 saw impressive changes in
     the foreign trade pattern of textiles with overseas
     investments jumping dramatically. Japanese firms
     operating overseas are covered by area.

229. "Overseas Investment by Japanese Textile Enterprises."
     Japan Textile News. 263 (Oct. 1976): 64-67.

     This article surveys the overseas operation of textile
     firms since the 1960's to the end of March 1975. The
     report is centered on Asia. The overseas investments
     of three major textile affiliated groups are discussed:
     Toray Industries Group, Teijin Group, and Unitika
     Group.

230. Ozawa, Terutomo. "Japan's Resource Dependency and
     Overseas Investment." Journal of World Trade Law.
     11.1 (Jan.-Feb. 1977): 52-73.

     The "oil crisis" of 1973-74 made Japan aware of its
     dependence on imported raw materials. This article
     analyzes the problems of Japan's dependence on overseas
     resources and notes the direction of her recent policy
     on natural resources. It continues then to discuss the
     new characteristics of her overseas investment in

extractive activities.

231. Phalon, Richard. "A Yen for New Markets." <u>Forbes</u>.
     134.15 (Dec. 31, 1984): 46-47.

     The "big 4" Japanese brokerage firms are becoming major
     players in international financial markets. Nomura
     Securities Co., with a net worth of over $2 billion, is
     the world's largest broker. The other major Japanese
     brokers - Daiwa Securities, Yamaichi Securities, and
     Nikko Securities - also had a highly profitable 1984
     because of high trading volume on the Tokyo Stock
     Exchange. The Japanese brokerage firms have helped
     channel money overseas in search of much higher returns
     than are available in Japan. The U.S. investment
     bankers are still dominant in Europe, but the Japanese
     are gaining. The "big 4" are now operating in New
     York, London, Frankfurt, and Zurich, besides their
     traditional outlets of Tokyo, Hong Kong, and Singapore.
     The rest of the world is now calling for an opening of
     Japan's financial markets.

232. "Raw Materials for Japan." <u>Economist</u>. 257.6898
     (Nov. 8, 1975): 80-81.

     Japan has a large need for import of its raw materials.
     The nature and size of this importation is discussed
     for the years 1965 and 1974. Japan's foreign
     investments in steel, aluminum, copper and oil
     production are outlined. There is also a consideration
     of the approved and actual direct investments overseas,
     for the period 1971/72 to 1974/75. The cumulative
     total of direct investments is then analyzed by sector.

233. Saito, Masaru. "Japan's Overseas Resource Development
     Policy." <u>Japanese Economic Studies</u>. 3.4 (Summer
     1975): 38-82.

     Japan's foreign dependency for resources is profiled
     for some of the key raw materials, for the years 1968,
     1970, and 1975. Investments in raw materials indust-
     ries are described by industry and also by region, for
     the period 1951-1969. The drive to stabilize supplies
     is noted, and the policies of the countries supplying
     Japan's resources are also considered. Various develop-
     ment contracts are outlined, and some attention is
     given to the cooperation with other firms and nations.
     Marine resources are also considered.

234. Sato, Takeshi. "The Sword Thrust of Musashi."
     <u>Euromoney</u>. (March 1985): 77-80.

     There has been significant change in the forms that
     foreign leasing, installment selling, and such forms of
     financing may take among Japanese firms. Starting in
     1984, the investment bank's intercession was skipped in
     an arrangement called a Musashi lease. Such trans-
     actions involve fixed rates for about 20 years
     duration. The Ministry of Finance does not consider
     these under their control. The demand for leasing for

such items as office equipment, electronics and
computers, as well as industrial machinery, has been
growing. Competition in the field, however, has kept
the rates of profitability relatively low.

235. "Securities Firms." Oriental Economist. 51.867
     (Jan. 1983): 16-26.

     This study characterizes the typical Japanese
     securities companies. Their locations and investing
     patterns are outlined. Foreign investment in Japanese
     securities is described, as is the Japanese investment
     in the securities of other nations. Foreign bond
     issues by corporations are outlined, by currency of
     transaction. There is an analysis of the business
     performance of fourteen securities houses. Statistics
     are offered for the period 1975-82.

236. Sekine, Fusao. "Special on Camera Industry." Japan
     Economic Journal; International Weekly. 18.920 (Sept.
     9, 1980): 25-29.

     This is a study of the camera industry, detailing
     product line developments and showing the present and
     future prospects of foreign investments. Some long
     range projections are offered, and electronic
     applications are described. Export data is offered for
     the years 1973, 1978, 1985, and 1990 projections.

237. Takeuchi, I. "Japanese Banks Overseas in 1974."
     Euromoney. (April 1975): 63-67.

     A review of Japanese overseas banking operations in
     1974. The articles discusses the international
     monetary situation for the year and the reaction of
     Japanese banks to changing events. An outline is given
     of Japanese banks' foreign networks and affiliation.
     The rate of worldwide expansion by the banks has slowed
     down.

238. Wright, Richard W. and Gunter A. Pauli. The Second
     Wave: Japan's Global Assault on Financial Services.
     European Services Industries Forum 2. New York: St.
     Martin's Press, 1987.

     This book draws together a comprehensive overview of
     the challenges posed to the West by Japan's move to
     become the dominant force in international financial
     services. Background information is offered on the
     dynamics of international financial services. The
     awesome capital surplus position of Japan is traced,
     with analysis of its origin and significance.
     Competitive advantages of Japanese banks are examined.
     The role of deregulation of the financial markets is
     pointed out as a tool of Japanese success. The Second
     Wave is depicted as a challenge with ominous
     implications for the West.

239. Yokoyama, Akinori. "Cosmo Plans Internationalization,
     Strengthens Osaka Market: An Interview with Yasuo

Bunya, President, Cosmo Securities Co., Ltd."
<u>Business Japan</u>. 31.2 (Feb. 1986): 28-29.

Yasuo Bunya, Cosmo Securities Co. Ltd., discusses the
company's response to the internationalization of
Japan's financial and capital markets. In February,
the company's name was changed from Osakaya Securities
Co. Ltd. to Cosmo Securities Co. Ltd., reflecting the
internationalization trend. Cosmo has 4 overseas
branches; of these, London and Hong Kong are locally
incorporated, while New York and Zurich will be locally
incorporated within the year. Cosmos is also
considering establishing more overseas offices.
Currently the company sells mostly Japanese stocks to
foreign investors; soon it will increase the sale of
foreign stocks and bonds to Japanese investors. With
its focus on imports, Cosmo will emphasize intracompany
(domestic) internationalization. While foreign
investors are now selling more than they buy, Bunya
expects that a balance will eventually be achieved.

240. Yoshioka, M. "Overseas Investment by the Japanese
     Textile Industry." <u>The Developing Economies</u>. 17.1
     (March 1979): 3-44.

An overview is given of the development and current
status of overseas investment of Japan's textile
industry. Characteristics of these direct foreign
investments are described with projections of future
trends in the industry. Statistics for Japanese
production are provided for 1952-1977, and for
worldwide production and trade for the years 1963-1974.
Major customers and suppliers are listed. Japan's
textile industry is playing a declining role in the
industrial structure of the Japanese economy.

II

NORTH AND
SOUTH AMERICA

This chapter covers North and South America. It is divided into three sections: Canada, United States, and Latin America. Additional references to individual countries, and to states within the United States, can be found in the Subject Index.

CANADA

241. Bilgin, B. "Japan's Changing Industrial Strategy and Its Implications for Japanese Investment in Canada." Pacific Affairs; An International Review of Asia and the Pacific. 55.2 (Summer 1982): 267-272.

This article is an explanation of the changing industrial structure of today's Japan and what kind of impact these reforms are having on patterns of Japanese import and export trade. There is a discussion of Canada's relationship to the anticipated growth in Japanese foreign investment and how this growth can directly benefit Canada. The issue of joint-venture capital between the two countries is also raised and delved into. There are statistics and data from 1965 to 1985.

242. Ferguson, Jonathan. "Canada: Japanese Intend Rapid Growth." Euromoney; Canada Supplement. (May 1987): 32-34.

Deregulation of Canada's financial services sector should result in rapid growth from foreign banks' consolidation and greater foreign investment. Proposed changes include permitting foreign banks 50% ownership of Canadian investment dealers by June of 1987 and 100% ownership by June of 1988, as well as a lifting of restrictions on cross ownership. This deregulation will be welcomed by Japanese and U.S. banks, which are prevented by domestic regulations from entering the

domestic securities business. Industry observers
predict a wave of large international Japanese banks
applying to establish operations in Canada. Already,
in January of 1987, four new banks with large Japanese
parents opted to set up Canadian operations.

243. Gherson, J. "Japanese Investment in Canada." Foreign
Investment Review. 3.1 (Autumn 1979): 4-7.

This work offers an evaluation of the Japanese
investments in Canada. Loans, minority holdings, and
joint ventures are the various methods of investment
encountered. The geographic distribution of the
Japanese presence in Canada is traced, and investments
are delineated by industrial sector.

244. Gray, Grattan. "Oh What a Feeling." Canadian
Business. 60.2 (Feb. 1987): 82-88.

Cambridge, Ontario, is the site of a new C$400-million
automobile plant for Toyota Motor Corp. Cambridge's
primary gain is employment: 800 in construction,
another 1,000 at the plant by 1988, and perhaps another
10,000 in related parts plants and service companies.
Toyota bought the site for over C$2 million from the
Ontario Land Corp., which had bought it from local
farmers under threat of expropriation. Many people are
seeking work in Cambridge, but some expect the high-
paying jobs will be retained by Japanese. Parts
companies are expanding facilities without contracts
from Toyota. Toyota has promised to reach 60% Canadian
content by the mid-1990s, but Toyota's president says
that Canadians will have to accept his definition of
"local content". Taxpayers will fund Toyota with
C$72.8 million in loans, infrastructure improvements,
and government-funded training.

245. "Japan and Canada Develop an Energy Alliance." World
Business Weekly. 3.49 (Dec. 15, 1980): 14-15.

Giving an overview of the relationship between Japan
and Canada in terms of their energy industries, this
work portrays the natural alliance between Japan, which
is rich in technology but poor in resources, and
Canada, with its reserves of untapped resources. The
various energy industries, from the petrochemical to
the nuclear, are all traced in detail. Japanese
investment in the exploration for oil and gas, the
interest in nuclear power and purchase of reactors, and
other potential trade areas between the two countries
are discussed.

246. "Japan's Overseas Investments: Canada." Oriental
Economist. 47.828 (Oct. 1979): 38-45.

Japan's investments in Canada during 1978 are
described. There is a consideration of the development
of natural resources by Japan, and particular projects
are discussed. The relation of Canada to the induction
of Japanese capital is noted.

247. Kirton, John and Michael Donnelly. "Japanese
     Investment: The Answer for Canada; Alternative to
     U.S.A., a Yen for a Dollar." International
     Perspectives. (March/April 1986): 3-7.

     The era when the U.S. provided Canada with its
     technology and investment capital has passed. Now
     there is a new relationship in which the U.S. no longer
     offers the only source of training and research for
     Canada. U.S. technology products have declined in
     market share throughout the world. Japan has begun to
     emerge rapidly as a leading producer and exporter of
     technology and capital. The article offers some
     practical, low cost proposals for solidifying the
     mutually beneficial relationship between Canada and
     Japan.

248. Kurosawa, Yoh. "Bonds between Canada and Japan."
     Canadian Business. 49.8 (Aug. 1976): 29-31.

     Between 1970 and 1975, Japanese direct investments in
     Canada more that doubled, reaching $440 million.
     Japan's need for raw materials fueled this rapid
     expansion. Japanese overseas investments decline after
     the recession precipitated by the 1974 "oil crisis".
     Large-scale development of overseas natural resources
     is central to the Japanese economy. When investment
     activity regains its former momentum, closer ties are
     expected between Canadian and Japanese governments.
     Private banks will coordinate project financing and
     capital export.

249. Lake, David. "Canada: Japanese Banks Crowd In."
     Euromoney. (Nov. 1985): 141-147.

     Japanese banks are seeking Canadian foreign bank
     status. Six banks have so far entered Canada's
     domestic market; others are waiting. Foreign bank
     status enables them to act for Japanese trade
     corporations, to lend to Canadian companies, and to
     participate in project financing. The Japanese banks
     have encountered some problems arising from their
     reluctance to be involved in the middle market by
     withholding deemed increases. Instead, some banks have
     hired aggressive Canadian credit staffs or promoted
     competitively priced middle market account services.
     The main interest of Japanese banks in Canada remains
     the Japanese trade corporation market. Competition for
     these corporations is complicated by asset ceilings.

250. Pearce, Jean. "Canada Looks Westward to a New
     Relationship with Japan." Business Japan.
     30.11 (Nov. 1985): 30-31.

     These are the comments of Barry Connell Steers,
     Canada's ambassador to Japan, relating to the opening
     of the financial market in Japan and Canada's
     acceptance of increased Japanese investment in Canada.
     Data about Canadian exports to Japan, and Japan's
     exports to Canada are considered, with improvements in

the balance of trade noted. Japan is occupying the
second most important place as foreign investor in
Canada. Problems between the nations are cited. Plans
and developments for increased communication about the
markets and needs in both countries are envisioned, so
that future prospects will include greater cooperation.

251. Ross, Alexander. "Some New Links in the Tokyo
     Connection." <u>Canadian Business</u>. 50.11 (Nov. 1977):
     68-76.

     In this treatment of the Canada-Japan economic
     situation, it is noted that a change occurred with the
     recent oil crisis. Though previously the aim of
     Japanese investment in Canada was a stable source of
     raw materials, Japan now became aware that its economy
     would probably shift to slower growth patterns for the
     future. With that realization, and with the high trade
     surpluses Japan amassed with countries other than
     Canada, certain difficulties have arisen. Some joint
     ventures have developed between the two countries in
     Canada, and the economic relations of Japan and Canada
     are expected to evolve in new ways.

252. "Rough Road Ahead for Toyota in North America."
     <u>Business Japan</u>. 31.3 (March 1986): 14-15.

     Toyota's plans for manufacturing large numbers of autos
     in the U.S. and Canada will have many ramifications.
     These plans include making a total of 300,000 cars in
     North America, some 50,000 of these in a joint venture
     with General Motors. The U.S. operation based in
     Kentucky will invest $800 million and 3,000 workers
     will be employed there. Expansion and competition
     possibilities are discussed. Toyota will meet with a
     tough situation requiring very high quality and low
     cost production techniques. Supplies of smaller cars
     by 1990 may become too large, and this could cause
     problems.

253. Semkow, Brian W. "Japanese Project Financing of
     Canadian Resources." <u>International Financial Law
     Review</u>. 4.2 (Feb. 1985): 18-22.

     There are several projects described which put together
     financing from Japan and from Canadian firms to develop
     Canada's natural resources. Some carefully designed
     legal relationships are outlined, in which the
     Canadians, primarily Canadian oil and gas firms,
     maintain a measure of control over their resources, as
     the Japanese provide necessary financing. Foreign
     ownership restrictions and provincial legislation's
     effects are explained. Case studies of particular
     transactions are offered.

254. Terry, Edith, Leslie Helm, and Maralyn Edid.
     "Asian Auto Makers Find a Back Door to the U.S.
     Market." <u>Business Week (Industrial/Technology Edition)</u>.
     2924 (Dec. 9, 1985): 52-53.

Asian car producers are planning to build plants in
Canada, enabling them to develop production and
marketing strategies similar to those used by U.S.
automakers. Hyundai, the Korean car manufacturer,
chose Bromont, Quebec, as the site for its $220-million
plant. They pledged to hire 1,200 Canadians and to
produce 100,000 cars by 1991. In return Hyundai
received: 1. free land and water, 2. job-training
assistance, 3. discounts on electric power, and 4. help
with financing. Both Honda and Toyota may expand their
parts manufacturing in Canada, helping to meet both
Canadian and U.S. provisions of a 1964 auto pact,
qualifying thereby for duty exemptions. Canadian
manufacturing costs have been cut since 1980, giving
Canada an $8-an-hour labor-cost edge over the U.S.

255. Wright, Richard W. "Investment for Japan: Small but
     Growing Rapidly." CA Magazine. 120.5 (May 1987):
     40-44.

     Japanese direct investments in Canada at the end of
     1988 totaled C$2.1 billion. This represents less than
     2% of total foreign investments in Canada, but Japan's
     Canadian investments in the years 1980-1985 grew by
     260%. Investments are primarily concentrated in
     natural resources, merchandising, and the automotive
     industry. British Columbia and Ontario are major
     benefactors of this investment, although there are
     spill over effects in the other provinces. Japanese
     investments tend not to be risk-taking, and it is not
     certain that these investments will continue to grow.
     The U.S. is a more attractive market for Japanese
     investors. It is recommended that Canada should adopt
     a 2nd-tier investment promotion strategy to attract
     small firms and manufacturers of specialty products.

256. Wright, Richard W. Japanese Business in Canada; The
     Elusive Alliance. Montreal, Quebec: The Institute for
     Research on Public Policy, 1984.

     This study chronicles and analyzes the Japanese
     business presence in Canada. The relationship of the
     two countries is largely complementary, with Japanese
     aims to secure a supply of raw materials matched by
     Canadian willingness to undergo productive development.
     But the fears of foreign intrusion among the Canadians
     do have some significance. Thus after an overview, the
     work treats the aspects of Japanese business in Canada.
     The economic impact on various business sectors is
     assessed. Then intangible effects are traced, noting
     how the financial presence of the Japanese is felt.
     Trends for the future and policy recommendations are
     offered.

257. Wright, Richard W. "Japanese Business in Canada:
     What's in It for Us?" Business Quarterly. 49.1 (Spring
     1984): 31-36.

     By 1982 Canada trade with Japan exceeded C$8 billion,
     however Canada's trade surplus with Japan has declined.

This has resulted from the increase in imports of
Japanese finished goods, while raw material exports
from Canada have risen. It is estimated that Japan has
C$387.6 million invested in Canadian businesses in
1981. Japanese managers see several barriers to
increased investment in Canada, including Canada's
foreign investment screening policies, bureaucratic
controls, and government conflicts. Increased Japanese
involvement in Canada requires more cooperation and
flexibility on both sides.

258. Wright, Richard W. "Japan's Investment in Canada."
     Business Quarterly. 41.2 (Summer 1976): 20- 27.

     Japanese direct investments in Canada are uncertain on
     account of the newly enacted Foreign Investment Review
     Act. Foreign investment in Canada is likely to become
     much more restricted. Japan is interested in investing
     in natural resources, particularly oil and coal.
     Canada will require foreign investors to do more
     processing within its borders. This may entail greater
     Canadian imports to Japan, since processing facilities
     have a long lead time. The alternative for Japanese
     firms is to supply Canadian resource firms with long-
     term loans or to become minority shareholders in these
     firms, thereby avoiding the restrictions of the new
     legislation.

UNITED STATES

259. Abo, Tetsuo. "U.S. Subsidiaries of Japanese Electronic
     Companies Enter a New Phase of Activities: A Report of
     On-the-Spot Observations." Institute of Social Science
     Annals 1984. 26 1985.1-32.

     This is a report on the characteristics and problems of
     four U.S. subsidiaries of Japanese electronic
     companies. Visits were made in 1981 to Toshiba
     America, Inc,; Sharp Manufacturing Co. of America;
     Sanyo Manufacturing Corp.; and Oki Electronics of
     America.

260. Alaska. Division of Economic Enterprise. Japanese
     Investment in Alaska. Juneau: Department of Economic
     Development, Division of Economic Enterprise, 1974.

     This is an analysis of current Japanese investment
     patterns in Alaska. There are many changes noted in
     the last three years. While investments used to be
     centered on natural resources extraction, there is now
     a trend toward investment in hotels, restaurants,
     banking, insurance, securities, and real estate.
     Manufacturing has not been an area of growth. Fishing
     and forest products investments have been important in
     Alaska. Some of the international factors that have
     led to the current level of investment in Alaska are
     identified.

261. "Alumax: Turning Aluminum Capacity Upside Down."

<u>Business Week</u>. (March 6, 1978): 72-4+.

This article discusses the joint venture of Mitsui and
Co., Japan's second largest trading company, and AMAX,
Inc., a small U.S. mining company. Known as ALUMAX,
the joint venture is the largest corporate partnership
between Japan and the U.S. The activities that are
planned appear highly aggressive, even risky. At a
time when others in the field are moving slowly, ALUMAX
is putting forward major investments. It will more
than double its capacity, bringing it to fourth place
from sixth among U.S. producers.

262. Armstrong, Larry, Leslie Helm, James Treece, et al.
      "Toyota's Fast Lane; Frugal, Reclusive Commanders of an
      Industrial Army." <u>Business Week (Industrial/Technology
      Edition)</u>. 2919 (Nov. 4, 1985): 42-46.

Toyota Motor Co. is determined to become the world's
leading automobile company by overtaking General Motors
Corp. Toyota controls 42% of the Japanese market and
currently sells more cars in the U.S. than any other
foreign car manufacturer. The firm has a joint venture
with General Motors to establish a just-in-time
production system in the U.S. and plans to open
manufacturing facilities in the U.S. and Canada.
Toyota City, Japan, is the headquarters of Toyota's
successful just-in-time production. The family
patriarch, Eiji Toyoda, is turning over his power to
Shoichiro Toyoda, who seeks to obtain 10% of the
world's auto market.

263. Arvan, Alice. "Big Bank in the Big Apple." <u>Bankers
      Monthly</u>. 105.1 (Jan. 1988): 40-42.

In this article, a description of the activities of the
Da-Ichi-Kangyo Bank Ltd. is offered. The scope of its
business includes providing assets in sovereign loans
to governments and supplying letters of credit and
municipal participation in public finance for local
governments. The focus on public finance has been a
deliberate strategy, and has made this the world's
largest financial institution. Other activities
include working with Fortune 500 firms and other large
U.S. corporations which are attracted to the Japanese
capital market because of its substantial size.

264. Arvan, Alice. "Class Act in International Banking."
      <u>Bankers Monthly</u>. 105.1 (Jan. 1988): 35-37.

This is a treatment of the business status of Fuji Bank
Ltd. It is the second largest bank, worldwide, with
assets running into the $23 billions as of 1986. Its
major emphasis is on the corporate finance area, and
for the future, it will be developing products for the
large Fortune 500 corporations. One technique is the
acquisition of Walter E. Heller, which gives Fugi the
opportunity to do business with the midsize firms that
form the nucleus of the Heller contacts. As a
subsidiary, the Heller section will be very profit

oriented, even in the competitive lending atmosphere of
today. Expansion and avoidance of risk will be other
key directions.

265. Arvan, Alice. "Wearing Different Hats at Bank of
Tokyo." Bankers Monthly. 105.1 (Jan. 1988): 38-39.

Giving a profile of the Bank of Tokyo, which has a New
York sector worth $16 billion, this article describes
the bank's U.S. direction. The primary focus is on the
corporate market. Real estate construction in the
eastern U.S. and financing for Japanese firms working
in the U.S. are key areas of interest, as well. Though
the bank was recently downgraded by Moody's from AA1 to
AA2, that was based on intense competition in the
bank's core wholesale banking franchise. There will be
a trend toward strengthening its focus areas, and also
some attempt at "broader-based" banking. When the
interstate banking laws are changed, the bank will be
in a good position for taking advantage of the more
open climate.

266. Baxter, John D. "Japanese Set Up Shop in U.S.A. in a
Big Way." Iron Age (Manufacturing Management
Edition). 229.15 (Aug. 1, 1986): 39-45.

Japanese direct investments in the U.S. are on the rise
even though their exports to the U.S. are slacking.
The increase in direct investment, particularly in
manufactures, is attributed to the rising yen,
protectionist sentiments in the U.S., potentially
constructive Japanese government policies, and special
incentives by many U.S. states seeking such
investments. These Japanese investments will create
greater job opportunities and promote technology and
management transfer, along with tougher competition for
U.S. manufacturers. Success of Japanese-owned firms in
the U.S. is linked to emphasis placed on quality,
customer service, good labor/management relations, and
new product development.

267. Beauchamp, Marc. "Buy American." Forbes. 138.7
(Oct. 6, 1986): 74,76.

Suntory Ltd., Japan's leading distiller, seeks more
U.S. businesses to buy. The Japanese market has given
Suntory some problems lately, including: 1. declining
consumption of blended whiskey, 2. liquor taxes
decreasing pre-tax profits, and 3. missing the boom of
shochu, a potent clear liquor. In addition, the
eventual removal of trade restrictions will further
damage domestic profit margins. Suntory has been using
diversification to combat these problems for years,
moving into such areas as beer, wine, soft drinks,
juice drinks, canned and frozen foods, and restaurants.
Currently, foreign operations account for only 5%-6%
of sales. Most of Suntory's U.S. profits come from
Pepcom Industries Inc., a Pepsi-Cola bottling company.
Suntory wants to expand its U.S. soft drink bottling
business, and it may buy a soda line.

268. Beauchamp, Marc. "Japan's Kodak." Forbes. 137.6
     (March 24, 1986): 90-93.

     Konishiroku Photo Industry Co. Ltd. (Japan) has had a
     history of product innovation but now suffers from
     marketing ineptitude. The firm's products have
     included Japan's first commercially produced camera and
     Japan's first X-ray film. However, Konishiroku's
     alliance with Fotomat in the U.S. has created problems.
     Konishiroku bought into Fotomat as a way of entering
     the U.S. market inexpensively. However, Fotomat sales
     declined as its market share dropped. Konishiroku is
     also faltering in the office equipment market in
     Europe, Japan, and the U.S. In the U.S., Konica
     Business Machines USA Inc. must meet strong competition
     from Canon, Sharp, and Xerox. In addition, the
     Konishiroku receive almost half its sales from exports,
     which have been hurt by the yen's appreciation.

269. Beauchamp, Marc, and John Heins. "We'll Send You VCRs
     -- You Send Us Stocks." Forbes. 140.3 (Aug. 10,
     1987): 60-62.

     While Americans may see the current stock market as
     high, Japanese consider these bargain times, with
     investments in U.S. equities expected to reach $20
     billion this year. In Tokyo, stocks trade at 70 times
     earnings; in the U.S., about 20 times earnings. Partly
     due to the Japanese government's recent move permitting
     more investments overseas, and also because the dollar
     is cheaper than the yen, Wall Street firms such as
     Morgan Stanley have tripled commissions at its Tokyo
     office from Japanese investments in U.S. stocks.
     Within its first 16 months a Tokyo-based trust
     subsidiary of New York's Chemical Bank brought in $1.5
     billion in assets. Yoshinari Morimoto of Nomura
     Securities Co., Ltd. reports that Japan's fund managers
     have limited experience with foreign equities.

270. Bellanger, Serge. "The Japanese Invasion." Bankers
     Magazine. 170.4 (July/Aug. 1987): 50-54.

     Japanese banks now have assets in the U.S. totaling
     over $200 billion and hold nearly 9% of U.S. industrial
     and commercial loans. Using low-priced products as a
     key to enter the market, Japanese entrants then move on
     to higher margin products. This is possible because
     Japanese banks, six of which are the largest in the
     world, have lower capital ratios than U.S. institutions
     and can offer low loan rates. Growth of assets is
     emphasized by their long-term interest in volume rather
     than return rates. On the down side, however, are
     Japanese bankers' sizable cultural and language
     barriers and a lack of creativity that limits
     instrument and mechanism development. In addition,
     Japan's economic success in the U.S. has creating
     growing support for protectionist legislation.
     Japanese involvement in U.S. financial institutions may
     prove beneficial in reducing the U.S. budget deficit.

271. Berry, Bryan H. "An American Work Force Produces
     Japanese Quality." Iron Age (Manufacturing Management
     Edition). 229.14 (July 18, 1986): 44-50.

     In 1983, Nissan Motor Manufacturing Corp. USA began to
     build light trucks at its new and highly successful
     plant in Smyrna, Tennessee. By the end of 1986 the
     Sentra will be in production with an expected total of
     240,000 units per year, possibly doubling by the year
     1990. The U.S.-built trucks are of the same or better
     quality than the Japan-built trucks, which has led to
     the plant's expansion. Its 2,170 hourly employees are
     all U.S. citizens, and only 15 of its 875 salaried
     workers are Japanese. Most employees do not favor
     joining the United Autoworkers union, citing job
     security and involvement in decision making as the
     reasons. A vehicle evaluation system checks for
     quality and about 88% of the autos need no reworking.
     In addition, plant equipment has an average 95% uptime,
     very high by American standards.

272. Berry, Bryan H. "Inside Honda's Plant in Marysville
     Ohio." Iron Age. 226.17 (June 15, 1983): 26-27.

     This year, Americans east of the Mississippi will buy
     50,000 Accords; all manufactured in Marysville, Ohio at
     its Honda of America Manufacturing, Inc. plant. Japan
     will supply those west of the Mississippi. In addition
     to the 4-door Accord, Marysville is the sole producer
     of Honda's top-of-the-line motorcycle, the Goldwing;
     147,000 since September 1979. Awaiting production are
     the Accord Special Edition and the Accord hatchback.
     Marysville may also begin making the Prelude, Civic and
     the new mini-car, the Honda City. As with most of its
     plants worldwide, Honda Engineering Co. supplies most
     of Maryville's special machine tools, but the plant
     handles its own metal stamping and plastic injection
     molding. Over 80% of the steel used is provided by
     U.S. steelmakers and Borg-Warner Chemicals supplies
     plastic. Employees are not from other auto companies
     and Honda is leaving the union decision up to them.
     Absenteeism is less than 2% and hourly wages are $9.80.

273. Billon, S. A. "Global Strategic Alliances and the
     Trade Deficit: Japan and the United States." Business
     Forum. 11.4 (Fall 1986): 22-25.

     The U.S. Congress has begun to act on Japan's continued
     reluctance to open its shores to U.S. products by
     introducing 400 pieces of pending legislation for
     retaliatory action. To avoid the problem of
     protectionism in its largest market, Japan has switched
     to direct investment, taking the focus away from
     exports. Japanese investments in the U.S. tripled to
     $16 billion during the years 1980-1985. In Japanese-
     owned, U.S.-based auto plants, the technology is all
     Japan's, prompting some analysts to warn of
     "screwdriver operations." Joint ventures are
     increasing between Japanese and U.S. companies,
     enabling both nations to overcome market barriers and

reduce costs of international marketing.

274. Blanden, Michael. "Foreign Banks Add a New Dimension."
     Banker. 131.668 (Oct. 1981): 117-119.

     Six of California's top ten banks are controlled or
     owned by foreign interests. Foreign banks have assets
     totaling over $43 billion or 17.7% of all California
     banks. This foreign growth has taken place mostly
     during the last ten years due to the state's easy
     supervisory climate, its strong economic growth, and
     expectation of stricter laws governing foreign banks in
     the U.S. Local banks cannot compete with foreign ones,
     with their huge international banking network back-up.
     Japan has the largest share of California assets, among
     22 other countries, including Lloyds and Barclays
     (England); Sumimoto, 25% of whose business lies in the
     Japanese community; and California First Bank, owned by
     the Bank of Tokyo. The latter is staffed mainly with
     Americans, as is Bank of the West, controlled by Banque
     Nationale de Paris.

275. Block, P. M. "Japan's Careful U.S. Investment
     Strategy." Chemical Week. 137.11 (Sept. 11, 1985):
     25-27.

     This article examines Japan's current foreign invest-
     ment strategy, focusing on U.S. activity but also
     discussing investments elsewhere. The chemical sector
     has been aggressive in its international investments.
     This is in large part due to Japan's desire to gain
     access to cheap feedstocks. The chemical companies
     seek to export a portion of the materials produced,
     shipping some back to Japan for use by its domestic
     industry. Statistics are collected from 1980 through
     1984.

276. Borrus, Amy, Mark Maremont, and William J. Hampton.
     "Japanese Car Wars Have Nissan Biting the Bullet."
     Business Week (Industrial/Technology Edition). 2976
     (Dec. 8, 1986): 52-53.

     Nissan Motor Co. reported its first loss since 1951 for
     the six months ending September 30, 1986. This
     operating loss of $121.9 million, precipitated by
     Toyota Motor Corp.'s cutting Japanese market prices and
     Nissan's tying up its U.S. profits in an ambitious
     international expansion plan, has made the company
     quite vulnerable. Cash flow is a problem, while Toyota
     holds approximately $5.4 billion. Nissan's U.S. plant,
     the first Japanese auto producer on American soil, was
     not as efficiently built as many of its Japanese
     rivals, and though its strategy is to build higher-
     priced cars to revive the U.S. market, its rivals are
     doing the same. With its market share failing both in
     the U.S. and at home, Nissan's best bet is to increase
     production in the U.K. from 24,000 cars to 100,000 and
     to export these vehicles to France, Italy and Spain by
     1988. There are tables illustrating these points.

277. Boyer, Edward. "Are Japanese Managers Biased Against
     Americans?" Fortune. 114.5 (Sept. 1, 1986): 72-75.

     There is a growing feeling among American manufacturers
     that Japanese companies with plants in the U.S. are
     biased against American suppliers, turning instead to
     Japanese suppliers located in the U.S. This practice
     is felt most strongly in the auto industry, where
     American managers claim the Japanese discriminate by:
     1. delaying sales visits, 2. providing only sketchy
     specs to prospective U.S. suppliers, and 3. expecting
     similar prices to those offered in Japan, even though
     orders are smaller. Inferior quality of U.S. goods is
     the claim made by managers of Japanese firms such as
     Honda of America. This is disputed by most experts,
     who feel that the Japanese prefer the exclusive,
     familial relationship existing between Japanese
     suppliers and automakers, where the 2 groups cooperate
     to lower costs and increase productivity. In the U.S.
     the situation is quite the contrary. The Big 3 U.S.
     automakers are now turning toward Japanese suppliers,
     and some are creating joint ventures with their
     Japanese competition.

278. Boyer, Edward. "Foreign Investors Still Love the U.S."
     Fortune. 113.10 (May 12, 1986): 93-96.

     Although the falling U.S. dollar has caused foreign
     investments in the U.S. to either dwindle or turn to
     losses, the international financial atmosphere still
     looks good for U.S. investment, with foreign activity
     actually increasing. Without these investments, the
     interest rate might rise, affecting the economy
     adversely and encouraging protectionist measures. 23
     Japanese insurance companies and 7 trust banks,
     including Nippon Life and Mitsui Bank, now hold U.S.
     securities. They take a long-term view, expecting to
     make more money if the dollar holds or drops only
     slightly. European net purchases of U.S. stocks
     increased in the latter half of 1985; $869 million to
     $2.8 billion. There is worldwide confidence that the
     dollar's decline will boost corporate profits and that
     U.S. assets will outshine other countries.' Japanese
     government regulation reforms will further encourage
     Japanese investors.

279. Brecher, Charles, and Vladimir Pucik. "Foreign Banks
     in the U.S. Economy: The Japanese Example." Columbia
     Journal of World Business. 15.1 (Spring 1980): 5-13.

     Japanese and other foreign banks have established
     offices in the U.S. for 3 major reasons: 1. many of
     their clients are American, 2. they want to
     participate in the international capital market,
     located in New York City, and 3. they wish to compete
     for services to domestic firms and consumers. The
     impact of the 89 Japanese banks and numerous other
     foreign banks in the U.S. can be discerned directly and
     indirectly. Directly, these banks create jobs for
     Americans, pay over $64 million in tax revenues, and

use office space, and purchase goods and services from
U.S. companies. Indirectly, these banks increase
innovation and competition, add to the flow of funds
into the country due to participation in Eurodollar
markets, and stimulate foreign investment. Growth may
be slowed in the future by increased regulation and a
decline in trade financing needs among the banks'
customers.

280. Bryan, Michael F., and Michael W. Dvorak. "American
     Automobile Manufacturing: It's Turning Japanese."
     Economic Commentary (Federal Reserve Bank of
     Cleveland). (March 1, 1986): 1-4.

     The value of the U.S. market has become at least as
     important to Japanese automakers as their home market.
     The fall of the dollar in relation to the yen has made
     Japan's U.S.-located assembly plants more lucrative,
     even though some production advantages are lost in the
     move to the U.S. The Japanese are attempting to bring
     their production methodology and ways of handling labor
     relations to their U.S. plants. Protectionist
     legislation, always a threat to Japanese firms, may
     become less frightening as nationality distinctions
     continue to blur, as they have with General Motors
     Corp. and its 38.6% interest in the Japanese auto firm,
     Isuzu.

281. Burr, Barry B. "Property: Japan Cuts Deals with U.S.
     Help." Pensions & Investment Age. 15.20 (Sept. 21,
     1987): S1,S46-S47.

     The $4.9 billion of U.S. equity real estate owned by
     Japanese firms has been purchased via relationships
     with U.S. real estate companies. This method has
     proven to be the most popular way for Japanese firms to
     invest in U.S. real estate, giving Japan access to U.S.
     real estate expertise while providing the U.S. with new
     foreign finance contacts. These deals, which take a
     variety of forms, including outright purchases of U.S.
     real estate companies, contractual agreements, and
     deal-to-deal transactions, are exemplified by: 1.
     Nomura Babcock & Brown Inc., a joint venture of Nomura
     Securities Co. Ltd. (Tokyo) and Babcock & Brown Co.
     (San Francisco, CA), which bought 50% of Eastdil Realty
     Inc. (NY), and 2. Sumitomo Trust and Banking Co. Ltd.
     (Tokyo), which has a 5-year contractual relationship
     with Richard Ellis Inc. (NY). As the Japanese learn
     more about the U.S. market, these relationships are
     expected to increase.

282. Bylinsky, Gene. "The Japanese Score on a U.S. Fumble."
     Fortune. 103.11 (June 1, 1981): 68-72.

     The semi-conductor industry, once U.S.-dominated, has
     been taken over by the Japanese, with a San Francisco-
     based Japanese company, Kyocera International, Inc.
     making 70% of the ceramic packaging for U.S. semi-
     conductors. Its parent, Kyoto Ceramic, supplies 70% of
     the world market. The company's success stems from

their responsiveness to the requests of domestic semiconductor makers who found American companies unwilling
to meet specifications. High quality and excellent
service make it difficult for U.S. companies to
compete, and they are reluctant to reenter the market,
despite encouragement from American silicon chip
manufacturers. Other Japanese firms are competing with
Kyocera, who are determined to dominate. By increasing
local ownership of Kyocera's stock,the U.S. may gain
control of some of the ceramic packaging market.

283. Byrne, John A. "Japan, U.S.A.: At Sanyo's Arkansas
     Plant the Magic Isn't Working." Business Week
     (Industrial/Technology Edition). 2955 (July 14,
     1986): 51-52.

     Not all Japanese-run U.S. plants are problem-free.
     Sanyo Manufacturing Corp. purchased its Forrest City,
     Arkansas, plant in 1977 from Warwick Electronics, Inc.
     After $60 million in design changes, the plant now
     produces a microwave and television line. 10 times the
     TVs are now produced with fewer employees. But, with
     no quality circles, and little compromise or trust
     between the Japanese managers and the American workers,
     tension is high. Sanyo claims that its Japanese plants
     are far more productive and blames its U.S. plant's
     problems on unsatisfactory worker attitudes. A strike
     in 1985 is still memorable in the minds of the workers,
     and there is a definite cultural gap between the
     Japanese executives and the local Forrest City workers,
     locals from this small, isolated, conservative town.
     Union leaders were not convinced that concessions and
     work-rule flexibility were necessary.

284. Calantone, Roger J. and Carolyn S. Looff. "Estimated
     Economic Impact of Toyota on Kentucky." Review and
     Perspective. 11 (Spring 1987): 3-7.

     The potential for increased employment, output and
     earnings is examined in the state as a result of Toyota
     locating in Scott County.

285. Cathey, Paul. "Japanese Managers Find Best Way to
     Direct U.S. Workers." Iron Age. 225.15 (May 21,
     1982): 69-74.

     The Japanese own over 240 manufacturing facilities in
     the U.S. and the Japanese system of managing employees
     is evident in most. Examples are Nissan Motor
     Manufacturing Corp., U.S.A., Sanyo Manufacturing Corp.,
     and Auburn Steel Co. Inc. Their training practices,
     which in Nissan's case cost $56 million, produces a
     competent, flexible and highly motivated workforce.
     Nissan's successful formula entails: 1. careful
     selection of employees, 2. very extensive training for
     workers, and 3. participative, Japanese-style
     management. U.S. labor unions have been a problem for
     the Japanese managers, though experience is helping;
     Sanyo faced a lengthy strike in its U.S. television
     plant and is now better prepared for future

negotiations. U.S.-based Japanese firms emphasize full
and consistent communications between management and
workers, and describe production, profits, and
personnel matters freely. Decision-making is not left
strictly to top management, as in U.S. firms.

286. Chernoff, Joel, and Marlene Givant. "Western Advisers
     Tap into $16 Billion from Japanese; U.S. Firms Serve as
     Mentors." Pensions & Investment Age. 15.16 (July 27,
     1987): 3,50.

     Non-Japanese money managers are both acting as advisors
     and running the investment of $16.84 billion in
     Japanese institutional and private assets, according to
     a recent Pensions & Investment Age survey. By
     establishing ties with Japanese firms, U.S. money
     managers have gained access to Japanese markets. With
     the Japanese government loosening restrictions on
     foreign activity, investors are anxious to invest
     American, due to the high value of the yen. Some U.S.-
     Japanese joint ventures are taking place in
     Batterymarch Financial Management, Wells Fargo
     Investment Advisors, and Putnam Cos. Quantitative
     investment techniques used in the U.S. are now being
     studied by the Japanese. Cigna Corp. is an example of
     a U.S. firm that acts as a mentor to Sumimoto Fire &
     Marine Insurance Co. Ltd., training its personnel.

287. Chernotsky, Harry I. "Selecting U.S. Sites: A Case
     Study of German and Japanese Firms." Management
     International Review. 23.2 (1983): 45-55.

     When reviewing the merits of locating in the U.S.,
     prospective foreign investors must assess which region,
     state, and community best serves their needs.
     Interestingly, priorities of different countries are
     quite varied. This article compares the 14 German and
     7 Japanese firms that operate in the
     Charlotte/Mecklenburg, North Carolina area. Overall,
     the decision to locate there is due to the area's: 1.
     accessibility to markets, 2. transportation and
     freight-forwarding services, 3. productive labor
     force, and 4. quality of life considerations. The
     most important factors for the Germans were quality of
     the local environment and availability of support
     systems. The Japanese had much more cost-conscious
     priorities, scrutinizing closely local operating costs
     and labor cost conditions.

288. Clarke, David. "Japan Survey: Japanese Banks in U.S.
     Mount a Multi-Pronged Assault." Asian Finance. 12.10
     (Oct. 15, 1986): 40-49,60.

     Led by The Bank of Tokyo, Japanese banks have made
     aggressive moves into the American market. While U.S.
     regulators are monitoring them and U.S. banks are
     annoyed at the Japanese strategy of high volumes and
     low spreads, Japanese banks have found acquisition in
     the American market to mean fast profits. Examples of
     these deals include Fuji's purchase of Walter E. Heller

& Co. (1984,) Sanwa's buying Lloyd's Bank of California
(1986,) and Mitsubishi's ownership of Bank of
California (1986.) Most important of all is a deal to
come: Sumimoto Bank has sought a limited partnership in
Goldman Sachs & Co. for a $500 million sum. This deal
challenges both the Glass Steagall Act and Article 65.
The Japanese boom in direct investment is being
encouraged by its government.

289. Corrigan, Richard. "Japan's Third Wave." <u>National
Journal</u>. 17.16 (April 20, 1985): 840-847.

First the Japanese exported their cars to the United
States and then followed with the establishment of U.S.
assembly plants. In the third wave, the Japanese
automobile producers are setting up U.S. based parts
suppliers, even as U.S. auto companies are moving out.
Emphasis is placed on Michigan. The incentive for this
move is that the Japanese cannot retain its share of
the lucrative U.S. market unless it brings its operation
to U.S. shores.

290. Courtis, Kenneth S. and Paul A. Summerville. "Beyond
Trade: A New Phase in the International Competitive
Expansion of the Japanese Automotive Industry."
<u>American Chamber of Commerce in Japan. Journal</u>. 24
(Oct. 1986): 24+.

Structural changes in the Japanese automotive industry
brought about by overseas investments are discussed, as
well as the experiences of Japanese factories operating
in the U.S. Also included is a discussion of U.S.
import quotas.

291. Covell, Jon Carter. "Japan Finds a Warm Climate for
Investment in Hawaii." <u>Asian Business</u>. 21.6 (June
1985): 84-86.

The beginnings of Japan's investment in Hawaii are
vague and little publicized, but it looks as though
1959 marked the first major flow of capital from Tokyo
and Yokohama. Hawaii's Japanese-American community and
the new opportunities provided by its becoming a U.S.
state made it a natural investment target for Japan.
The majority of Japanese money went into Oahu property,
but during the 1970's Maui and Hawaii itself are being
invested. After hotels, golf-course land and
surrounding building areas have been the most desirable
areas for investors. Today's Japan-Hawaii monetary
axis has been largely pioneered by the president of
Kyo-ya Co., Tokyo billionaire Kenji Osano, who acquired
and poured billions into Waikiki Beach tourist
property. Among his conquests are the Princess
Kaiulani and Moana Hotels. In 1974 he paid a whopping
$105 million for three more Hawaii hotels.

292. Covell, Jon Carter. "The Japanese Economic Invasion of
Hawaii." <u>Asian Business</u>. 21 (June 1985): 84-86.

Japanese investments in Hawaii have greatly increased.

Real Estate is the prime target for investments,
including hotels, golf courses, and resorts.

293. Derven, Ronald. "Japanese Interest in U.S. Market
     Expected to Rise; Investors Not Deterred by Economic
     Uncertainties." National Real Estate Investor. 30.3
     (March 1988): 84-95.

     The interest of Japanese investors in U.S. real estate
     remains very strong, in spite of recent difficulties in
     the currency and stock market situation. There will be
     an estimated $10 billion invested in U.S. real estate
     in 1988. There are some key tendencies that can be
     seen: an increased interest in office buildings, a
     continuation of the domination of the U.S. northeast, a
     desire for premium sites, and price-sensitivity. The
     opportunities for investment are quite numerous, with
     good return. Hot spots include Boston and Guam, which
     seem to attract heavy Japanese interest.

294. Derven, Ronald. "Japanese Investors Dominate Action
     from Overseas; European Sources Shift Strategy to
     Smaller Deals." National Real Estate Investor.
     29.10 (Sept. 1987): 61-72,146.

     Japanese investment in U.S. real estate has risen so
     significantly that it now dominates all other foreign
     sources. T. Welch, Equitable Real Estate Investment
     Management, points out that the Japanese financed 3
     times as much as they acquired in 1986, if guarantees
     on a credit enhancement type of vehicle are counted.
     J. Montanari, Cushman & Wakefield, claims that the
     Japanese come to the U.S. looking for higher yields and
     portfolio diversification. J. Schaffer, Sonnenblick-
     Goldman, adds that the Japanese seek prime real estate
     and focus on central business district property. Also,
     they seek top properties in the top markets, despite
     growing price sensitivity. Keen interest in U.S. real
     estate continues among other overseas investors,
     particularly Dutch pension funds and money pooled by
     German banks.

295. Downs, Anthony. "Foreign Investors Paying More for
     U.S. Real Estate." National Real Estate Investor.
     29 (Dec. 1987): 42+.

     This articles examines the causal factors involved in
     payment of very high prices for premium quality U.S.
     property, particularly by Japanese investors.

296. Eason, Henry. "The Corporate Immigrants." Nation's
     Business. 75.4 (April 1987): 12-19.

     Direct foreign investment in the U.S. is estimated at
     over $200 billion. The U.K. is the largest investor,
     followed in order by the Netherlands and Japan, but
     recent investment patterns indicate Japan is rising in
     relation to the others. The more than 10,000
     affiliates of foreign companies operating in the U.S.
     employ almost 10 million people and are responsible for

over $600 billion in annual sales. The fear of pro-
tectionism and currency fluctuations are the major
reasons for foreign companies to operate in the U.S.
Japan, particularly, is having a strong impact on
management techniques used in the U.S. by minimizing
waste, maximizing quality, and developing team
concepts. Foreign firms, such as Hitachi Ltd. (Japan)
and Siemens (Germany), are seeing the growth potential
of an immense market, the availability of high technology, and many other factors.

297. Edid, Maralyn. "Why Mazda Is Settling in the Heart of
Union ‛Territory." Business Week
(Industrial/Technology Edition). 2911 (Sept. 9,
1985): 94-95.

Mazda Motor Corp. will build its $450-million
automobile plant in the heavily unionized state of
Michigan, and has recognized the United Auto Workers
(UAW.) Mazda expects output from its plant in Flat
Rock (Michigan) to boost its market share (now under
2%) as well as help ease trade frictions between the
U.S. and Japan. Mazda's deal with the UAW calls for
lower benefits and temporarily lower wages than other
UAW members receive; the union also agreed to flexible
work rules. In exchange, laid-off UAW workers will get
top priority when the plant starts hiring. Mazda chose
Michigan for its favorable location, transportation
facilities, and the state's $120 million in financial
and other incentives. Flat Rock also agreed to a 12-
year property tax abatement. State leaders plan to use
Mazda's decision to help lure other firms to Michigan.

298. Ehrlich, Edna E. "Foreign Pension Fund Investments in
the United States." Federal Reserve Bank of New York
Quarterly Review. 8.1 (Spring 1983): 1-12.

Investment in the U.S. of pension funds of the U.K.,
the Netherlands, Canada, and Japan reflects a
significant increase in the flow of foreign pension
funds into the U.S. During the last 3 years, foreign
pension money may have increased from $2 1/2 billion a
year to approximately $4 billion. The relative
stability and performance of U.S. assets, and a trend
toward broader geographical diversification has
contributed to this interest in U.S. assets. Analysis
of the increasing internationalization of pension fund
portfolios indicates that: 1. the effects of the value
of the dollar in the exchange markets are
insignificant, 2. the depth and liquidity of U.S.
securities and real estate markets are enhanced, and 3.
both foreign and U.S. pension funds are able to develop
better portfolios than if restricted to domestic
investments.

299. Ely, E. S. "Foreign Banking in America: Dawn of a New
Age?" Institutional Investor. 21.3 (March 1987):
245-255.

In 1986, foreign banks appeared more competitive with

U.S. banks by tighter pricing and clever deal making.
They moved into investment banking and began
challenging Washington regulators. Japan's Sumitomo
Bank purchased a substantial interest in Goldman, Sachs
& Co., while Union Bank of Switzerland raised $100
million in 30-year bonds for Allied-Signal through UBS
Securities Inc., its U.S. investment bank subsidiary.
Union Bank was the first foreign bank to lead or manage
a U.S. domestic offering. Also in 1986, Schroders PLC,
a U.K. investment bank, acquired a 50% interest in New
York's Wertheim & Co. In the future, foreign banks
will play a growing role in underwriting U.S. corporate
debt. Observers expect more acquisitions like the
Goldman deal, for ties with a Wall Street house may be
crucial for prestige as a global banking power. Buying
a U.S. firm offers a foreign institution instant market
share and credibility.

300. Encarnation, Dennis J. "Cross-Investment: A Second
     Front of Economic Rivalry." California Management
     Review. 29.2 (Winter 1987): 20-48.

     The practice of cross-investment between the U.S. and
     Japan is examined. Historically, U.S. industrial power
     caused Japan to erect foreign trade barriers and
     capital controls to limit foreign investor expansion in
     Japan. The few U.S. multinationals who invested in
     Japan diversified horizontally with their assembly and
     manufacturing plants. Early Japanese investments meet
     their need for natural resources, and later investments
     aided Japan's export strategy. Direct investment in
     the U.S. by Japan remained small for 30 years after
     World War II. During the late 1970s, Japan's current
     account surpluses grew, changing the scale and scope of
     their foreign investments. Growing similarities in
     U.S. and Japanese cross-investment patterns are
     reflected in the corporate strategies of investors, but
     important differences in government policies and
     corporate strategies still persist. The greatest
     threat to bilateral relations is the increasing
     asymmetry of investments. In 1984, Japanese
     investments in the U.S. were nearly 2 times the U.S.
     investments in Japan.

301. "Financial Centre -- New York: The Slow March on Big
     Apple." Banker. 138.745 (March 1988): 31-33, 37-61.

     This is a treatment of the Japanese role in U.S.
     financial markets. The general conclusion is that the
     Japanese presence is significant and growing. There is
     a description of the factors which encourage such
     growth, such as the dollar's weakness, the yen's
     strength, and the protectionist U.S. trade posture.
     The amount of direct Japanese investment has reached
     $10.2 billion. Yet Japan moves with caution, often
     preferring to invest in minority holdings rather than
     full takeovers. The Big Four securities houses have
     one fourth of the long-term U.S. government bond
     trading, and are moving in on the equity market and
     other areas such as real estate finance. There is a

listing of foreign banks in New York and other U.S.
cities.

302. Finn, Edwin A., Jr. "In Japan We (Must) Trust."
     Forbes. 140.6 (Sept. 21, 1987): 32-34.

     U.S. financial markets and the U.S. economy are
     increasingly dependent on Japanese investment capital.
     Japanese banks and life insurance companies dominate
     international bond markets, affecting rates for
     business loans, mortgages, and consumer credit. By
     buying bonds in the U.K. and Germany instead of the
     U.S., the Japanese made it cheaper to borrow there than
     in the U.S. In the U.S., this has meant: 1. losses in
     bond and mortgage securities trading, 2. higher
     interest rates, and 3. lower economic growth. Finally,
     the Japanese Ministry of Finance exerted pressure on
     Japanese institutions to stop speculating against the
     U.S. dollar because further devaluation would have a
     negative impact on Japanese exports and existing
     Japanese investments in the U.S. As Japan's foreign
     investments approach $700 billion by 1990, U.S.
     interests will depend on the Japanese government for
     deft use of its financial power.

303. Finn, Edwin A., Jr. "The Quiet Invasion." Forbes.
     137.13 (June 16, 1986): 30-31.

     Japanese banks are now control about 8% of the U.S.
     banking market. The Japanese gained a foothold in the
     U.S. by: 1. offering better short-term loan rates than
     U.S. banks, 2. using their high credit rating to back
     municipal bond issues, and 3. buying loans from U.S.
     banks through silent participation. Japanese banks can
     offer cheaper rates because they have to maintain
     capital equal to only about 2% of assets, compared to
     5.5% for U.S. banks. In addition, they pay low
     interest on consumer deposits in Japan and have close
     relationships with large Japanese manufacturers. The
     Japanese began by pursuing large multinational
     companies but are now targeting smaller firms. The
     Federal Reserve Board is studying the advantages held
     by Japanese banks but has not taken action to minimize
     those advantages.

304. Flint, Jerry. "What Fraser Fears." Forbes. 128.5
     (Aug. 31, 1981): 37-38.

     The new Nissan truck-building plant in Smyrna,
     Tennessee is a must for the United Auto Workers (UAW)
     to organize. If the Japanese can operate the plant at
     lower cost and without the union, then the UAW's
     bargaining power with Ford and General Motors will be
     weakened. The average cash wage for an auto worker is
     $11 an hour. Social Security and liberal fringes bring
     labor cost to $19-$20 per hour. The UAW fears the
     results on present contracts if Nissan and Honda are
     able to avoid UAW's benefit package. The greatest
     concern for UAW President Douglas Fraser is the
     increasing use of foreign parts in U.S.-assembled cars.

The UAW is pushing a law that requires cars sold in the
U.S. to be made mostly from U.S.-made parts. Automakers are using the threat of buying more foreign
parts as a lever in lowering the 1982 UAW contract
costs.

305. Frank, John N., and Larry Armstrong. "The Japanese Are
     Elbowing into Chicago's Futures Pits." Business Week
     (Industrial/Technology Edition). 3001 (June 1,
     1987): 106-107.

     Japanese investors are becoming involved in Chicago's
     booming futures and options markets. Seat prices on
     the exchanges are soaring, office vacancies are
     disappearing, and traders are working extra shifts to
     accommodate their new Japanese customers. The Japanese
     Finance Ministry has given the go ahead for Japanese
     brokerage firms, banks, insurance companies, and money-
     management firms to trade futures for their own
     accounts. Japan's massive investment in U.S. Treasury
     issues and U.S. stocks may make it a major player in
     bond and stock-index futures. Japan's focus on
     Chicago's financial markets may help continue the rally
     in agricultural commodities. Currently, foreigners
     account for less than 10% of the trading volume. The
     Japanese are sending their U.S. traders back to Japan
     to teach them how these markets operate.

306. Freedman, Audrey, and David Bauer. Japanese
     Investment in the United States: An Opinion Survey of
     Elected Officials. Research Bulletin 142. New York:
     Conference Board, 1983.

     For the most part, elected officials in the U.S.
     welcome the investment by Japanese firms that is taking
     place in the U.S. Many states seek foreign investment,
     seeing the capital inflow as a stimulus to technolog-
     ical advance and employment rates. The prevailing
     attitude is that foreign investment in U.S. facilities
     tends to reduce trade conflict. Some officials,
     however, feel that a reciprocity should be promoted to
     encourage equal opportunity for U.S. investment in
     Japan. This survey report details the major benefits
     envisioned by U.S. officials to the inflow of Japanese
     investment.

307. Gaffney, Charles, and Scott Scredon. "Why the No. 2
     Photo Company Is Snapping Up Fotomat." Business Week
     (Industrial/Technology Edition). 2872 (Dec. 10, 1984):
     64.

     A discussion of the experience and plans of Konishiroku
     of Japan in the U.S. photography markets, this study
     traces the relationship of Konishiroku with its U.S.
     partner, Fotomat. Since Fotomat found it necessary to
     close many of its outlets, the impact was felt by
     Konishiroku, whose film processing products were
     mostly marketed by Fotomat. In response, Konishiroku
     plans to increase its holdings in Fotomat to provide
     needed capital for its operations. Konishiroku will

also increase its sales of film and cameras directly in U.S. markets. The status of Konishiroku in the U.S. however will depend in part on whether it will be able to restore Fotomat's profitability.

308. Gary, Richard. "The Japanese Connection." <u>Financial Planning</u>. 13.1 (Jan. 1984): 129-131.

Large Japanese companies' stocks are being actively traded in the U.S., and 8 Japanese companies are listed on the New York Stock Exchange. American Depository Receipts are certificates issued by a U.S. bank, representing shares physically held overseas. The Japanese do not allow shares to leave the country, but many U.S. investors have arranged for U.S. banks to issue American Depository Receipts.

309. Gemmell, Art. "Fujitsu's Cross-Cultural Style." <u>Management Review</u>. 75.6 (June 1986): 7-8.

The cross-cultural experience of Fujitsu Ltd. is discussed. Its successful U.S. subsidiary uses a blend of U.S. and Japanese practices. Its employees and some management techniques are American, while its manufacturing, R&D, quality control, and customer service are Japanese. It generates a family-like atmosphere for employees, and has a turnover rate under 5%, partly the result of encouraging individual responsibility and monitoring morale. Technology transfer and the teaching of U.S. personnel in Japan have produced an American-based company with many of its roots in Japanese organizational methods.

310. Ginzberg, E., C. Brecher, and V. Pweik. "Impact of Japanese Business Community in U.S.; Business Assigned Japanese in America Totals about 30,500." <u>Japan Economic Journal</u>. 17.881 (Dec. 4, 1979): 28-29.

Japan's influence in the U.S. has been significant since the 1970s, largely through trade relationships. The role of Japanese trading companies, and Japanese marketing and distributions firms is explored. The economic impact of Japan's activities in the U.S. is assessed.

311. Glasgall, William, Barbara Buell, Richard Melcher, and Mike McNamee. "Japan on Wall Street." <u>Business Week (Industrial/Technology Edition)</u>. 3015 (Sept. 7, 1987): 82-90.

This is a discussion of the big four Japanese brokerages, all of which are working on an increased presence in the U.S. financial market. At present they account for 20% of long-term U.S. government bond trading. They are moving into stocks, corporate finance and other areas. They will be a challenge to U.S. firms, entering the field of mergers and acquisitions, as well. Some obstacles for the big four include the need to spend half their revenues in the U.S. on personnel

expenses, and worry about the effect another drop in
the dollar might have.

312. Glasgall, William, and James Treece. "Japan, U.S.A.:
     Japanese Capital Finds a Home in Middle America."
     Business Week (Industrial/Technology Edition). 2955
     (July 14, 1986): 52-53.

     Japan's banks and securities investors are increasing
     their role in the U.S. They act as banks to affiliated
     suppliers which come from Japan, and they also match
     commitments from U.S. firms that need capital and
     technology with Japanese firms that want to enter U.S.
     markets. Another role for the Japanese is lending to
     middle-market U.S. firms which are trying to expand.
     Examples of Japanese activities are discussed. Often
     the Japanese banks are offering cheaper capital to both
     Japanese and U.S. firms and industries. Japanese banks
     have certain advantages which enable them to offer
     competitive rates.

313. Greenberg, Karen. "Japanese Subsidiaries Offer Job
     Security, Product Quality." Advanced Management
     Journal. 48.3 (Summer 1983): 52-54.

     The New York Stock Exchange commissioned a study to
     find how difficult it would be for U.S. industries to
     adopt Japanese management styles. A comparison was
     made of the management and workforce of 13 U.S. based
     Japanese firms and 13 corresponding U.S. firms.
     Results indicate the major difference between the 2
     groups is the Japanese emphasis on job security. The
     Japanese avoid layoffs through wage reduction and job
     rotation. They stress product quality rather than
     quantity, and job satisfaction ranks higher in the
     Japanese firms. Compared with U.S. firms, the Japanese
     have lower firing rates, more management participation,
     and more emphasis on company-sponsored activities.
     However, the Japanese firms provide limited opport-
     unities for women, and stress group conformity.

314. Harris, Diane, and Andrea Rock. "The Japanese Are
     Here to Stay." Money. 16.5 (May 1987): 140-158.

     The U.S. government appears ready to take protect-
     ionist measures against Japan for unfair trade
     practices. These measures however may produce the
     opposite results, making Japan a tougher world
     competitor with greater investment in U.S. manufact-
     uring facilities. Japan has surplus funds and the U.S.
     is a good place to invest. The further the dollar
     falls and the greater the protectionist sentiment, the
     quicker the Japanese will start U.S. ventures. In the
     automobile industry, estimates project that Japanese
     factories in the U.S. will cut the big 3 U.S. auto-
     makers' market share from about 70% to 50%-60% by the
     early 1990's. Other areas likely to be penetrated by
     Japanese investments are the computer industry and the
     financial services sector. Presently, Japanese money
     is pouring into U.S. equities and real estate.

315. Hayashi, A. M. "Semiconductors: The Year of Living
     Dangerously." Electronic Business; The Business
     Magazine for the Electronics Industry. 13.5 (March 1,
     1987): 50-53.

     1986 was an eventful year for the leading worldwide
     semiconductor companies. The proposed Fujitsu
     acquisition of Fairchild and the Toshiba joint venture
     with Motorola highlighted the industry's move toward
     consolidation and alliances among the top players. The
     U.S.-Japan semiconductor trade pact agreement forced
     many companies to redesign their corporate strategies.
     And major swings in exchange rates shifted the
     competitiveness of companies doing business in foreign
     markets. Worldwide semiconductor production is given
     along with the top 10 semiconductor companies and the
     top 10 integrated circuit manufacturers.

316. Hector, Gary, and Alison Rea. "The Japanese Want to
     Be Your Bankers." Fortune. 114.9 (Oct. 27, 1986):
     96-104.

     The large Japanese financial firms are becoming a
     powerful force in world finance. At U.S. Treasury bond
     auctions, the Japanese firms sometimes buy 60% of a new
     offering. Japanese commercial banks now hold 8.4% of
     all commercial loans in the U.S. Even the smaller
     Japanese securities firms have more equity than most of
     the large U.S. investment banks. Underwriting bonds at
     extremely low prices, the big Japanese securities
     houses led an assault on the Eurobond market. Their
     U.S. trading staffs are becoming primary dealers in
     U.S. government securities. Japan's commercial banks
     also are seeking customers around the globe with low
     interest rates.

317. Heins, John. "A Mixed Blessing." Forbes. 141.4
     (Feb. 22, 1988): 63-65.

     The impact of Japanese investment and tourism in Hawaii
     is assessed. There has been a 9% growth in Hawaii's
     economy in 1987, and part of that is accounted for by
     the Japanese investment in construction and real
     estate there. The flight time from Japan is only six
     hours, so Hawaii is becoming a desirable vacation spot,
     as Japanese working people begin to focus more on
     leisure. About 20% of tourists come from Japan. The
     good and bad effects of Japan on Hawaii are discussed.
     While there is a need for economic growth, some
     Hawaiians note that steep rate increases in the hotels
     may discourage U.S. mainland visitors. The state is
     trying to encourage high-technology industry, to help
     avoid too much dependence on Japanese spending.

318. Heller, Heinz Robert. "The Hawaiian Experience."
     Columbia Journal of World Business. 9.3 (Fall 1974):
     105-110.

     The Hawaiian-experience with Japanese investments
     indicates that foreign-investors can respond quickly to

investment opportunities. The political leaders of
Hawaii provided the strong economic incentives needed
for a surge in Japanese investment. This is shown by
investments being selectively concentrated in the
tourist industry. This industry had good growth
potential and profit opportunities, offering the
Japanese investor the opportunity to cater to the
increasing number of Japanese tourists visiting Hawaii.
As the size of Japanese firms increase, more local
personnel is hired than Japanese nationals.

319. Heller, Heinz Robert, and Emily E. Heller. The
Economic and Social Impact of Foreign Investment in
Hawaii. Honolulu: Economic Research Center,
University of Hawaii, 1973.

This report analyzes the trade situation of the state
of Hawaii, especially in regard to Japanese direct
foreign investment. The trade standing of Hawaii is
first documented. Then the inflow of capital is
detailed, with a discussion of the effects. The causes
of increased Japanese investment are sought, and data
on the extent of the investment are offered. Opinion
within Hawaii about Japanese investment is assessed.
Some analysis of the opinions presented is offered.

320. Heller, Heinz Robert, and Emily E. Heller. Japanese
Investment in the United States; with a Case Study of
the Hawaiian Experience. New York: Praeger
Publishers, 1974.

This study was conducted in response to a request from
the Hawaiian Senate, and was conducted with an
international team, which provided interviews of
managers and directors of participating firms. The
incentives for foreign investment activities are
discussed, and identification of key features of the
process is made. There is then a treatment of Japan's
foreign investment posture. The status of the U.S. as
host to Japanese investments is delineated. The
specifics of Japanese investments in Hawaii are then
traced, with statistics on the legal situation, lack of
state regulation, and reasons for the increases in
Japanese investment explained. The size and impact of
the investment in terms of capital and labor force is
outlined. The conclusion offers some comments on the
attitudes toward the investment by Japan in Hawaii.

321. Hemmerick, Steve. "Property: Pools Making a Splash."
Pensions & Investment Age. 16.6 (March 21, 1988):
P17.

There is a trend toward creation of commingled real
estate pools, to fund the investment by Japanese and
U.S. firms in real estate. Traditionally an area that
Japanese investors have preferred, real estate
opportunities with somewhat more risk can be taken on
through investment pools. Limited partnerships offer
some advantages, in sharing the investment risk in each
property and opening up the way for larger deals. One

of the companies which are cooperating with Japanese
investors is Metropolitan Life. The returns are mostly
stable, and the operating costs are minimized to each
investor.

322. Herzstein, Robert E.   "Japanese Investment in the U.S.:
An American Perspective." Texas Business Executive.
6.2 (Fall/Winter 1980): 19-22,27.

There is substantial growth of Japanese direct
investment in the U.S. A number of factors have
produced this investment surge: 1. the cheap U.S.
dollar, 2. exports from Japan are promoted, 3. U.S.
firms' ease of purchase, 4. Japan's dependency on
imported natural resources, and 5. protection against
import restrictions. Because of the closed nature of
the Japanese economy, U.S. investors have difficulty in
making direct investments in Japan. The restriction of
capital flows into Japan are creating adverse reactions
in the U.S. Options for U.S. action are considered.

323. Hochi, Shozo.   "Japanese Auto Companies: At Home in
America." Business Japan.   31.4 (April 1986): 24-29.

The establishment of U.S. based production facilities
by Japanese automobile manufacturers shows their
determination to reduce trade friction between the two
countries. The Honda of America Manufacturing Inc.
plant in Marysville, Ohio, houses stamping, painting,
plaster injection molding and assembly lines. The
majority of workers are American. Management-labor
relations are going smoothly with only three employees
having joined the union, and community relations are
very good. At the Nissan Motor Manufacturing Corp.,
USA plant in Smyrna, Tennessee, American employees seem
content with management, which combines Japanese and
U.S. styles, and with training and benefits. It
appears that the New United Motor Manufacturing Inc.
plant in Fremont, California, has already gained a
strong product and management reputation.

324. Hodges, Michael. "The Japanese Industrial Presence in
the USA: Trading One Source of Friction for Another?"
Multinational Business. 1 (Spring 1988): 1-14.

In assessing the impact of the investment by Japan in
U.S. manufacturing, this article offers insights about
the possible long term effects. Many have been
encouraging Japanese ventures to locate in the U.S.,
because of the trade friction and the weak dollar. But
little concern has been shown for the tendency for
Japan to increase market share and reduce costs by
relocating to the U.S. Often the suppliers for
Japanese manufacturing also move overseas, so there is
little gain in business for the U.S. host. Japanese
firms are also providing a great deal of the financing
for the ventures located in the U.S.

325. Holden, Dennis. "Japanese Bank Strategy in the United
States." United States Banker. 93.5 (May 1982): 40-44.

Japanese banks are interested in the U.S. for greater
stability with top U.S. corporations and for long-term
profit growth in retail and wholesale banking. Twenty-
three Japanese banks are located in the U.S. with their
aggregate outstanding loans estimated at over $16
billion. They have branches in all important U.S.
money and commodity centers and are ideally positioned
for nationwide banking. They emphasize responsiveness
to changes in the marketplace and in consumer
preferences. Japanese banks will expand North American
operations to strengthen their profit base and to
follow the rising level of direct foreign investment by
Japanese multinationals. They also seek to replace
losses from slow growth in capital spending and loan
demand in Japan. They expect large Japanese investment
to come to the U.S. They also are interested in
acquisitions, with depressed Wells Fargo a possible
choose.

326. Holden, Dennis. "The Mitsubishi-BanCal Deal: A
Japanese Perspective." United States Banker. 95.2
(Feb. 1984): 50-52.

Japanese banks continue to penetrate the U.S. market
through acquisitions of banking assets. The recent
takeover of two subsidiaries of Walter E. Heller
International Corp. by Fuji Bank and Mitsubishi's
purchase of BanCal Tri-State illustrates the
determination of Japan's drive to build up an asset
base in the U.S. This aggressiveness of the Japanese
banks may stem from their recognition that the U.S.
market is more important than the international market.
The big attraction is promising loan demand, easy
access to domestic dollar financing, and the politic-
ally safe haven the U.S. offers for all types of
investments. It is easier for a foreign bank to take
over a U.S. bank than it is for a U.S. bank to take
over a Japanese one. The Fuji and Mitsubishi
acquisitions may awaken U.S. bank regulators to the
unfair advantages accruing to foreign banks in such
takeovers.

327. Hollerman, Leon. "Japanese Direct Investment in
California." Asian Survey; A Monthly Review of
Contemporary Asian Affairs. 21.10 (Oct., 1981): 1080-
1095.

This article examines the factors working to promote
Japanese direct foreign investment within and out of
Japan. It reviews the positive and negative aspects of
the California climate for Japanese direct investment,
particularly the role of administrative intervention
and regulation by the state government.

328. Hollerman, Leon. "Japan's Direct Investment in
California and the New Protectionism." Journal of
World Trade Law. 18.4 (July/Aug. 1984): 309-319.

Japan's direct investment in California is conditioned
by the new protectionism and welfare state system. The
new protectionism threatens Japan with Trade restrictions unless it invests directly in the U.S. It appears
that this new protectionism of the U.S. welfare system
has had a heavy impact on California, while the state's
own policies have reinforced the adverse effects. By
trying to preserve jobs in declining and obsolete
industries, by promoting labor-intensive, low technology, low productivity types of production, the
welfare state preserves an inappropriate forms of
production. While the U.S. resists Japanese exports,
it insists that Japan export its declining industries
to provide employment in the U.S. California is one of
the main destinations of these declining industries.
Thus, alongside a high-technology sector, California is
promoting the growth of a backward sector.

329. Hollerman, Leon. "Japan's Economic Impact on the
     United States." Annals of the American Academy of
     Political and Social Science. 460 (March 1982): 127-
     35.

     In this general treatment of the impact of Japan's
     economy on the U.S., there is a consideration of the
     motives and determinants of the economic policy of
     Japan. While it needs to correct for its unbalanced
     physical endowment, Japan has an unbalanced trade
     structure. To overcome the many protectionist
     tendencies in the U.S., Japanese investments are
     increasingly moving into the U.S. Voluntary export
     agreements are discussed, and cartel arrangements are
     examined. The repercussions of Japanese policy on the
     U.S. are analyzed.

330. Holstein, William, Larry Armstrong, Robert Neff, and
     Richard Brandt. "Japan's Bigger and Bolder Forays
     into the U.S." Business Week (Industrial/Technology
     Edition). 2973 (Nov. 17, 1986): 80-81.

     The strong yen has made U.S. investments attractive to
     the Japanese. The Japanese at first moved cautiously
     into U.S. acquisitions by entering joint ventures in an
     industry and then by buying ailing firms or becoming
     minority owners. Now, Japanese companies wish to
     acquire large U.S. manufacturers. Impetus is added to
     this movement by the fact that Japanese firms find it
     easier to diversify in the U.S. than in Japan. Some
     observers worry that the Japanese tend to concentrate
     in specific industries. For instance, in 1986, the
     Japanese made about 400 investments in the trouble-
     plagued U.S. electronics industry. So far, the
     Japanese have preferred to make friendly purchases and
     have not been involved in raiding.

331. Holstein, William, Pete Engardio, and Dan Cook.
     "Japan, USA." Business Week. 2955 (July 14, 1986):
     45-55.

     A new wave of Japanese investment is sweeping across

America. It is creating Japanese industrial centers
and is giving failing U.S. companies a fresh start
through infusions of Japanese capital management. This
second wave promises to be one of the most important
economic forces reshaping America; it is creating jobs
in depressed areas and dozens of states and cities are
eagerly competing for it. Americans hope the
investment will dramatically increase productivity and
revive aging industries. It is hoped that it will
diminish trade friction and make the U.S. and Japanese
economies more alike. Also discussed are the Japanese
auto-industry in America, the difference Japanese
management makes, and the lending of Japanese capital
to the U.S.   Statistics provided for 1982-1990.

332. Horovitz, Bruce. "Honda: Not So Simple Any More."
     Industry Week. 217.1 (April 4, 1983): 45-47.

     Honda Motor Co. Ltd. has had more success in the U.S.
     than in Japan. It is presently the only Japanese
     carmaker to build a production plant in the U.S. With
     the added production of the Marysville, Ohio, plant,
     Honda expects to increase its U.S. market share more
     than 2% during the next 2 years. In Japan, Honda could
     not find dealers willing to give up their loyalties to
     Toyota and Datsun. In the U.S., Honda has had no
     problem recruiting dealers. Ranking third in the world
     for customer satisfaction, Honda's quality will not be
     affected by U.S. production. Tetsuo Chino, president
     of American Honda Motor Co. Ltd., credits Honda's
     quality to management's equal treatment of employees.
     Although only 4 of the 1,000 workers at the Marysville
     plant are union members, Chino claims the decision to
     unionize belongs strictly to the workers. At present,
     the Marysville plant is protecting quality by producing
     at about one-sixth of capacity.

333. Horovitz, Bruce. "How 'Old Toyota' Views the Sibling
     Rivalry." Industry Week. 217.2 (April 18, 1983):
     47,50-51.

     The new cars produced by the proposed Toyota/General
     Motors (GM) joint venture in the U.S. will be sold
     through GM's Chevrolet Motor Division. The Toyota/GM
     cars will be made in GM's currently idle Fremont,
     California, plant. If the Toyota/GM cars are
     successful, they could replace GM's Chevette compact
     model. A successful Toyota/GM venture would further
     solidify Japanese engineering in the U.S. automobile
     industry. Toyota/GM will compete with Toyota Motor
     Sales USA, the "old Toyota." Norman Lean, chief
     operating officer of Toyota Motor Sales USA, was not
     selected to head the new joint-venture company. Lean
     views the joint-venture company as a competitor. The
     new, jointly made car will be part American and part
     Japanese, although the engine and transmission are
     likely to be Japanese-made. The venture is expected to
     create about 3,000 jobs at the Fremont plant.

334. "The Increase in Japanese Direct Investment in the

United States." LTCB Research. 31 (Sept. 1978): 4-
8.

This article describes Japanese investments in
manufacturing facilities in the U.S. It follows the
changes in Japanese objectives and forms of investment.
Also presented is the trend in site locations in the
U.S. for Japanese direct investments. Speculations are
given of future developments.

335. Ioannou, Lori. "Venture Capital: What Trade War?"
Euromoney. (Aug. 1987): 105-111.

Since 1982, Japanese investments in the U.S. venture-
capital industry have reached an estimated $500
million. Japanese investors are drawn by the prospects
of high returns on equity and by the opportunity to
gain access to developing U.S. technology. American
start-up companies are agreeable to working with the
Japanese, and many see it as the only path to growth.
U.S.-based consultants are often used to assist
Japanese investors in reaching the venture-capital
market. Successful partnerships between portfolio
companies and Japanese investors include: Montgomery
Pacific Technology Partnership, Orien I, and Concord
Partners Japan. U.S. venture-capital assoications have
also proven to be useful in gaining access to U.S.
technology.

336. "Japan: Electronic Industries Versus Unitary Taxation."
Bulletin for International Fiscal Documentation. 38
(April 1984): 162-165.

An analysis is presented on the effects of unitary
taxation on Japanese investments in the electronics
industries in the United States. The implications of
for U.S.-Japan economic relations are discussed.

337. "Japan: The Impact of Japanese Investment in the
U.S./Sogo Shosha Can Help You." Nation's Business.
70.6 (June 1982): 13-18.

In 1981, Japanese businesses devoted $5 billion to
overseas investment, 23.3% of which went to the U.S.
By 1979, some 1,100 Japanese businesses were operating
in the U.S., including more than 200 manufacturing
subsidiaries. Japanese firms hired more than 100,000
American employees with compensations of $20 billion,
and Japanese firms have paid U.S. taxes of $1 billion.
Japanese electronics manufacturers have the largest
presence, but there is a wide range of other products
made in the U.S. The Japanese view their commitment to
the U.S. market as a partnership, including sharing
manufacturing technologies and management practices.
General trading companies are directly involved in
importing and exporting, as well as in overseas investments and joint ventures. In partnership with general
trading companies, U.S. firms may be able to establish
themselves in Japan by finding markets, overcoming
red-tape, and suggesting joint ventures.

338. "Japan: The Trading Giants Shift to Investment."
     Business Week. 2615 (Dec. 10, 1979): 46.

     Mitsubishi International Corp. seeks to enlarge its
     holdings in energy resources and raw materials in the
     U.S. in its changing role from trader to investor. Its
     overseas investments of $185 million range from
     operating grain elevators to strip mining and steel
     fabrication. It recently invested in a project in
     Malaysia to produce liquified natural gas. Production
     of steam coal in New South Wales and an Australian
     smelting plant are among other investments. Mitsubishi
     and the 5 other major Japanese trading houses are
     increasing their overseas investments, particularly in
     the building industry. No longer are these trading
     companies just selling the materials for projects but
     they are actually getting involved in their
     development.

339. "Japan in America: Special Report." Business Week.
     (July 14, 1986): 44-55.

     In these five articles chronicling the Japanese
     investment in the U.S., there is a discussion of the
     "second wave" of Japanese industry in the U.S. The
     effect of Japanese management is analyzed, and there is
     a case study of the Arkansas Sanyo plant. The articles
     also consider the interplay of Japanese and American
     cultures and values in determining the success of the
     ventures.

340. "Japan Is Here to Stay." Business Week (Industrial
     Edition). 2614 (Dec. 3, 1979): 81-86.

     This is a treatment of the Japanese semiconductor
     industry. It has successfully captured much of the
     world market, and continues to grow at an increasing
     rate. Several manufacturers are already located in the
     U.S., and various incentives for increased presence in
     the U.S. are discussed. The possible impact of heavier
     protectionist limits on imports has tended to spur
     Japanese direct investment. The importance of Japanese
     quality assurance in its winning of the large market
     share is noted, and the reliance of U.S. manufacturers
     on Japanese computer memory chips is observed.
     Possibilities for U.S. government regulation to support
     U.S. industry are weighed.

341. "Japan, U.S.A." Business Week. 2955 (July 14,
     1986): 44-55.

     The growing presence of Japanese investments in the
     U.S. will have a deep impact. It may create jobs in
     depressed areas, raise productivity, and reduce trade
     friction. Various U.S. states are competing for the
     introduction of new investment from Japan. Cultural
     distinctions are becoming evident, as a distinctive
     management style is brought in. Questions about
     whether the new investment wave will stimulate US
     manufacturing, and include Americans in the decision-

making process are asked. The response of unions will
be another key to the impact of the investments. A
case study of Sanyo is offered. Some consideration of
the methods the Japanese are using to raise capital is
given, and questions are asked about the cultural and
political attitudes toward Japan.

342. "Japanese Brokerage Firms Broaden Their Horizons."
      World Business Weekly. 4.36 (Sept. 14, 1981):
      46-47.

At the time when Nomura Securities first joined the New
York Stock Exchange, the movement toward increasing the
flow of Japanese money into foreign markets was in full
swing. The company is an example of the trend which
attempts to hedge against fluctuations on the Japanese
market. Eurobond coupons and U.S. stocks and bonds
offer this hedge. As the yen appreciates, foreign
investment becomes more attractive. There will be
significant competition among Japanese investment firms
emerging.

343. "Japanese Cars at the Crossroads." Economist.
      280.7193 (July 11, 1981): 76-77.

This is a study of the role of the Japanese car
industry in the markets of the U.S. and Western Europe.
With some possibilities lurking for greater restrictions
on imports, the Japanese are looking toward increased
direct investment. Relocation abroad comes with
various pitfalls and benefits. The investment plans of
some of the larger auto makers are discussed.
Statistics are offered for the period 1975-1980.

344. "Japanese Firms Going into Production in U.S."
      Oriental Economist. 45 (June & July 1977): 6-9 &
      10-15.

This is a reflection on the Japanese entry into
typically U.S. production fields like TV's, chemicals,
and autos. It offers a sweeping survey of how Japanese
corporations are advancing in the U.S. markets.
Obstacles to the Japanese moving into U.S. fields are
noted, and progress for Japanese firms is cited.

345. "Japanese Foreign Direct Investment: Love and Hate in
      America." Economist. 306.7542 (March 19, 1988):
      74-75.

This is a general treatment of the debate on the
advantages and disadvantages of Japanese investment in
the U.S. For the most part, U.S. states encourage the
investments as they create jobs. No federal regulation
exists, so the states can offer financial incentives
and cut red tape to bring in the ventures they seek.
There are, however, some problems to expect between the
Japanese employers and U.S. workers. These are
considered worth the effort, since the investments will
bring rewards to the U.S. communities in which they are
located.

346. "Japanese Foreign Direct Investment: The Moneymen's
     Pursuit of Money." Economist. 306.7540 (March
     5, 1988): 83-84.

     The motives for Japanese financial institutions to
     invest abroad are examined, and the reasons why they
     succeed are described. The Japanese bankers are
     following their domestic clients who wish to invest
     abroad. The large capital supply moves into world
     markets, and there are business that bankers may enter
     overseas which are closed to them domestically because
     of regulations. The strong yen encourages outward
     movement. And market share can be gained abroad quite
     readily. This is just as important as returns in the
     short run. Some of the attributes of Japanese banks
     that make for success include their ability to provide
     low-cost, low-profit, high-volume loans, and their good
     Japanese business connections. There are many Japanese
     financial institutions now interested in entering
     brokerages houses in the U.S.

347. "Japanese Investment Abroad." Columbia Journal World
     Business. 8.4 (Winter 1973): 19-33.

     The structure and conditions for Japanese investment in
     the U.S. are examined. Various strategies can be taken
     by Japanese companies who wish to compete in the more
     expensive labor market of the U.S. Recent acquisitions
     in the U.S. are identified. The Japanese management
     system will face different conditions in the U.S.
     Strengths and weaknesses are considered. A case study
     of the Hitachi America's investment in the U.S. is then
     outlined.

348. "Japanese Investors Say Real Estate Is Most Critical
     Buy." National Real Estate Investor. 30.2 (Feb.
     1988): 26, 28.

     This article surveys the Japanese investors in the U.S.
     to determine the importance of real estate as a mode of
     direct investment. Decision makers at 45 large
     Japanese firms were interviewed. There were high
     ratings given by a majority of the respondents as to
     the importance of real estate. 57% expect to increase
     their holdings, and 64% indicated they would remain
     very important for the next two years. The attraction
     of U.S. real estate seems to be its availability and
     the good returns it offers. The Northeast and West are
     preferred areas, and office buildings and complexes are
     also popular. Most firms use U.S. intermediaries when
     they make such investments.

349. "Japan's Overseas Investments: The United States."
     Oriental Economist. 47.824 (June 1979): 37-50.

     The Japanese direct investments in the U.S. are
     examined for the year 1977. A comparison of the dollar
     and yen is made, and the type of Japanese sales and
     branch office structures in the U.S. is described. The
     Japanese role in the U.S. industrial sector is

considered, as well as sales, production and business
ties of Japanese investors to U.S. business.

350. "Japan's U.S. Plants Go Union: Labor-Relations Methods
that Work in Japan Are Not Easily Transplanted."
Business Week. (Oct. 5, 1981): 70+.

The campaigns for unionization of Japanese plants in
the U.S. are crucial for U.S. and Japanese industry.
There are large numbers of Japanese plants in the U.S.,
with a workforce of about 110,000 Americans. Some are
beginning to unionize, and this poses problems to
Japanese managers in some cases. Often the Japanese
have difficulty gaining worker acceptance of their
approach to labor relations, without causing friction.
Japanese methods are not always easy to transplant.
Wages and production standards can become issues.

351. Jenks, Craig. "Leasing: The Yen for American Clients."
Euromoney. (Jan. 1986): 105, 108.

The lease product which dominates Japanese leasing
activities is the yen-denominated conditional sales
contract, with a low interest rate and 15 to 18 year
terms. The constant mergers and acquisitions in this
volatile industry are discussed. Through this
activity, Japan is able to penetrate the U.S. leasing
market with both yen-denominated and dollar debt forms,
through the Japanese subsidiaries in the U.S. The
strongest growth for both Japanese and American leasing
operations is in factories and facilities.

352. Johnson, Richard W. "The Japanese Have Hit the Beaches
in Hawaii." Fortune. 92.3 (Sept. 1975): 130-144.

The presence of Japanese investors in the hotel
industry of the U.S., particularly in Hawaii has
grown. From 9% to 18% of the hotel rooms on the
island of Oahu are owned by a single investor, and
about another 9% are owned by other Japanese investors.
While reaction in Hawaii to the Japanese owners has
been mixed, public sensibilities have had limited
power.

353. Jones, Susan R., Anne Watzman, James Schwartz, Shota
Ushio, and Jon Joseph. "Auto Parts Makers Gird for
War." Chemical Week. 138.14 (April 2, 1986): 8,10.

Japan is offering increased competition to the chemical
process industries which supply parts to the auto
industry in the U.S. The creation of Japanese plants
in the U.S. brings with it an influx of Japanese parts
technology and suppliers. While Japanese manufacturers
operating in the U.S. have pledged to use local suppliers, the technology to make the parts needed may often
lag in the U.S. Then the Japanese suppliers step in.
Often quality becomes an issue with the purchase of
U.S. made parts.

354. Kaletsky, Anatole. "Living on Borrowed Money."

Financial Planning. 13.12 (Dec. 1984): 53-55.

This offers an analysis of the significance of the use
of Japanese investment to finance activities in the
U.S. With more than $100 billion per year, capital
influxes from Japanese and other investors bolster the
value of the dollar and keep U.S. interest rates down.
At the same time, it produces a negative influence.
There is a trade deficiency as a result of the
investments, and this hurts U.S. manufacturers. If
there is a loss of confidence among the foreign
investors in the U.S. economy, a collapse could result.
Some projections for the future are considered.

355. Kawata, Makoto. "Making It Work: Japanese Direct
     Investment in the United States." Journal of Japanese
     Trade & Industry. 3 (Jan./Feb. 1984): 25-27.

A look is taken at Japanese investments in the U.S.
with emphasis on the operations of Nissan Motor
Manufacturing Corporation, near Nashville, Tennessee,
and Sharp Manufacturing Company, in Memphis, Tennessee.

356. Kendall, Richard M. "Safety Management: Japanese-
     Style." Occupational Hazards. 49.2 (Feb. 1987): 48-
     51.

This treats the safety and health issues arising in
Japanese plants in the U.S. The automakers Honda and
Nissan are studied through interviews of participants
at Ohio and Tennessee plants. Characteristics of
Japanese safety concerns are as follows: workers
participate in safety decisions; managers take a
visible interest in safety; concerns can be addressed
quickly, because of the lack of hierarchy and
bureaucracy; peer influence tends to work toward safe
practices; housekeeping problems are minimized by
scheduling materials delivery well; communications are
open; and job rotation alleviates the dangers of
boredom. Some other features however, lead to some
possibilities for accidents. There is a strong
emphasis on productivity, and this can mean that
workers take more risks.

357. Kennedy, Kim. "Japan on Main Street, U.S.A." Corporate
     Design & Realty. 4.8 (Oct. 1985): 62-64.

Japanese investments in the U.S. are centered 38% in
the Western states, and total 715 companies nationwide.
In the Northeast there is also a significant concentration. Real estate is a sphere of investment
that has a greater amount of increase for Japan than
for any other country since 1979. Construction and
development is also a major area, with over 26
companies involved. Often they have worked for other
Japanese firms' development needs, gaining a
familiarity with U.S. markets. The location of
manufacturing is tending to be placed nearer to the
actual markets, and joint ventures with U.S. firms are
taking place. The Japanese employ about 90,000

Americans in manufacturing processes.

358. Kim, Youn-Suk. "Japan's Direct Investment in the
     United States." Seoul National University Economic
     Review. 13.1 (Dec. 1979): 124-137.

     In a theoretical model of trade barriers, this work
     deals with the function of multinationals in the U.S.
     Japan's direct investment activities are analyzed, and
     the viewpoint is offered that the nature of foreign
     investments is essentially defensive in motivation.

359. King, Paul, ed. M & A: For Richer, for Poorer.
     Euromoney Publications, 1987.

     This publication was issued as a supplement to
     Euromoney and Euromoney Corporate Finance. It recounts
     the state of hostile and friendly corporate takeovers
     in the U.S., Great Britain, Australia, and Western
     Europe. It also details some trends in Japanese
     acquisitions of U.S. firms, especially as the strong
     yen makes U.S. companies look attractively priced. The
     Japanese attitude, however, is portrayed as cautious.
     Most acquisitions are expected to take place on a
     strictly friendly basis. A listing of buyers and
     potential targets is offered, with comments on the
     various players in the field.

360. "Komatsu Digs Deeper into the U.S." Business Week
     (Industrial/Technology Edition). 2862 (Oct. 1,
     1984): 53.

     Komatsu, the largest construction machine manufacturer,
     is characterized in terms of its U.S. production plants
     and its overall position. The higher labor costs in
     the U.S. will have to be borne, but there is an
     advantage in insulating Komatsu from possible U.S.
     protectionism and currency fluctuations. The
     competitive strength of Komatsu has forced Caterpiller
     to lower prices in order to keep its share of the
     market. Plans for Komatsu to establish U.S. plants are
     discussed, to produce bulldozers, hydraulic excavators,
     and dump trucks. Dealer networks will be built. Sales
     by 1984 should reach $300 million.

361. Kotkin, Joel. "A Yen for Lending." Inc.. 10.4
     (April 1988): 107-110.

     This is an examination of the role of foreign banks in
     the U.S. There are now foreign banks which control
     about 22% of the U.S. commercial loans, especially
     important for midsized companies. These companies
     offer an easy entrance for the foreign bankers, and
     yield steady returns. There is also a partnership
     attitude among these firms, so the banks obtain
     potential customers and partners through them. Japan
     holds 8% of the U.S. commercial loans, and controls
     about 20% of California's assets. Chinese banks will
     be growing in competitive force, having formed 45 banks
     in the past 10 years.

362. Krauss, Alan. "Japanese 'Land Rush' Seen." Pensions
     & Investment Age. 13.23 (Oct. 28, 1985): 3,71.

     Japanese institutions investments in U.S. real estate
     could double that of 1984, reaching $1.5 billion in
     1985. As a rule, Japanese institutional investors
     purchase large blue-chip properties, thereby competing
     with U.S. pension fund investors. Although there are
     no direct real estate investments by Japanese pension
     funds, it is believed that a considerate portion of the
     estimated $60 billion in Japanese pension assets has
     come to the U.S. through trust banks and insurance
     companies. The pension funds are seeking the diversity
     that they cannot find in Japan. Japan lacks investment
     opportunities and has lower rates of return. Cultural
     and political reasons also play a role in rise of
     Japanese investments in the U.S.

363. Krisher, Bernard. "A Different Kind of Tiremaker Rolls
     into Nashville." Fortune. 105.6 (March 22, 1982):
     136-146.

     Japan's Bridgestone Tire Co. will be manufacturing
     tires in the U.S., and is arranging to purchase a plant
     in Nashville, Tennessee, from Firestone for $52
     million. Bridgestone needs overseas investments to
     maintain growth. In order to compete with Goodyear and
     Michelin, it must have a manufacturing base in both the
     U.S. and Europe. It is vital for Bridgestone's plans
     to reach an accord with the United Rubber Workers. The
     company has a strong commitment to research and
     development and has been a forerunner in tiremaking
     technology. However, the company will probably give
     more care to the wording of advertise- ments in the
     future, after agreeing to a consent decree with the
     Federal Trade Commission in 1975.

364. Kujawa, Duane. Japanese Multinationals in the United
     States: Case Studies. New York: Praeger, 1986.

     Case studies of Japanese multinationals operating in
     the U.S. are offered, analyzing differing corporate
     strategies and industrial relations. Each firm is
     reviewed in light of technology transfers from the
     Japanese parent. Corporate strategies are classified
     as product-, process-, and/or management-centered
     technology oriented. Management-centered firms are
     more likely to oppose unionization, to prefer a less
     stratified workforce in terms of job classification and
     assignments, to maintain flexibility in workforce
     management, to conduct cross-training, and to strive to
     avoid layoffs of production workers. Product life
     cycle and risk-aversion models are used to analyze
     corporate behavior.

365. Kujawa, Duane. "Technology Strategy and Industrial
     Relations: Case Studies of Japanese Multinationals in
     the United States." Journal of International Business
     Studies. 14.3 (Winter 1983): 9-22.

Eight case studies of U.S. manufacturing subsidiaries
of Japanese multinationals are analyzed for variations
in competitive strategies and industrial relations
practices. Based on 1980 data, each firm's technology
contributions coming from the Japanese parent is
categorized as having product-, process-, and/or
management-centered technology strategies. Findings
center on firms with management-centered strategies.
Results are interpreted in light of product life cycle
and risk-aversion models of firm behavior.

366. Lake, David. "Japanese Custodian Business in New York
Is Ripe for Expansion." Asian Finance. 12.5 (May 15,
1986): 48-51.

Japanese custodian banks are growing due to a weak U.S.
dollar, a strong U.S. economy, and a liberalized
environment. The custodian business, in which banks
are paid a fee to hold and process securities for large
institutional clients, is booming over the short term
along with Japanese investment in U.S. securities.
Japanese pension funds are entering the U.S. market
seeking higher returns and diversified portfolios. The
Bank of Tokyo and Daiwa Bank control over 85% of this
business, but are facing stiffer competition from other
Japanese banks and big U.S. institutions. In the
custodian business, technology has become a key factor
in meeting the volume and global requirements of
clients.

367. Lake, David. "Life Companies Make Big Inroads into
U.S." Asian Finance. 13.4AI 76-79.

Japanese life insurance companies are buying billions
of dollars of U.S. bonds, real estate, and equities.
Japanese investment rose to $49 billion in 1986, with
another $30 billion in U.S. Eurobonds and $16 billion
invested by the Bank of Japan in U.S. treasuries. Over
half of these life insurance company foreign investments is in U.S. treasuries. Japan's life companies
are the fastest growing financial service firms
worldwide. Improved cash flow led the insurers to
invest abroad. The Ministry of Finance recently raised
its foreign investment limit for life companies to 30%
of total assets overseas in order to stop the fall of
the yen. Equities investment is increasing, while
investment in the real estate market tripled in 1986.
Meanwhile, the short-term liabilities of Japanese banks
rose by over $90 billion last year. The banks are
investing heavily in long-term U.S. bonds while financing with short-term U.S. dollar borrowings.

368. LeCerf, Barry H., and Bryan H. Berry. "Nissan's Truck
Plant: People and Robots Under One Roof." Iron Age.
225.26 (Sept. 15, 1982): 29-33.

This is an analysis of the Nissan auto plant in
Tennessee, which assembles 156,000 trucks per year and
can handle up to 240,000 with additional machinery.
Robots are an important element in the production

process there. And off-line processes are used to a
larger degree than is generally found in American
plants.   Automated control and monitoring systems are
described. The expenditure for training employees has
been quite significant. There are expectations that
work will be offered for a lifetime, though no guarantees are to be offered. The company is hoping to avoid
any unionization.

369. Lindner, Russell C. and Edward L. Monahan, Jr.
     "Observations on Understanding and Working with
     Japanese Investors." Real Estate Review. 17.4
     (Winter 1988): 31-36.

     An overview of Japanese investments in the US is
     offered, with analysis of trends. Japan's affluence
     and surplus of capital is described. There is a need
     to stimulate the Japanese economy while diversifying
     investments. The Ministry of Finance wishes to ease
     restriction of foreign investments, to accomplish its
     aims. Japanese investors are persistent and tend to
     remain for steady periods of time, rather than opening
     and closing ventures quickly. Patience and profession-
     alism are the hallmarks of Japanese investors, and U.S.
     counterparts have much to gain from adopting similar
     attitudes.

370. Long, Donald R. "More Foreign Firms Putting Money in
     U.S. Plants." Industry Week. 179.1 (Oct. 1, 1973):
     30-35.

     Most U.S. businessmen agree that direct foreign
     investments in the U.S. is good for the economy. The
     U.S. is becoming an attractive location for foreign
     investment because of the cheap dollar, wage
     advantages, and success with exports. The Japanese
     government has recently removed restrictions to
     overseas investments and this is expected to further
     encourage investments in the U.S. By 1972, 537 foreign
     firms in the U.S. employed more than 400,000 people in
     819 subsidiaries with a book value exceeding $13
     billion.

371. Majumdar, Badiul A. "Technology Transfers and
     International Competitiveness: The Case of Electronic
     Calculators." Journal of International Business
     Studies. 11.2 (Fall 1980): 103-11.

     This paper draws a link between innovations,
     diffusions, and international competitiveness in
     electronic calculators. The aim is to provide a
     greater understanding of the process. Changes in
     factor intensities were responsible for international
     migrations of electronic calculator technology between
     the U.S. and Japan. There is an association between
     technology transfers and international trade.

372. Martin, James A. "Big Dreams, Strong Yen."
     Computerworld. 20.46 (Nov. 17, 1986): 146,122.

Fujitsu Ltd., Japan's largest computer maker, announced plans to acquire 80% of Fairchild Semiconductor Corp. The Japanese are interested in shopping for struggling U.S. chip companies. This could give the Japanese a new dominance in the world chip market and an edge in the hardware and software markets. Fairchild's business is in bipolar gate-array chips that are used in U.S. defense weapons. Key U.S. semiconductor vendors have met to discuss the ramifications of a Fairchild-Fujitsu merger. While Japan has production capacity and manufacturing expertise, the U.S. has architectural innovation. Both countries working together could improve the plight of the semiconductor industry.

373. Matsumoto, Yutaka. "Future Car Competition Centers on America." Business Japan. 30.9 (Sept. 1985): 22-23.

In an overview of the automobile manufacturing interests of Toyota in the U.S., there is a consideration of the size and impact of the Japanese operations. Dealerships in the U.S. generally face difficulties with steady supplies, and usually trade in other brands of cars too. Manufacturing in the U.S. now amounts to about 200,000 for all Japanese firms building cars in the U.S., but should increase to more than 1.3 million per year. Competition and activities of dealers at up-coming dealers' conventions are discussed. The future sales plans of the Toyota management will be revealed at the convention.

374. McCarthy, James E. "The Germans, the Dutch, the Japanese, the French, the Swiss, the Canadian, the British Are Coming: One Reason They Are Investing Here Is That the U.S. Is Becoming a Low-Cost Country." Across the Board. 13.12 (Dec. 1976): 21-29.

This brief article offers a general explanation for the rise in direct foreign investment in the U.S. Factors considered are costs, resources, and confidence. This simply means that the labor costs in the U.S. now are declining relative to other advanced countries, and the supply of natural resources is ample in many categories. Confidence in the political stability of the U.S. is high, as is the confidence that many firms are developing in their own ability to locate in the U.S. As they grow, such firms begin to feel ready for the move. Statistics about the 100 largest foreign- owned firms, including many from Japan, are offered.

375. McClenahen, John S. "Cultural Hybrids: Japanese Plants in the U.S." Industry Week. 200.4 (Feb. 19, 1979): 73-75.

With investments of nearly $2 billion in the U.S., Japanese manufacturing and other investment activities are growing more and more in significance. The reasons for the Japanese incursion are outlined. Some characteristics of the management style of the Japanese firms are noted, with an emphasis on stable markets

and stable employee bases. Consensus management is
discussed, with pros and cons of the decision-making
process outlined. The importance of communication
within the production team is also noted.

376. McClenahen, John S. "Who Owns U.S. Industry?"
     Industry Week. 224.1 (Jan. 7, 1985): 30-34.

     This is an assessment of the significance of foreign
     investment in the U.S., in which Japan has a major
     role. Total investment by other countries in the U.S.
     has increased more than 4 times over 10 years.
     Statistics on the magnitude of foreign investment are
     offered. Some of the largest holders are the U.K., the
     Netherlands, Japan, Germany, Switzerland, France, and
     Canada. There is a non-profit group seeking to reduce
     the proliferation of foreign investment in the U.S.,
     and while its concerns might overstate the dangers, it
     is clear that the control of U.S. industry is at issue.
     Monitoring is proposed for foods, chemicals, petroleum,
     electrical, electronics, cement, banking, and defense
     products.

377. Menzies, Hugh D. "Can the Twain Meet at Mitsubishi?
     To Boost Business in the U.S., the Giant Trading
     Company Is Trying to Attract Smarter Americans."
     Fortune. 103 (Jan. 26, 1981): 41-44+.

     The American executives who work for Mitsubishi
     International Corporation, MIC, encounter a set of
     special demands from their employers. First, the
     corporation is unusually large by American standards
     and the trading services it provides earn very thin
     profits. Americanization policies call for the use of
     Americans in key executive positions, but qualified
     people who understand the requirements of the sogo
     shosha are difficult to find. The recruitment and
     training activities at MIC are described.

378. Meyers, Laura. "Tokyo California." Madison Avenue.
     28.9 (Sept. 1986): 64-66.

     Increasing the market share of Japanese auto makers
     based in Southern California is a major goal of the
     Japanese manufacturers. They now have 20% of the U.S.
     car market, and gains in market share are put above
     profitability in terms of corporate goals. There is a
     discussion of the components of the business which are
     Americanized and those which have the typical Japanese
     style. Advertising has been created in the U.S.,
     promoting products rather than corporate image, through
     television and magazines primarily. On the other hand,
     management practices such as quality circles are being
     brought in from Japan.

379. Meyers, William. "Japanese Landlords." Institutional
     Investor. 21.3 (March 1987): 143-152.

     The Japanese entry into the real estate markets in the
     U.S. has been growing. Acquisitions such as the Arco

Plaza in Los Angeles and Exxon's headquarters in New
York are among the almost $6 billion in U.S. holdings
by the Japanese. It is possible that Japanese trust
banks may obtain permission to invest pension funds
in U.S. property as well. Regions where Japanese real
estate purchases are concentrated include the East and
West coasts, plus cities such as Chicago and Atlanta.
Reasons for the increase in activities are offered.
Weakening of the yen and political pressure would be
factors that could slow the trend of acquisitions by
the Japanese in the U.S.

380. Meyers, William. "Shuwa's Great American Gamble."
Institutional Investor. 22.2 (Feb. 1988): 136-140.

This treats the case of Shuwa Investments Corp., a
phenomenally fast growing real estate investor. It led
the way in purchases of major U.S. office buildings
acquisitions, and bought a large number of properties
between 1985 and 97. There was a question as to their
continuing in this pattern of investment after the
October stock market crash. Shuwa discontinued
negotiations on three prospective purchases at that
time. However, there are signs that the company will
continue to invest. It has entered into a deal to buy
a Manhattan office building for $250 million. The
large number of holdings of Shuwa will require the
development of significant expertise in building
management.

381. Misawa, Mitsuru. "Financing Japanese Investments in
the United States: Case Studies of a Large and a
Medium-Sized Firm." Financial Management. 14.4
(Winter 1985): 5-12.

In this study of the large and mid-size firms which are
a product of Japanese "global financial engineering",
there is an assessment of the motives for Japanese
foreign investment. A shift from basic resource areas
such as petroleum and toward autos, electrical-
electronic products and other manufacturing has been
seen. The internationalization of finance includes
using government financial incentives, leasing
arrangements, and a multiple currency basis. Two case
studies of the Japanese firms in the U.S. are offered,
from the automobile sector. The financing arrangements
are detailed for each.

382. Miskell, J. T. "Japan Discovers the U.S." Modern
Asia. 8.2 (March 1974): 33-35.

This is a general examination of the issues involved in
the recent movement for Japanese investment in the U.S.
Traditional investment patterns are shown to be
altering, and profitability in the U.S. sites is
investigated. Some consideration is given to textiles,
and the expectations of future expansion plans.

383. "Mitsubishi: Japanese Giant's Plans for Growth in the
U.S." Business Week. 2697 (July 20, 1981): 128-132.

Mitsubishi is a firm with major plans for growth in the
U.S. Its activities are outlined, both in Japan and in
the U.S. Some of its concerns are automobiles,
especially linked with Chrysler, and aircraft. It has
an electric subsidiary which manufactures
semiconductors in the U.S. It uses its diverse
organization as a basis for a trading company, which is
the worlds largest. Banking is another area of
interest, and its assets in the U.S. amount to $4
billion. Some of the Mitsubishi sectors are growing
faster than others, as it is observed. The directors
of the corporation meet regularly with Getty Oil Co.,
Monsanto Co., and Westinghouse Electric Corp. Still
other U.S. firms are associated with the Mitsubishi
group, as well. Competition with U.S. firms and trends
in Americanization are noted.

384. "Mitsubishi Electric America Develops a Higher
     Profile." OEP Office Equipment & Products. 13.69 (July
     1984): 24-25.

     This is a treatment of the Mitsubishi operations in the
     U.S. The various parent-subsidiary relationships are
     outlined. A consideration of the history of the firm's
     move into foreign markets is given, showing that after
     a slow beginning, the company increased its foreign
     revenues by almost 43% in 1983. The growth of its
     investments was paralleled by certain other changes.
     Product lines were developed, and American production
     facilities increased. Computers manufacturing is
     outlined. The maintenance of R & D operations is
     described. New products and projects are also
     outlined, with plans and prospects for the future
     assessed.

385. Mogi, Yuzaburo. "The Conduct of International
     Business: One Company's Credo -- Kikkoman, Soy Sauce
     and the U.S. Market." Columbia Journal of World
     Business (Commemorative Issue). 20.4 (1986): 93-94.

     As a special case the activities of the Kikkoman
     Corporation of Japan are investigated. The Kikkoman
     experience demonstrates many facets of the interplay
     between a foreign investor and a host country. While
     the firm is marketing its food projects in the entire
     U.S., it sells its soy sauce in several countries, as
     well. The company has developed methods of harmonizing
     with the host culture. One technique is the adaptation
     to laws and customs. Also there is an effort to employ
     local citizens, to participate in activities of the
     localities, to see that Japanese employees mix with
     local citizens, and to employ U.S. suppliers. Some-
     times it is effective to delegate authority to local
     managers.

386. Mooney, James L. "International Real Estate: While Far
     Eastern Investment in U.S. Real Estate Slowed in '84,
     Interest Is There to Spur Its Growth." National Real
     Estate Investor. 27.1 (Jan. 1985): 70,72.

Japanese investors are likely to increase their
investments in the U.S. real estate market as they
become more familiar with it. Japanese insurance
companies have been involved in U.S. real estate,
usually through joint ventures with U.S. firms. Other
Far East investors include Hong Kong, where a weak real
estate market has not decreased interest in the U.S.
market, and Singapore, where a strong economy has
encouraged investors to invest locally. However,
Singapore's interest in the U.S. will most likely
increase. In general, Far Eastern real estate investors prefer prime properties - office buildings and
shopping centers - in central business districts on the
West Coast and in the Sun Belt. These investments
function to preserve capital, protect against
inflation, and provide cash flow.

387. Morris, John. "Japan Enters the U.S. a Step at a
     Time." Euromoney; M & A Supplement. (Aug. 1987):
     30-36.

     This year does not expect a strong rise in Japanese
     purchases of U.S. firms, even though there has been a
     steady increase. While a strong yen encourages
     acquisitions, Japanese management still maintains a
     conservative view. Wall Street dealmakers expect an
     increase in merger activity and are making attractive
     offers to acquire companies. Some experts believe the
     Japanese want to start small in order to gain exper-
     ience, while others believe this is a mistake because
     of missed opportunities. The number of deals being
     explored is on the increase. Japanese firms are
     consulting merger and acquisition firms to find them
     appropriate targets. Hostile takeover bids may present
     the Japanese with some trouble since they lack the
     expertise to defend themselves.

388. Mushakoji, Kinhisa. "The Process of
     Internationalization at Asahi Glass Co."
     International Management (Europe Edition). 41.3
     (March 1986): 73-80.

     Asahi Glass Co. (Tokyo) is the world's 4th-largest
     producer of flat glass and the biggest producer of
     automotive glass and television tube glass. Glass
     constitutes 54% of 1983's global turnover of $2.6
     billion, while chemical products accounted for 39% of
     sales. In 1954, Asahi Glass entered the international
     market by building a soda chlorine plant in Indonesia;
     now, it also has companies in India, Thailand, and
     Malaysia. Recently, the firm began investing in
     industrialized countries, such as the U.S., Belgium,
     and the Netherlands. Asahi Glass' International
     operations are characterized by a liberal policy in
     regard to technology transfer, a great deal of
     independence from the parent company for the
     affiliates, and frequent job rotation among groups and
     industrial fields.

389. Nathans, Leah. "Then Came Kawamura." Business

Month.   130.4 (Oct. 1987): 40-42.

Shigekuni Kawamura, of Dainippon Ink and Chemicals
Inc., has successfully won two hostile takeovers in the
U.S. In 1986, he gained control of Sun Chemical
Corp.'s big graphic arts division; in August 1987,
after a two month battle, his offer for Reichhold
Chemicals Inc. was accepted. Kawamura believes he can
make Reichhold's profitable in 3-4 years and he wants
to hold the $765- million (sales) company together,
since its specialty- chemical businesses are inter-
related. Dainippon may even be able to save the dying
product lines. Some analysts think that Dainippon will
keep only those segments that fit with its printing ink
business. Kawamura is unique in Japan's business
community for his understanding of Western ways. He
prefers Japanese-style management but realizes that
Japanese lifelong employment and seniority systems will
not work in the U.S. However, he is critical of the
American practice of delegating authority.

390. Niesyn, Betsy. "U.S. and Japanese Ventures Need Common
     Ground." High-Tech Marketing. 3.7 (July 1986): 51.

     Japanese-U.S. joint operations in the U.S. often
     experience problems because the involved companies do
     not understand each other clearly. This was the
     finding of a study completed by Bain & Co. They inter-
     viewed key managers at 13 major U.S. and Japanese firms
     that have had business relations in the past five
     years. The study's principal conclusions included 1.
     operations built from scratch were the most successful,
     2. each party needs to understand the other's
     objectives and management needs, 3. one partner needs
     to have final decision making authority, and 4. at the
     beginning it must be decided whether American or
     Japanese culture will prevail. Communications problems
     often arise from different management styles.

391. "Overseas Factories Are All-or-Nothing Gamble for
     Japan's Auto Makers." Business Japan. 32.4 (April
     1987): 79-85.

     Japanese auto manufacturers' struggle for survival
     centers around the yen's appreciation and overseas
     production in North America. The rising yen has
     deteriorated profits from exports and weakened the
     competitive pricing in foreign markets. Domestic sales
     still remain strong. All Japanese car producers have
     started to build factories in North America. Ten
     plants are expected to be completed by 1989 by 8
     passenger car makers. The U.S. auto industry is
     fighting this development by insisting on including
     locally produced cars in the export quota. Japanese
     auto producers are investing $500 million to $800
     million in the U.S. Failure to establish North
     American factories seriously threatens the survival of
     any Japanese firm.

392. Ozawa, Terutomo. "Japan's New Industrial Offensive in

the United States." <u>MSU Business Topics</u>. 21.4
(Autumn 1973): 23-28.

Japanese firms are increasingly attracted to direct
investment in the U.S. to circumvent protectionism and
prevent the loss of their export markets. The Japanese
are free to establish wholly owned subsidiaries in the
U.S., unlike their American counterparts who are
restricted by the Japanese government policies on
foreign direct investments. In fact, Japanese
investments are welcome in the U.S. as a measure for
improving the balance-of-payments and employment.
States are even sending missions to Japan to attract
investments to their locality. The yen's appreciation
has been another strong incentive for Japanese
manufacturers to invest in the U.S.

393. Packard, George R. "The Coming U.S.-Japan Crisis."
<u>Foreign Affairs</u>. 66.2 (Winter 1987/1988): 348-367.

The potential for serious friction between Japan and
the U.S. exists, in spite of the developing ties
between the two. There is a tendency toward
protectionism. This can develop into retaliatory
action, and a search for new partners. Japan may turn
to China and the Soviets, and may attempt to protect
its dominance in Asian economics. The balance of power
could become fragile, with confrontational
interactions. This would be a negative outcome, one
that should be avoided. The article proposes a
"Wisemen's Commission" to be formed, consisting of
senior staff from both countries. They could work out
mutual policies to insure good trade practices and
envision long range directions.

394. Palmer, George. "Japanese Banks Abroad: California,
Here We Come." <u>Banker</u>. 138.746 (April 1988):
49, 51-53.

This is a treatment of Japanese banking influence in
the state of California. As almost 9% of total U.S.
banking is controlled by Japan, the role they occupy is
significant. California First Bank, the largest of the
nine Japanese owned banks in the U.S., uses competitive
pricing and sales techniques. The strong yen helps
these institutions to gain momentum and to grow. Some
of the methods the Japanese banks are using to gain
their market shares include higher rates for deposits,
charging lower rates for loans, and keeping the details
of each transaction in careful order. These techniques
are building customer satisfaction and loyalty.

395. Patterson, William Pat. "Japan's Economic 'Grand
Design'." <u>Industry Week</u>. 214.6 (Sept. 20, 1982):
46-48,50-54.

Japan's trade relationship with the U.S. has been
showing the effects of its national trade policies.
The trade imbalance has made U.S. policymakers consider
greater use of the principle of reciprocity in market

access for future trade agreements. There is a
consideration of the elements contributing to the
Japanese trade superiority. An important factor is the
MITI's role in international trade and policy
direction. The plans for Japan to expand its
investments in U.S. territories are assessed. Joint
ventures as the means to this new investment move are
described.

396. Patterson, William Pat. "Planting a Japanese 'Hybrid'
     on U.S. Soil." Industry Week. 212.6 (March 22,
     1982): 74-75,78.

     In this study of the NEC Electronics USA, a subsidiary
     of Nippon Electric, there is consideration given to the
     management and planning techniques that have been very
     successful at the outset. The executives of NEC
     envision a blend of Japanese and American professional
     skills and styles. Restructuring is taking place to
     achieve this amalgam. The motives for establishing the
     U.S. operations, which may reach revenues of up to $500
     million by 1985, are complex. Avoiding the protection-
     ist regulations of U.S. policy is only one of the
     factors. Making closer contact with markets for better
     product design and service is also important. Long-term
     planning is the key to initial gains, as NEC has
     captured 70% of the U.S. market for high density
     computer chips.

397. Pendleton, Jennifer. "Will Americans Buy an 'Ohio
     Honda'?" Advertising Age. 54.36 (Aug. 29, 1983):
     M-4, M-5, M-26.

     Nissan Motor Co. Ltd. and Honda Motor Co. Ltd., the 2nd
     and 3rd largest automobile importers in the U.S.,
     respectively, have opened up U.S. plants. Vehicles
     produced here are not subject to the voluntary import
     restrictions. Protectionistic sentiments in the U.S.
     could severely limit Japan's trading activities.
     Opening these plants has a good public relations value.
     Both Honda and Nissan have done little to promote the
     domestic origin of its U.S. produced cars. While both
     companies want to reinvest their money in the U.S.
     economy, they must deal with the stigma attached to the
     "Made in America" label.

398. Pugel, Thomas A., ed. with Robert G. Hawkins. Fragile
     Interdependence; Economic Issues in U.S.-Japanese Trade
     and Investment. Lexington, Mass.: Lexington Books,
     1986.

     This book is designed to bring together experts from
     Japan and the U.S. to analyze areas of stress on the
     interdependence of the two countries. Three major
     areas are identified: 1. the access to import markets,
     2. the issue of international investment as financial
     liberalizations proceeds and large two-way flows of
     direct investment, and 3. the question of international
     technology competition. The authors discuss specific
     problems and attempted solutions. The goal is to

promote information which can lead to significant
policy recommendations. The points of view are
diverse.

399. "Real Estate: A High-Water Mark?" Institutional
      Investor. 22.1 (Jan. 1988): 129-136.

      The Japanese interest in U.S. real estate has been
      continuing. The Dai-Ichi Mutual Life Insurance Co.
      acquired parts of the Citicorp complex, in the largest
      deal of 1987. The real estate industry estimates that
      Japanese investors have bought as much as $1 billion in
      California. Some U.S.-Japanese partnerships include
      one between Nomura Securities and Eastdil Realty. Some
      of their ventures have been quite large. Activity may
      be tapering off, but there is no sign of a major
      slowdown in Japanese buying.

400. Regeling, Henry, C. J. Bartram, and Takahide Moribe.
      "Foreign Investors in the United States: A Symposium."
      Real Estate Review. 14.3 (Fall 1984): 34-42.

      This symposium on foreign investments in the U.S. looks
      at three countries active in U.S. real estate, the
      Netherlands, Scotland, and Japan. While Dutch firms
      are often seeking diversification, many have already
      obtained large real estate portfolios in their home
      country. The Scottish Amicable Life Assurance Society
      holds about $80 million in U.S. real estate, with a mix
      of about 50% in office properties, 30% in retail, and
      20% in industrial warehouses. Japanese investors, who
      find a scarcity of land at home and high capital gains
      taxes on recent acquisitions, also have a strong
      interest in U.S. property. Life insurance and real
      estate companies are both active investors.

401. Rehder, Robert R. "Japanese Transplants: A New Model
      for Detroit." Business Horizons. 31.1 (Jan./Feb.
      1988): 52-61.

      A characterization of the Japanese impact on U.S.
      automaking is given. Some of the major partnerships
      which have been formed include General Motors and
      Toyota, Chrysler and Mitsubishi, and Ford and Mazda.
      These operations have profited from the Japanese
      management techniques which depend on the understanding
      of how each subsystem in the plant relies on every
      other system. Interrelationships are key to the
      constant improvements and frequent speed-ups that are
      planned as part of an on-going productivity push.
      Often the team approach is used to bring these
      management practices about.

402. Reich, Robert, and Eric Mankin. "Joint Ventures with
      Japan Give Away Our Future." Harvard Business
      Review. 64.2 (March/April 1986): 78-86.

      Japanese joint ventures in U.S. investment arise from
      the need to avoid protectionist regulations. The U.S.
      firms enter into joint ventures to obtain high-quality

product lines at low cost. Nonetheless, the opinion is
offered that the U.S. industries are suffering because
Japan keeps the better projects, with more advanced
processes in Japan. American workers receive less
crucial experience, and lose the opportunity to be
innovative. Suggestions of ways the U.S. government
could promote the innovation process are offered.

403. Reier, Sharon. "Japanese Investors Come of Age."
      Institutional Investor. 19.12 (Dec. 1985): 131-136.

      Beginning slowly, Japan's move toward U.S. real estate
      investment is expected to increase its pace. The MITI
      just granted permission for such investments 5 years
      ago. Already there are insurance companies and private
      real estate firms entering the U.S. market. Banks are
      also being drawn in. The Japanese style of negotiation
      is characterized by very deliberate and careful
      planning and decision-making. The type of real estate
      they prefer to acquire is premier properties with low
      risk.

404. Rescigno, Richard. "Here Comes Honda: It's Now No. 4
      Among U.S. Car Makers ... And Pushing." Barron's.
      65.48 (Dec. 2, 1985): 13,48-49.

      This interview with Honda of America's president,
      Tetsuo Chino, offers his views on the role of his
      company. As the fourth largest manufacturer of cars in
      the U.S., Honda has ambitious plans. New product lines
      are discussed. The plan is for 60% of the parts to be
      locally obtained. Production at its Marysville, Ohio
      plant will increase. Profits and the dollar exchange
      rate are discussed. Mr. Chino offers the view that it
      would be desirable to make Honda of America an American
      corporation.

405. Rice, Faye. "America's New No. 4 Automaker -- Honda."
      Fortune. 112.9 (Oct. 28, 1985): 30-33.

      This offers details of the role of Honda in the U.S.
      auto market. As the 4th largest producer, Honda has
      passed American Motors but still has does not nearly
      equal any of the big three. Relative to Nissan and
      Toyota, Honda is doing well. Profit for the year
      ending February 1986 will be $665 million, and $125 of
      the profit comes from U.S. built autos. New product
      lines are discussed. The future prospect for more U.S.
      investment is outlined and possibilities for another
      U.S. plan emerge.

406. Richman, Louis S. "The Japanese Buying Binge: Real
      Estate Shoguns, Propelled by a Huge Trade Surplus and a
      Land Boom at Home, Are Driving Up Property Prices in
      the U.S.; Your Next Landlord May be Japanese."
      Fortune. 116.13 (Dec. 7, 1987): 77+.

      This article describes some of the effects of Japanese
      competition for major commercial properties on the U.S.
      real estate market. Some of the activities of key

Japanese investors are outlined, including Mitsui
Fudosan, Shwa Corp., and Dai-Ichi Mutual Life.
Commentators believe the Japanese are the driving force
in the first-tier markets for U.S. real estate. U.S.
Institutional investors are often surprised by the high
prices the Japanese are willing to pay. The role of
Japanese developers is also examined, along with trends
in the real estate industry as a whole.

407. Roehl, T. W., M. M. Amano, V. W. Rapp, et al. "Trading
in the New World Economy." Journal of Contemporary
Business. 8.2 (1979): I-133.

In this collection, economic relations of Japan, the
U.S. and Asian countries are discussed. Trade and
investments are described. The control of trade by
Japan is outlined. The investments and climate in Asia
and the American Pacific Northwest are examined. The
case of one company's investments in Indonesian raw
materials production is offered. The capital markets
of Asia are characterized. In general, statistics
cover the period from 1971-1978. There are fourteen
contributors in all.

408. Russell, Sabin. "The Yen for Capital: Japanese
Companies Look for Direct Venture Investments."
Venture. 7.11 (Nov. 1985): 134,137.

There has been a growth in investment by Japanese firms
in U.S. investments. Often the Japanese supply capital
and the technology is not transferred. Instead a long-
term relationship is evolving. There has been a 30%
rise in Japanese investment in U.S. firms in 1984.
Some examples are offered. A genetic engineering
operation and a brewery are profiled. The nature of
the financial deals is discussed, and the marketing and
direction of the firms are explained.

409. Savage, Peter. "Houston Woos Far East Companies."
Chemical Week. 142.3 (Jan. 20, 1988): 24.

Houston, Texas has been actively seeking investments
from Japan, notably in the chemical process industry.
The Houston Economic Development Council has estimated
that about 40% of the new U.S. petrochemical activity
is taking place in the Houston area. Some of the
Japanese firms include Kaneka Texas, Nippon Pigment,
and Shintech. Mitsubishi Metals also has a copper
smelting project which Houston would like to attract.
There are favorable labor supplies and other good
connections in the region which make it competitive as
a location for foreign investment.

410. "Saving the Auto Industry from Itself: Will Japanese
Know-How Do the Trick?" Dollars and Sense. (April
1987): 6-9.

This article concentrates on the joint venture between
General Motors and Toyota in the establishment of New
United Motors Manufacturing, Inc. (NUMMI) in Fremont,

California.

411. Sears, Cecil E. "Japanese Real Estate Investment in
the United States." Urban Land. 46 (Feb. 1987): 6-
11.

Conditions favoring Japanese real estate investment in
the U.S. are analyzed, including Japanese preferences.
A discussion is also included of what it is like
working with Japanese investors.

412. Senia, Al. "Japanese Automaking Lands in America --
What It Means to U.S. Suppliers." Production. 98.5
(Nov. 1986): 42-49.

The efficiency of the three Japanese car assembly
plants in the U.S. is investigated. High technology,
harmony among workers, and good management are
identified as factors in the performance success. Cost
effectiveness and high motivation of the workforce also
have an impact. The employees are treated with special
respect, as a valued resource, and responsibility for
the work is transferred to the individuals involved.
Many of the parts are imported, but American suppliers
may be able to overcome quality problems to meet more
of the demand by these Japanese plants.

413. Setzer, Steven W. and Richard Korman. "Japanese Bring
More than Money in Their Quest for U.S. Market Share."
ENR. 220.9 (March 3, 1988): 30-36.

This gives an overview of the Japanese role in the U.S.
construction market. Firms are beginning to enter the
field, primarily in the form of subsidiaries of
established Japanese firms working in the U.S. Kumagai
Gumi Co. Ltd. is an example. Many of the Japanese
construction firms have very strong relationships with
clients, in which a verbal system of contract negoti-
ation prevails, as it did for U.S. firms 40 years ago.
The Japanese firms aim for customer satisfaction, and
each takes the role of research very seriously, with
expenditures of 1% by each on in-house laboratories.
There is an assessment of the opinions of Japanese
construction research and market impact.

414. Siegel, Jay S. "The Japanese to New England: Are
Unions the Sticking Point?" New England Business.
4.10 (June 7, 1982): 65-66.

Honda Motor Corp. is the first major Japanese company
to locate in the New England area. A $9 million parts
distribution center is to be build this spring in
Windsor Locks, CT. and expects to employ about 100
workers. This may result in a confrontation between
the company and union over organizing attempts,
particularly by the Teamsters Union which has been
successful at several Toyota parts centers. Different
management- employee ideologies separate the Japanese
companies from American unions; and it is questionable
how the Japanese will respond to U.S. union efforts.

It may deter the Japanese from investing more in New
England, or they may view it as a challenge and try to
instill Japanese-like attitudes in the American worker.

415. Simon, Ruth, and Andrew Tanzer. "Fiasco at Fujitec."
     Forbes. 139.6 (March 23, 1987): 60-61.

     Fujitec Co. (Osaka, Japan), the Japanese elevator
     company, is running 2 1/2 years behind schedule in the
     construction of a $50 million plant in Lebanon, Ohio.
     The company made a number of miscalculations and
     failures in entering the U.S. market. First, they
     failed to develop a U.S. market through imports.
     Second, construction was begun before it received its
     first order and eventually plant size was cut to 2/3
     its original goal. Third, having under bid its
     competitor to gain market share, it found itself unable
     to deliver on time. The company ran into problems with
     union work rules, problems in the factory, and
     unfamiliarity with U.S. suppliers. Techniques developed
     in Japan were unable to be transferred simply to the
     U.S. And lastly, the overbuilt commercial real estate
     market leaves even established U.S. firms with low
     expectations for the next several years.

416. Smith, Joel, and William Childs. "Imported from
     America: Cooperative Labor Relations at New United
     Motor Manufacturing, Inc." Industrial Relations Law
     Journal. 9.1 (1987): 70-81.

     The New United Motor Manufacturing Inc. (NUMMI), a
     joint-venture between Toyota and General Motors, is
     discussing labor relations with union representatives.
     In a letter of intent signed by NUMMI and the United
     Auto Workers, it was agreed to reduce substantially the
     number of skilled trade and production line class-
     ifications. In return, the union understood, although
     not in writing, that NUMMI would provide stable,
     long-term employment. A team concept is used at the
     plant which holds the employees responsible for the
     quality of the cars with management and the union
     working together to solve problems.

417. Snyder, Jesse. "Subaru Drives into New Niches."
     Advertising Age. 57.35 (June 16, 1986): S33-S34.

     Subaru of America has been seeking markets other
     importers ignored and using low-key advertising. The
     announcement that Isuzu Motors and vehicle supplier
     Fuji Heavy Industries Ltd., which owns 49% of Subaru,
     would build an assembly plant in the U.S. acknowledges
     that Subaru is being affected by competition and trade
     issues. Subaru sells over 150,000 cars a year and is
     building a retail network capable of selling 250,000-
     300,000 units annually. Company strategy involves
     finding good dealers, insuring customer satisfaction,
     and picking the right market niche.

418. Stavro, Barry. "Made in the U.S.A." Forbes. 135.8
     (April 22, 1985): 50-54.

Foreign auto manufacturers are building plants in the
U.S. These include Volkswagen, Honda, Nissan, and
Toyota. Mazda will begin production in 1987 and
Mitsubishi is looking for sites. It is projected that
in 10-20 years foreign manufacturers will be producing
major components and designing cars for the local
market. By 1989, four Japanese firms expect to produce
one million vehicles in the U.S.. Currently 30
Japanese auto parts suppliers are setting up operations
in the U.S. The possibility of future trade
restraints, cheaper land, and higher U.S. profits make
the U.S. an attractive production site. Competition is
likely to intensify; new jobs will be created, while
holding down labor costs; and a new challenge will be
given to the autoworkers' union.

419. Storck, William J. "New Incentives Are Spurring Growth
of Foreign Investment in U.S. Chemicals." Chemical &
Engineering News. 56.9 (Feb. 27, 1978): 12-16.

Since 1973, the U.S. Dept. of Commerce reports that
investment in the U.S. chemical industry by foreign-
owned firms has increased by more than 50%. During the
same period, foreign investments in all U.S. industries
increased by 46%. Reasons for this surge of foreign
investment include the size of the U.S. market, better
supplies of raw materials, declining dollar, less
government regulation, and less labor unrest. Most of
the foreign investment in the chemical industry comes
from Europe, particularly West Germany. The lack of
Japanese investment stands out as the major exception.
It appears that Japan's good labor relations at home do
not provide the incentives for U.S. investment that it
provides for Europe.

420. Suby, C., and L. Stallmann. "Japan Leads the List of
Top Foreign Firms in the U.S." Electronic Business;
The Business Magazine for the Electronics Industry.
11.20 (Oct. 15, 1985): 85-87.

Although the high-tech industry in the U.S. is growing
slowly, foreign investment in electronics continues to
climb. The Japanese, especially, have been very active
by setting up joint ventures, acquiring and expanding
existing companies, and establishing U.S. manufacturing operations and sales and distribution channels
for parts or products produced abroad. The current
influx of foreign capital played an active role in the
U.S. economic recovery. Statistics are provided for
the year 1984.

421. Takitani, Kenyi. "A Prototype for Japanese Investment
in the U.S." Columbia Journal of World Business.
8.4 (Winter 1973): 31-33.

Japanese corporations are expected within the next 10
years to become the largest group of foreign investors
in the U.S., surpassing the U.K., West Germany, and
France. The case of Hitachi Metals America is offered
as an example of Japanese activity. This firm is a

subsidiary of Japan's Hitachi Metals Ltd, which in turn
is part of Hitachi, Ltd Group, Japan's largest
industrial conglomerate. In 1973, Hitachi invested $10
million in a magnetics business in Edmore, Michigan,
renaming it Hitachi Magnetics Corp. The author
examines the experience of this case from a number of
viewpoints.

422. Tanzer, Andrew. "Beer Wars from Across The Pacific."
      Forbes. 141.8 (April 18, 1988): 33-35.

The Japanese beer industry is reviewed. Kirin Brewery
Co. has been having a decline in the share it holds of
the total market. Plans are being made to purchase a
large European brewery and re-enter the U.S. market
more competitively. Some of the reasons for the slow
performance of Kirin, while it yet retains good
profitability, are presented, with the need to develop
new products. A possible move into Canadian production
sites is being considered. Other plans include
acquisition of more Coca-Cola Bottling Co. entities.

423. Tanzer, Andrew. "Deukmejian's Dilemma." Forbes.
      135.2 (Jan. 28, 1985): 62-63.

Three leading Japanese companies have decided to build
new plants in Oregon, rather than in California because
of its hostile tax climate. California governor George
Deukmejian is being urged to reform that state's
corporate tax code. The central issue is the unitary
tax, which takes an average of a corporation's
California payroll, assets, and sales as a percentage
of worldwide figures and imposes California's taxes on
that basis. One of the problems of reforming the tax
code is providing equitable treatment for U.S. inter-
nationals, compared with foreign ones. In addition,
California receives $500 million a year from this
taxation method. Any position Deukmejian takes will
hurt someone, but meanwhile the state is losing
millions in investments.

424. Tanzer, Andrew. "The Silicon Valley Greater Co-
      Prosperity Sphere." Forbes. 134.14 (Dec. 17, 1984):
      31-32.

California's Silicon Valley, the center of U.S.
electronics industry, is receiving growing investments
from Japanese trading companies and venture capital
firms. Although current investments are not large, the
implications are long-term. A Japanese venture
capital investment with an American startup company
provides them with a "strategic partnership" that gives
exclusive product distribution rights in Japan and
access to advanced technology. Furthermore, Japanese
banks get underwriting and lending opportunities in the
U.S. that they can not get in Japan. There is mixed
opinion among U.S. high-technology firms about Japanese
involvement. It could however open Japanese markets to
U.S. products and the possibility of licensing
technology for manufacturing in Japan.

425. Tanzer, Andrew. "With Friends Like These." Forbes.
     137.14 (June 30, 1986): 31-32.

     Dainippon Ink & Chemicals Inc., a producer of printing
     inks, synthetic resins, and specialty chemicals, is the
     first Japanese firm to attempt a hostile takeover of a
     U.S. corporation. Dainippon has offered $85 a share
     for Sun Chemical Corp., which recently brought $63 a
     share. Although Dainippon licenses Sun's printing-ink
     technology, it is fighting the takeover. Dainippon has
     always been interested in acquiring Sun and decided to
     bid on the firm before a competitor did. Dainippon
     seeks to acquire a 30% share of the global printing-ink
     market and has already made 2 smaller acquisitions. Sun
     executives can block Dainippon's bid because they own
     51% of the firm's stock. Kawamura, president of
     Dainippon, believes more Japanese firms will launch
     hostile takeover bids for U.S. firms as Japanese
     interest rates stay low and the yen appreciates.

426. Tomisawa, Konomi. "The Auto Parts Industry of Japan;
     Facing the Challenge of Internationalization and
     Technical Innovation." LTCB Research; Quarterly
     Review of Japanese Industry. 74 (July/Aug. 1984): 1-
     13.

     This article explores the internationalization of the
     Japanese auto parts industry and the technological
     transformation it is undergoing. The inroads Japanese
     car producers and parts manufacturers have made
     overseas are described. Pros and cons of overseas
     operations are given with a description of auto parts
     companies' activities in the U.S. A look is taken at
     the direction auto technology is moving, particularly
     technology for improving engine performance. Responses
     of auto parts manufacturers to these changes are given.
     Statistics and projections provided for 1960-1990.

427. Treece, James, Sarah Bartlett, and Amy Borrus.
     "Mighty Nomura Tries to Muscle In on Wall Street."
     Business Week (Industrial/Technology Edition). 2925
     (Dec. 16, 1985): 76-77.

     Nomura Securities Co., the world largest brokerage
     house, is aggressively going after the U.S.
     institutional market. Until now, they have operated
     almost exclusively in Japan with only 3% of its after-
     tax new income coming from the U.S. In the next 1 to 3
     years, the firm plans to increase this to 10%. This
     year Nomura had over $1 billion in pre-tax profits and
     huge retail sales force that sells bonds and mutual
     funds door-to-door. It is questioned whether Nomura
     can adapt its Japanese marketing strategy to Wall
     Street. It currently has no mergers operation and its
     equities research has been criticized.

428. "TRW: Fujitsu's Key to the U.S." Business Week.
     (May 19, 1980): 118+.

     Fujitsu, Japan's largest computer manufacturer, and TRW

have jointly formed a Los Angeles based marketing
company. TRW is a U.S. firm with software and
distribution knowledge. Fujitsu views this combine
effort as an inroad to the large U.S. market.

429. Tsubota, Yasuhiro. "Where to Buy; Where to Build?"
     Chief Executive. 39 (Spring 1987): 42-43.

     Japanese manufacturers are investing in the U.S. on
     account of a rising yen and the fear of protectionism.
     Epson America Inc., a subsidiary of Seiko Epson Corp.,
     plans to produce in the U.S., France, and the U.K.,
     selecting each site on its relative merits. Portland,
     Oregon, was finally chosen, offering the best site for
     financial and psychological reasons. Initially the
     firm will assemble parts manufactured in Japan, but
     later calls for the development of local teams to
     purchase local components and increase engineering
     capacities. Japanese companies are expected to locate
     more of their production operations in the U.S.

430. Tsurumi, Yoshi. "The Strategic Framework for Japanese
     Investments in the U.S." Columbia Journal of World
     Business. 8.4 (Winter 1973): 19-25.

     Japanese corporations are recognizing opportunities of
     investing overseas, particularly in the U.S. Sony,
     NMB, and Fuji are among the Japanese manufacturers
     interested in direct investments in the U.S. It has
     been the strategy of U.S. multinationals to move with
     the international product technology cycle, while small
     to medium-sized companies have chosen smaller
     specialized product markets. These strategies have
     limited U.S. firms' marketing capacity, and open the
     possibility for the Japanese to inject a new
     competitive spirit. Japanese direct investments in the
     U.S. should change the anti-foreign investment attitude
     prevailing Japan. Both countries should benefit from
     the merger of management and innovation methods.

431. Unger, Harlow. "The Japanese Style Scores U.S.
     Successes." Industrial Management. 9.5 (June 1985):
     13.

     The number of Japanese manufacturers now operating in
     the U.S. is reaching 700. Columbia University Graduate
     School of Business has produced a study showing that
     these Japanese companies are performing better than
     their U.S. counterparts. Their success is attributed
     to product quality, good management-labor relations,
     and Japanese culture with its strong work ethic. The
     study concluded that the Japanese management style
     could be adapted to almost any industry in any country.
     Japanese management methods seek to make workers feel
     as though their are a member of a corporate "family,"
     involving them in various activities and soliciting
     their ideas. By placing emphasis on teamwork and
     cooperation, the Japanese encourage American workers to
     become competitive more productivity.

432. United States. Congress. House. Committee on Energy
     and Commerce. Subcommittee on Commerce,
     Transportation, and Tourism. Future of the Automobile
     Industry: Hearing, February 8, 1984.. 98th Congress,
     2nd Session. Washington, D.C.: U.S. Government
     Printing Office, 1984.

     In light of the recent tentative approval of the
     Federal Trade Commission of the proposed joint venture
     between General Motors and Toyota, the issue calls
     forth discussion. The current testimony reflects the
     views of public interest groups, auto manufacturers
     such as Lee Iacocca, chairman of Chrysler, and
     professors from New York University School of Law,
     Harvard, and George Washington University. The
     committee chairman, James J. Florio, submitted comments
     to the effect that the future of American manufact-
     uring, as well as the trends toward increasing
     corporate mergers must be considered, in addition to
     the present position of the automobile industry. The
     high interest rates, currency imbalance, plant
     closings, and sagging productivity in auto manufacture
     seem to threaten the industry.

433. United States. Congress. House. Committee on Ways and
     Means. Subcommittee on Trade. Task Force Report on
     United States-Japan Trade, with Additional Views.
     Washington D.C.: GPO, 1979.

     This report finds that bilateral trade would be
     normalized between Japan and the U.S. with the
     elimination of certain trade barriers. Japan is moving
     toward opening markets other than high technology and
     agriculture. The introduction of more Japanese
     investment in the U.S., creating more jobs, is regarded
     as desirable. American structural problems are
     identified as causes of the trade imbalance, and
     Japanese trade barriers are considered of secondary
     importance.

434. "Unveiling the Global Car." Economist. 306.7539
     (Feb. 27, 1988): 54-55.

     Japanese investment in automobile manufacturing in the
     U.S. is discussed. The reasons for the increasing turn
     to overseas investment are sketched. While the yen is
     strong, U.S. factories can be acquired at a bargain.
     The Honda approach has been to work on their own, while
     most others have used joint ventures. There had been
     some worry that the U.S. would see its plants overtaken
     by foreign interests and that little of the value would
     be produced locally. But this has not materialized.
     The Honda forecast is that about 65% of the value of
     its cars will be U.S. in origin. Direct investment
     will also be increased in Europe, as trade restrictions
     need to be overcome.

435. "VTR Wars: VHS Beats Beta, Sets Up Local Production in
     Europe." Business Japan. 30.11 (Nov. 1985): 55-59.

Since 1984, the sales of VHS models of videotape recorders has risen sharply, while Sony's beta models have declined. Sony is now turning to deluxe models and 8 mm VCR's. Competition is intensifying among VHS producers, including sales of camera-VCR combinations which have risen steeply. Sony is expected to challenge the VHS mode with its own 8-mm camera-VCR. As a result of European restrictions on Japanese imports in 1983, Japanese producers have established operations in Germany and the U.K. The high cost of buying parts locally is causing these Japanese firms to consider local production of electronic parts also. The U.S.-Japanese trade dispute has made Japanese producers consider manufacturing in the U.S. as well.

436. Waddell, Harry. "Japanese Banks Seek (Cautiously) to Enlarge U.S. Correspondent Networks." <u>Banking</u>. 69.7 (July 1977): 106-108.

For a number of reasons, Japanese banks are establishing correspondent relationships with U.S. banks. 1. They anticipate increased trade with the U.S. as well as increased investments in the U.S. 2. Preparations need to be made in order to grow with growing businesses in the U.S. 3. In Southeast Asia, they seek to make better deals for U.S. trade financing. 4. Dealing with regional banks may prove to be more satisfactory than with dealing with major money center banks. Advice is given to U.S. banks that want to establish a correspondent relationship with a Japanese bank.

437. Watanabe, Soitsu. "Trends in Japan's Manufacturing Investment in the United States." <u>EXIM Review</u>. 7.2 (1987): 32-87.

Japanese investment trends in the U.S. are discussed and the effects they will have on U.S.-Japan relations. Investments are given by industry type, coupled with an appraisal of the investment environment in the U.S.

438. Welch, Randy. "Getting a Piece of the Yen." <u>Oil & Gas Investor</u>. 5.10 (May 1986): 22-26.

A small group of Japanese investors are considering where to invest in U.S. oil business. The U.S. oil industry has the advantage of being a relatively good place to find oil, has a stable political system, and is a good place place to train their engineers, geologists, and moneychangers. Currently only 2% of Japan's oil exports come from the U.S. Japan National Oil Corp., a government funded agency, is the major investor, often providing up to 80% of capital for exploration. Although some deals have not worked out, Nippon Oil Co., Ltd has been able to survive. The Marubeni trading house and Japan Petroleum Exploration are two firms actively committed to ongoing investments in the U.S. Tax-oriented financial angles, risk acceptance, and oilfield variety are factors that act as barriers to Japanese oil investments in the U.S.

439. Whitman, Karen. "Portland Markets Itself at U.S.-Japan
     Meeting." Marketing News. 20.10 (May 9, 1986): 7.

     In 1985, Portland, Oregon, hosted an annual conference
     of mayors and chamber of commerce presidents from Japan
     and the U.S. Oregon has had a longstanding cultural
     and economic relationship with Japan. The Whitman
     Advertising & Public Relations Inc. (Portland) was
     responsible for making the conference a success.
     Japanese consultants were employed, and the conference
     staff took an 8-week course on Japanese culture. A
     public education campaign was introduced to educate
     Oregonians, and statewide tours, social activities, and
     cultural events were given to influence Japanese
     opinions about the Oregon marketplace. A technology
     tour highlighted Oregon's industry and facilities. The
     conference was success, and it should help to increase
     Japanese tourism and investment in the Pacific
     Northwest.

440. "Why Japanese Auto Makers Hesitate to Go to the United
     States?" Oriental Economist. 48.80 (April 1980):
     6-9.

     This article offers some insight as to the reasons why
     Japanese auto manufacturers are somewhat hesitant to
     set up production facilities in the United States. The
     attitudes of the U.S. car industry are part of the
     situation, and the economics of competing in the U.S.
     are another part. Though the U.S. manufacturers cannot
     adequately supply the U.S. market with compact models,
     there is resistance on the part of American labor
     leaders to the increased sale of Japanese cars in the
     U.S. Attitudes of key U.S. auto executives are
     presented.

441. Wilkins, Mira. "American-Japanese Direct Foreign
     Investment Relationships, 1930-1952." Business
     History Review. 56.4 (Winter 1982): 497-518.

     The history of U.S. multinational investment in Japan
     and Japanese multinational investment in the U.S. is
     presented. The period from 1930-1952 is considered.
     This time is significant because it covers the
     depression, war, and return to peace. The institutions
     are shown to adapt to a changing environment. Data is
     offered to support the observation that the cross-
     investment was not symmetrical.

442. Wilson, John, and Steven Dryden. "Semiconductors:
     What the Fairchild Fiasco Signals for Trade Policy."
     Business Week (Industrial/Technology Edition). 2991
     (March 30, 1987): 28.

     The Reagan Administration and U.S. chipmakers pressured
     Schlumberger Ltd. to withdraw its deal to sell Fair-
     child Semiconductor Corp. to Fujitsu Ltd. (Japan.) This
     may signify the end of a U.S. open market to foreign
     investors. Last year, the International Trade
     Commission found the Japanese guilty of dumping chips

in the U.S. Semiconductor executives felt that
permitting the deal would be rewarding the Japanese for
unfair trade practices. In addition, Commerce
Secretary Malcolm Baldrige is calling for a government
policy to prevent foreign takeovers that would harm
national security or other vital interests. U.S.
officials also charge Japan is violating the
Semiconductor Trade Agreement, especially in Southeast
Asia.

443. Wood, Bill. "Hasegawan Komuten's Big Stake in Hawaii."
     Hawaii Business. 26 (Feb. 1981): 34-36.

     This article discusses Hasegawan Komuten, a Japanese
     owned company, that has become one of the largest
     condominium developers in the Hawaiian islands.

444. "Yaohan's Carves Its Niche in U.S. Market." Chain
     Store Age Executive Edition. 63.2 (Feb. 1987): 48,52.

     Yaohan's will open a 50,000 sq. foot supermarket/
     department store in Edgewater, N.J., in fall 1987. It
     will cater to the Asian population, importing much of
     the food and merchandise from Japan. The store is owned
     by Yaohan's Department Store Co. in Japan. Edgewater
     was chosen because of the diversity of the population
     in the surrounding area: 65% Asian, 30% Caucasian, and
     5% "other." There are also two other Yaohan store in
     Los Angeles county, California. Each store adapts to
     the specific needs and wants of the population in its
     area.

445. Yasaki, Edward K. "Japanese Investments in the U.S.
     Computer Industry." Datamation. 24.12 (Nov. 15,
     1978): 72,76,81.

     During the 1980's, Japanese computer equipment will
     increasingly enter the U.S. market. The recent rise of
     sales was produced by the depressed value of the dollar
     against the yen and and other currencies. This shift
     in the exchange rates, and the U.S. lead in semi-
     conductor technology, has also caused a flood of
     foreign investments in the U.S. semiconductor industry.
     If Americans continue to accept Japanese computers
     because of their reliability and price-performance,
     they will open manufacturing operations in the U.S.
     This will enable them to escape possible import
     barriers to their products, to study more closely
     American marketing and management techniques, and to
     gain favorable public opinion by contributing to the
     U.S. economy.

446. "Yearning for Yen." Forbes. 121.6 (March 20, 1978):
     64.

     The Japanese finance ministry is encouraging Japanese
     nationals to investment in foreign stocks and bonds.
     Investors are expected to make large purchases in the
     U.S. stock market as soon as it begins to rise. This
     should make a difference to the depressed U.S. stock

market. Japanese brokers are expected to receive most
of the new business, but American stockbrokers will
receive new business also. Japanese investment is
likely to be concentrated in the Sunbelt, where their
studies indicate it to be the most dynamic area. This
rise in Japanese investment will result from Japan's
finance ministry dropping its rules requiring
permission to buy U.S. dollars and forbidding
speculation in foreign currency.

447. Yoshida, Mamoru. Japanese Direct Manufacturing
     Investment in the United States. New York: Praeger,
     1987.

     This book attempts to investigate the decision-making
     processes and the control systems of Japanese companies
     in high-tech industries operating in the U.S. The
     high-tech industries offer an example in which
     competition is intense, and there is an emphasis on the
     structural adjustment of the Japanese economy toward
     these industries. The impact of Japanese industrial
     policy in the hi-tech area is also felt significantly.
     It is also an aim of the work to provide some new
     insights into the subject of the government-business
     relationship in Japan, with particular concern for the
     effects on business strategies in Japan.

448. Zweig, Phillip L. and Richard Meyer. "Banzai Bull."
     Financial World. 157.4 (Feb. 9, 1988): 20-21.

     New developments by Nomura Securities and Daiwa
     Securities are described. As brokerage firms in Japan,
     they are seeking outlets to promote U.S. stocks to
     Japanese individual investors. Never before have these
     investors been attracted to U.S. equities, but there is
     now a possibility for this type of investment. Some of
     the reasons why it has become a possibility are
     discussed. Incentives to the Japanese investor will be
     growing, particularly for U.S. stocks involved in
     manufacturing, for machinery, pharmaceuticals and
     chemicals.

LATIN AMERICA

449. "Argentina Seeks Big Growth in Japanese Investment."
     Latin America Economic Report. 7.39 (Oct. 5, 1979):
     306.

     Argentina's trade with Japan is described for the 1969-
     1978 period with wheat, meat, and fruit being
     Argentina's major exports. Argentina would like an
     increase of Japanese investment in their country.
     Japanese companies are presently engaged in major
     investment projects in steel, railways, and fishing.

450. "Brazil - Japan's Investment Ardor Cools Off - Panama -
     High Economic Hopes If Ratification Comes." Business
     Week. 2503 (Oct. 3, 1977): 54-55.

The Japanese, who were counting on big profits from
their investments in Brazil, are pulling out for 3 main
reasons: 1. an across-the-board reining in of foreign
activity, 2. Brazil's ballooning trade deficit, and
3. world recession. In 1975, Brazil decided to require
importers to deposit for 360 days without interest the
equivalent of the F.O.B. cost of imported materials and
components, to cut back its enormous import bill.
This, plus the cost of locally borrowed money - up to
53% - has discouraged foreign activity in Brazil. The
ratification of the recently initiated Panama Canal
treaties is likely to greatly increase opportunities
for growth and development in Panama. Real estate and
transportation facilities would be ceded to Panama by
the treaties, and Canal leasing and related services
would create additional income for the country.

451. Frank, Allan Dodds. "Everyone Wants Us." Forbes.
      139.4 (Feb. 23, 1987): 37-38.

      The Panama Canal is shaping up to be a major economic
      and foreign policy problem for the U.S. In 1999, the
      U.S. bases there and the Canal will revert to the
      Panamanians, and the U.S. will want to lease back the
      bases. However, the Japanese have proposed to finance
      over $400 million to widen the Canal and upgrade the
      trans-Isthmus railroad. Japan's exports to Panama have
      risen 7-fold since 1980 to $641 million in 1985,
      making Panama more fiscally independent from the U.S.
      It is reported that goods from such countries as
      Colombia and Cuba are offloaded and recertified in
      Panama's Free Zone to ease their entry into the U.S.
      The U.S.S.R. has a strong but unofficial presence in
      Panama. With the Soviets on the political front and
      the Japanese on the economic front, the U.S. should
      have its hands full in Central America.

452. Houghton, Lyal. "Getting to Grips with Debt-Equity
      Swaps." Euromoney. (March 1987): 151-154.

      Japanese banks intend to set up a jointly owned
      institution to handle loans to developing countries.
      The Ministry of Finance is considering the plan. It
      would help reduce the debts of developing countries
      such as Malaysia and the Philippines. Japanese
      companies are buying up the debt of Mexico and the
      Philippines to swap for local currency needed for
      investment projects. A U.S. investment bank buys a
      loan from a commercial bank that fears it will never
      collect from the debtor nation. The investment bank
      then sells the loan to an investing company that needs
      the currency of the debtor nation. The investor
      tenders the loan to the central bank of the debtor
      country for about 80%-90% of its local currency value.
      Japanese manufacturing firms' acceptance of this method
      of financing acts as a catalyst for direct investment
      in the Philippines and Mexico. Investment banks
      promoting this debt repurchase system stress that the
      money is being recycled for its original purpose.

453. "Japanese Overseas Investments: Brazil 1." Oriental
     Economist. 48.832 (Feb. 1980): 32-43.

     This is a statistical treatment of the characteristics
     of Japanese investments in Brazil. A consideration of
     the nature of the corporations investing, and the
     capital that is involved is given.

454. "Japanese Overseas Investments: Brazil 2." Oriental
     Economist. 48.833 (March 1980): 54-61.

     A continuation of an article in last month's issue,
     this is a further development of the treatment of
     Japanese investment in Brazil. The investors and the
     nature and extent of the capital from Japan are
     considered.

455. "Japanese Rate Brazil Top of the Investment League."
     Latin America Economic Report. 5.46 (Nov. 25, 1977):
     223.

     This is a study of the rating of Brazil as compared to
     other investment locations from the point of view of
     the Japanese investor. Classifications are made
     according to market-oriented industries. The year of
     focus is 1977.

456. Kung, S. W. "Brazil and Japan: Partners for Economic
     Growth." Oriental Economist. 46.812 (June 1978):
     30-36.

     Brazil reassembles Japan in the size of its population
     and growth rate of its economy. Its developmental path
     may follow that of Japan in some key respects. The
     state of Japanese investment in Brazil is noted, with
     attention to the sectors of its concentration. Steel
     and infrastructural growth are described. The scope of
     Japanese investments is quite wide, with manufacturing
     and mining in the lead. A discussion of Japan's
     capacity to invest abroad is also offered.

457. Kung, S. W. et al. "Japanese Investment in Latin
     America: (1 & 2) Mexican and Brazilian Experiments."
     Oriental Economist. 48.835, 836 (May & June 1980):
     28-31 & 35-38.

     Japan has found a receptive partner in Latin America.
     While Japanese investments are less welcome in
     Southeast Asia, where Japan's political history has
     created obstacles, in Latin America there is a vast and
     growing market for Japanese exports and investments,
     providing good access to markets of other advanced
     nations, as well. Attitudes and patterns of investment
     by Japan in Brazil and Mexico are delineated as
     examples of the region as a whole.

458. "Milestones of Japanese Affiliated Spinners in Brazil."
     JTN; The Most Comprehensive Textile Magazine. 366 (May,
     1985): 42-45.

This details the history of Japanese investment in
Brazil since 1951. Data is offered by type of
industry. Brazilian spinning equipment is portrayed,
and features of the Japanese affiliated spinning
operations are examined. Competition is heating up,
and should be expected to be increasing in the future.

459. Okita, Saburo. The Developing Economies and Japan.
      Tokyo: University of Tokyo Press, 1980.

These essays focus on the question of promoting
economic development without threatening national
integrity and traditions. Some essays consider the
problem of food production and transfer of resources to
developing countries. Others rely on the Japanese
experience as an example of rapid growth. A third
section details Japan's relations with the developing
world, in terms of the north-south dialogue, Japan and
Latin America, and specifically a comparison of Japan
and Brazil. The Japan ASEAN relationship is also
examined.

460. Ozawa, Terutomo, M. Pluciennik, and K. Rao. "Japanese
      Direct Investment in Brazil." Columbia Journal of
      World Business. 11.3 (Fall 1976): 107-116.

An historical overview of Japanese investments in
Brazil is offered. The 1969-1974 period saw a relative
increase in Japanese investments in Brazil compared
with those of other countries. Reasons are presented
for this increase. The first wave of Japanese
investment occurred in the 1955-1960 period. A lull
and then a new surge took place in the sixties. The
1970's has seen increased cooperation with the
Brazilian government. A ranking of Japanese ventures
by invested capital in Brazil's industry is given for
1974. Some large projects underway are described with
suggestions for future prospects.

461. Pearce, Jean. "Firm Relationship Built on Mutual
      Benefits: An Interview with Luiz Paulo Lindenberg
      Sette, Ambassador of Brazil." Business Japan
      31.12 (Dec. 1986): 50-52.

In an interview, Brazil's ambassador to Japan discusses
the relations between Brazil and Japan. Numerous
Japanese nationals are living in Brazil, and many have
settled there for generations, contributing to the
culture greatly. Some of the achievements of the
Japanese investing in profitable Brazilian enterprises
are discussed, as well as problems in continuing the
investments at the present time, with the specter of
Brazil's debt situation. Prospects for more
cooperation and understanding, with diverse trade
developments, are envisioned.

462. Sieniawski, Michael. "South America Giant Seeks
      Stronger Links with Asia." Asian Business. 21.11
      (Nov. 1985): 30-32.

Brazil is seeking stronger economic ties with Asia on
account of a growing fear of protectionism by
industrialized nations and its high level of foreign
debt. Japan is Brazil's third largest foreign investor
with an estimated 400 companies employing 10,000
workers with a total of $2,000 million in assets. No
Japanese cars are imported and only Toyota has
manufacturing facilities to produce high-cost jeeps.
Brazil's two-way trade with the Peoples' Republic of
China is expected to reach $1,000 million by the end of
1984 with a favorable balance of trade for Brazil.
China has purchased two Brazilian lumber mills, and
their products will be shipped to China. Brazil's
strict import regulations have made trade with China
difficult.

463. Wiegner, Kathleen K. "How to Mix Sake and Tequila."
     Forbes. 139.6 (March 23, 1987): 48-51.

     Japanese firms, such as Sanyo Industries America Corp.,
     are moving their assembly facilities across the border
     into Mexico. Components are brought into Mexico
     in-bond (duty free), assembled, using cheaper Mexican
     labor, and then exported into the U.S. Union leaders
     are seeking measures to slow down the moves into
     Mexico, but the U.S. Dept. of Commerce feels the
     in-bond program helps create jobs since many of the
     components are produced in the U.S. Further, the move
     of labor- intensive operations to Mexico may cause U.S.
     factories to be converted to the production of more
     technically advanced products. The only Japanese
     concern is the high rate of employee turnover in the
     in-bond market and its effect on product quality.

464. Yamada, Mitsuhiko. "A Study on Divestitures by
     Japanese Corporations in Foreign Countries." Japanese
     Economic Studies. 14 (Spring 1986): 3-51.

     Changes in the pattern of direct foreign investment by
     Japanese firms are outlined for the period since 1970,
     when the quantity of investments began to grow rapidly.
     There is some emphasis on experiences in the ASEAN
     countries, the Middle East, and Brazil. There is then
     a treatment of the reasons for divestiture, after a
     careful terminological discussion. Several case
     studies are then outlined.

III

EUROPE AND AFRICA

This chapter covers Japanese investments in Europe and Africa. The European section is divided into Continental Europe and the United Kingdom and Ireland. For individual country listings, the Subject Index should be consulted.

EUROPE

Continental Europe

465. Beresford, M. "And Now, Le Defi Japonais." European Business, Paris. 42 (Autumn 1974): 17-27.

This article focuses on the onslaught of Japanese investment in Europe. European fund managers, unfamiliar with Japanese business practices, must hone their skills and sharpen their understanding of the way the Japanese work, learning their competitive strengths and advantages. This knowledge can assist in developing a coherent strategic response to continuing Japanese challenges and can prepare the way for the multinational joint venture, in which Europe and Japan can work together to strengthen both economies.

466. Burton, F. N., and F. H. Saelens. "Direct Investment by Sogo-Shosha in Europe." Journal of World Trade Law. 17.3 (May/June 1983): 249-258.

This article provides an overview and examination of the role of the Japanese general trader in Europe, focusing on investment activities that have been taking place in third world countries. Regional management offices are discussed, as are trading subsidiaries, sales, service, and manufacturing companies. Information is provided concerning ownership of sales companies, founded by overall statistics concerning the years 1971 through 1981.

467. Burton, F. N., and F. H. Saelens. "The European
     Investments of Japanese Financial Institutions."
     Columbia Journal of World Business. 21.4 (Winter
     1986): 27-33.

     The diversification of Japanese financial activity in
     Europe has come about partially because of restrictions
     at home, but also because of inducements abroad. In
     Japan there are fewer banking opportunities and
     numerous domestic controls. In Europe, Japanese
     investors have the opportunity to achieve higher rates
     of return in unregulated overseas markets by using
     supranational subsidiaries. Also, Japanese banks wish
     to follow corporate customers overseas by establishing
     host-country subsidiaries. Through these worldwide
     subsidiaries, the Japanese also acquire vast amounts of
     knowledge in preparation for wider deregulation of
     domestic markets. They are gaining experience overseas
     in activities from which they are barred at home.

468. Burton, F. N., and F. H. Saelens. "Investment in
     Trade; The Japanese General Traders in Western Europe."
     Gestion 2000, Louvain-la-Neuve. 3.3 (1985): 49-72.

     The sogo-shosha, Japanese general traders, have
     established a huge network of sales subsidiaries in
     Western Europe. An increase in this direction is not
     expected in the future, as it is widely believed that
     the traders worldwide are now in a period of
     consolidation, not expansion. This piece includes an
     outline of the general traders' basic characteristics
     and their associated industrial groupings, of foreign
     direct investment (an overview of Japan's largest
     foreign direct investors), and of direct investment in
     Western Europe. These investments are classified into
     regional management offices, trading subsidiaries, and
     sales, service, and manufacturing companies. There is
     a description of owner characteristics and statistics
     from 1982.

469. Burton, F. N., and F. H. Saelens. "The Structure and
     Characteristics of Japanese Foreign Direct Investment
     in West Germany." Management International Review.
     20.4 (1980): 7-16.

     Japan's deficiency of natural resources and its
     burgeoning cost of industrial land contributed to the
     large expansion of the country's direct foreign
     investment drive from 1968-1974. Pollution became a
     concern as well, and Japan wisely shifted away from
     heavy industry and into knowledge-based endeavors.
     Foreign investment was encouraged by the government
     through loan and tax concession programs. The initial
     foreign investors in West Germany were general traders,
     although from 1955-1978 this trend was replaced by the
     manufacturer, with product emphasis shifting from
     consumer to industrial goods. Innovative Japanese
     technology changed the strategy of cheap labor and
     economies of scale. Having developed their markets
     first with exports, Japanese direct investors now tend

to be huge oligopolies, basing their strength on
production efficiency and technological innovation.

470. Burton, F. N., and F. H.   Saelens.   "Trends in the
Growth of Japanese International Banking in Western
Europe." Intereconomics; Monthly Review of
International Trade and Development.   18.4 (July/Aug.
1983): 172- 176.

A general account is given of the development of
Japanese international banking with special attention
to performance in Western Europe.   The Japanese banking
system is analyzed to show the effects internationalization and economic changes have brought.   Japanese
investments in European financial institutions is
presented with statistics provided for 1963-1979.

471. Crabbe, Matthew.   "Japanese Eurobond Houses: Wa Means
Harmony -- Or Does It?"   Euromoney.   (June 1986):
31-33.

Historically, Euromarket subsidiaries of Japanese
securities houses and banks have been keen rivals.
However, "wa," Japanese for harmony, is becoming
characteristic of the Japanese approach in the
international capital markets.   Syndicate managers are
predicting that the first Eurodollar deals with an all-
Japanese co-management group may occur soon.   Japanese
lead managers once paid foreign houses for their
nominal participation in Sushi bond issues, but now
the Japanese desire their own placing power.   Japanese
bank subsidiaries in London, such as Mitsubishi Trust
International and Taiyo Kobe International, are
interested primarily in trading among themselves.   This
could result in the formation of a Japanese Euromarket
association.   However, some Japanese houses are not
convinced that the old competitive ways are being
superseded by a more sophisticated and streamlined
business ethic.

472. Fodella, Gianni, ed.   Japan's Economy in a Comparative
Prospective.   Tenterden, Kent, England: Norbury, 1983.

Two articles in the collection touch upon the role of
Japan as an investor abroad, one in comparison with the
role of Italy.   The financial structures in Italy and
Japan are found to be similar, while the underlying
productivity and government relations are quite
different.   In its direct foreign investment in Asia,
Japan has some unique characteristics.   The rate of
increase and the degree of motivation for Japanese
direct foreign investment are distinctive.   The
Japanese role is often that of tutor, encouraging
industrialization.   Its prospects as an overseas
investor are assessed.

473. "A Foreign Aid Program for Energy Research."   Business
Week (Industrial Edition).   2553 (Sept. 25, 1978):
60.

Negotiations are occurring with the West Germans and
the Japanese for financial backing of a $700 million
plant to be built by Gulf Oil Corp. to demonstrate
solvent refined coal technology. The process converts
coal into boiler fuel to be burned in existing oil-
fired power plants. West Germany has agreed to $30
million in direct financing, and government officials
hope to increase this to $175 million or 25% of the
full project cost. A similar deal is being made with
the Japanese, who want to include fusion research as
part of the package. The Japanese accept the principle
of a "balanced approach" to fusion and coal technology
cooperation. The Energy Dept. plans to finalize the
agreement within the next few months.

474. Gregory, Gene. "The Future of Japanese Investment in
Europe." Euromoney. (June 1975): 64-69.

Japanese investment in Europe is analyzed in this
article. The Japanese are switching for importation to
direct investment in manufacturing. Also examined are
the Japanese financial and marketing substructures in
Europe. The balance of foreign investment is given by
region.

475. Gregory, Gene. "Japan: Finding a Toehold in Europe."
Far Eastern Economic Review. 86.48 (Dec. 6, 1974):
67-69.

Changing conditions of Japan's trade and economy are
forcing Japanese investments in European manufacturing
to enter a new phase. Reasons are given for this new
phase and the lack of Japanese investment. The areas
of marketing and finance are being given greater
priority.

476. Gregory, Gene. The Japanese Challenge in Europe.
Geneva: Business International S.A., 1973.

This analytical series of articles focuses on Japanese
industry as a competitor to European firms. The
components of "Japan, Inc." are examined to determine
it success on the world market, to dispel myths about
its power, and to analyze the impetus behind its export
thrust, both in general and on an industry-by-industry
basis. In addition, Japanese direct investments and
joint ventures in Europe are discussed, along with the
effectiveness of countervailing forces such as
protectionist policies, the E.E.C., and Japanese self-
restraints. Suggestions are presented on how Western
companies can effectively meet the Japanese challenge.

477. Gregory, Gene. "The Japanese Euro-Strategy."
Management Today. (July 1975): 54-60.

Leading priorities are outlined for Japanese overseas
investment. The Japanese investment strategy of
building for the long term is described. Japanese
investments are made in European production only where
there is no alternative for securing and expanding

markets. In addition, joint ventures and takeovers are
discussed along with the adaption of Japanese
management methods. Japanese criteria for selecting a
factory site are given.

478. Hideo Hirata. "A Management Philosophy on Overseas
Operations." <u>Management Japan</u>. 9 (Summer 1976): 12-
15.

This article concentrates on the situation of Yoshida
Kogyo K.K. in Japan, and its motives for foreign
investment in the area of fasteners. A description is
given of its current state of overseas operations,
outlining its overseas strategy. The factors
contributing to the success of Yoshida Kogyo K. K. are
sketched. Yoshida Kogyo K.K.'s operations in Western
Europe are discussed.

479. Ikeda, Masahito. "Japan's Direct Investment in Europe:
With Emphasis on Investment in Manufacturing
Industries." <u>EXIM Review</u>. 6.2 (1985): 97-137.

Japanese investments in Europe include manufacture of
color televisions, video cassette recorders, integrated
circuits, machine tools, and automobiles. Topics
discussed are the Japanese positioning of direct
investment in Europe; Management environment for
investment in manufacturing industries in Europe; and
prospects and problems for the future.

480. "Japanese Challenge Grows as Investment Buildup Gathers
Momentum." <u>Business Europe</u>. 20.11 (March 14, 1980):
81-83.

Investments of the Japanese in the U.K., Spain and
France are detailed in this study. Attitudes toward
the Japanese investor are changing. The case of France
is given particular attention.

481. "Japanese Investment Concentrates Less on Asian
Opportunities." <u>Business Asia; Weekly Report to
Managers of Asia/Pacific Operations</u>. 12.44 (Oct. 31,
1980): 349-350.

The role of Asia as the recipient of Japanese direct
investment is considered. Data from 1951-1979 are
offered. The efforts of Japan to build production
facilities in Europe as well as Asia are outlined. A
treatment of Asian investments by Japanese firms is
given industry by industry.

482. "Japanese Overseas Investments: France, Italy,
Netherlands & Belgium." <u>Oriental Economist</u>. 48.831
(Jan..1980): 43-53.

The article offers statistics on the location and
nature of Japanese direct investments in France, Italy,
Netherlands, and Belgium. The names, date of
operation, amount of capital and number of employees
are given. There is also a description of the major

business lines, annual sales, partner firms, and site
locations.

483. "Japan's CPI Gears Up for Yen Invasion of Europe."
     Chemical Week. 115.12 (Sept. 18, 1974): 45-46.

The level of direct investment by Japanese chemicals
and plastics manufacturers remains small in the
European community. While there are expectations of an
increasing Japanese presence, that presence is not
expected to be an overwhelming one. Belgium and the
Netherlands will be seeing increased Japanese
development, but not to the extent that Japan will be
in any sense taking over the industries.

484. Kapstein, Jonathan, Mark Maremont, Thane Peterson, et
     al. "Now Europe Is Hooked on Japanese Imports, Too."
     Business Week (Industrial/Technology Edition). 2956
     (July 21, 1986): 80-81.

The significance of Japanese exports of capital to
Europe is explored. Since the E.E.C. has received a
53% increase in Japanese investment in 1986, this
represents a major shift for European consumers. They
are buying Japanese exports and threatening the health
of local industries such as photocopiers and semiconductors. The success of Japan in making this market
penetration comes in part from the need to make up for
lost markets in the U.S. and China, and in part from
currency fluctuations and lack of general agreement in
Europe on policies to restrict Japanese entry. The
increase in Japanese plants in Europe is seen as a
reaction to the prospect of trade barriers.

485. Krause, Axel. "Europeans Wrestle with Surge in
     Japanese Investment." Europe. 254 (March 1986):
     28-32.

Japan's increasing presence as an investor in the
European Economic Community nations is discussed.
While Japan is expecting to avoid the protectionist
barriers of Europe through establishing local plants,
there are some obstacles for Japanese firms. There is
a high rate of turnover among employees in Europe.
Often it is hard to find parts of the necessary
quality, and some of the workforce is unaccustomed to
the Japanese management system with its high premium on
production. Other problems are also identified, and
European based firms are learning to meet the Japanese
competition by following the Japanese example. Often
the Japanese are asked to purchase at least 45% of
their parts and supplies from European manufacturers.
Joint ventures are also discussed.

486. Lewis, Vivian. "French feutre." Banker. 137.738
     (Aug. 1987): 26-27.

In this treatment of the reciprocal agreements reached
between France and Japan, it is shown that the
securities dealings of both countries will be

normalized. Two major Japanese securities firms will
be able to become fully licensed operations in France
as a result. At the same time, French banks will be
allowed to open up operations in Japan. One 1987
agreement will be a deal creating a new status for
Banque Nationale de Paris in Japan and for Mitsubishi
Bank in France. This arrangement will allow the two
countries to exchange paper without dollar-exchange
interference.

487. Loeve, A., J. de Vries, and M. de Smidt. "Japanese
     Firms and the Gateway to Europe; The Netherlands, as a
     Location for Japanese Subsidiaries." Tijdschrift voor
     economische en sociale geografie. 76.1 (1985): 2-8.

     The Japanese presence in Europe is discussed, with
     attention given to the way companies are building
     European headquarters and distribution centers. The
     Netherlands' position as a base of operation is
     described. The pattern underlying the growth of these
     Japanese direct investments is analyzed. The pattern
     reveals the role of the sales agent and then the
     coming of manufacturing installations, concluding with
     the forming of national submarkets. The Japanese seem
     to seek a more cosmopolitan location of trade
     operations and a non-metropolitan site for
     manufacturing.

488. Martin, Jurek. "E.C. and Japan Should Be Better
     Friends." Europe. 259 (Sept. 1986): 24-25.

     A number of factors prevent a closer tie between Japan
     and the European Economic Community (E.E.C.) The
     closeness of the Japan-U.S. relationship seems to
     hinder Japan and the E.E.C. sees it as a potential
     threat to its future. Although the E.E.C. has
     followed a more consistent trade policy, Japan feel it
     must follow the lead of the U.S. Their future
     relationship depends on the civil service and the
     business community. Japan's growing international
     sophistication and adaption of Western standards should
     improve their relationship. Japanese firms are
     considering more foreign investment and technology
     transfer.

489. McFatridge, Joe. Fujitsu in Spain; Technology and
     Tradition. Bulletin, Sophia University Socio-Economic
     Institute. Tokyo: Sophia University, 1977.

     In 1972, Spain's National Institute of Industry sought
     prospects for licensing of computer technology.
     Fujitsu was chosen because of its international
     position and its refusal to operate on a technical tie-
     up basis. This study focuses on the human problems
     encountered in the Japanese-Spanish relationship. It
     takes a look at two investments in Spain, discusses the
     transfer of technology as well as culture, and examines
     the learning process.

490. Mitsuhashi, Tadahino. "Brussels Grows in 'Stature'."

Japan Economic Journal. 17.849 (April 24, 1979): 8-9.

This is a focus on the role of Brussels in international trade activity. Many exchanges of visits between Tokyo and Brussels have spelled new relationships. Foreign investments find Brussels a central location. Prospects for future development are considered.

491. Mitsuhashi, Tadahiro. "Nation Is Vital International Center Japan Economic Journal. 15.746 (April 19, 1977): 11-13.

In this consideration of the role of Belgium in international trade, a general overview of the Belgian situation is offered. As foreign capital arrives, there is a development of economic growth as a result. Also there is a major money market located in Belgium, and many of the Japanese investors are centering attention there. Some consideration is also given to the wages and workforce situation.

492. Obayashi, K. "Japanese Investment Is Eagerly Sought Special on Belgium." Japan Economic Journal; International Weekly. 19.952 (April 28, 1981): 25-26.

Belgium economic mission went to Japan to explore the possibilities of future Japanese investments in Belgium. The Belgian government is reviewing wage-price spiral, social security, cost inflation, wage freezes, and their policy against Japanese car importation. There is also discussion of expanding the Zeebrugge-port to accommodate increased commercial traffic. Statistics are given for 1980-1981.

493. "PPC Movements in European Markets." OEP Office Equipment & Products. 17.114 (March 1988): 88-89.

This is a status report on the plain paper copier industry, which details Japan's role in Europe. In 1987, demand for the product had not grown substantially enough to meet suppliers' goals. Japan began developing lower priced models, which were charged a 20% anti-dumping tax in the E.E.C. Some makers concentrate on conventional dealerships, and others are taking on the general household market. Japanese manufacturers feel that the Europeans have fallen behind in the technology, and are willing to supply them with copiers on an original equipment manufacturer basis.

494. Pearce, Jean. "Spain and Japan Share Rich History of Early Contact." Business Japan. 32.2 (Feb. 1987): 30-31.

Spain's Ambassador to Japan, Camilo Barcia Y Garcia-Villamil, noted that ties with Japan dates back to the 16th century. Recently, Spain has become aware of its need to strengthen relations with Japan. Spain imports

over $900 million from Japan but exports only $274
million. Spain wants to keep its imports from Japan,
but it finds the Japanese market closed for its
important export items. The imbalance must be solved
by increasing exports to Japan. Spain is satisfied
with the progress of Japanese investments, but would
like to the flow of investments in Spain consolidated.

495. Peterson, Thane, Joyce Heard, Amy Borrus, and Larry
     Armstrong. "Tokyo's End Run Around Protectionism in
     Europe." Business Week (Industrial/Technology
     Edition). 2921 (Nov. 18, 1985): 108D-108G.

     Japan's
     strategy of circumventing tariffs by building plants in
     Europe is helping Europe's lagging economies, but it is
     harming major sectors of European industry. The
     European Economic Community's (E.E.C.) trade deficit
     with Japan has grown considerably over the past 5
     years. Japanese firms control 85% of the European
     market for small copiers and videocassette recorders.
     Calls for trade measures to limit Japanese imports are
     increasing, but Japan is skillful in dealing with trade
     sanctions. In addition, some governments offer
     incentives to attract Japanese investments. Japanese
     and European firms are now competing for Europe's
     semiconductor market. European companies are spending
     heavily to regain market share. Nonetheless, more
     European firms cooperate with rather than fight the
     Japanese.

496. Rafferty, Kevin. "Japanese Corporate Finance Goes
     Global." Institutional Investor. 20.11 (Nov. 1986):
     289-293.

     Japanese financial subsidiaries in Europe number more
     than 40, and the experience of its executives is
     offering them the opportunity to become more
     sophisticated and aggressive in the money markets. As
     the yen rises, the Japanese have noted a squeeze on
     their profits from the usual sources. Now they are
     actively seeking more sources for lower cost funds and
     better returns on investments. One place they have
     turned is toward the commercial paper market, and while
     there is resistance to the idea, prospects are good for
     such moves. Experience with the Euro-commercial paper
     market has been instructive.

497. "Trying to Turn a Rival into a Partner." Business Week
     (Industrial/Technology Edition). 2864 (Oct. 15, 1984):
     56.

     France is trying to attract Japanese investment to
     obtain new technology and jobs. President Mitterrand
     sees Japan as a key factor in France's struggle against
     inflation and unemployment. Although the French have
     attempted to limit Japanese imports and investment in
     Europe, the French Trade Ministry will seek increased
     access to the Japanese market. Several French
     companies have already established deals with Japanese

firms. French interest in attracting Japanese
investment may have resulted from the Japanese
expansion in other European countries. While the Trade
Ministry encourages increased French exports to Japan,
it does not intend to reduce limitations on a wide
range of Japanese imports. The proposed expansion of a
joint venture between Henri Ernault-Somua, an ailing
French machine tool maker, and Toyota Motor Corp. is
testing the developing Franco-Japanese relationship.

498. Tsoukalis, Loukas, and Maureen White, eds. Japan and
Western Europe; Conflict and Cooperation. New York:
St. Martin's Press, 1982.

This book is a collection of essays which examine the
Japanese-European relationship, with some attention to
the American influence as well. Beginning with the
history of European influence in Japan and mutual
images and stereotypes, the main emphasis is on the
economic dimension. Japan's economy, industrial policy
and politics are treated. Trade imbalance between the
European Economic Community and Japan, its adjustment,
industrial policies, and foreign direct investment are
then examined as they affect bilateral relations.
Working toward more cooperation, the final chapter
discusses future prospects.

499. "What's Behind the Rebirth of Dunlop in Europe? The
Japanese Arbose." Jules International Management.
42.7/8 (July/Aug. 1987): 65-68.

Since Sumitomo Rubber Industries Ltd.'s purcase of
Dunlop, it has been thriving. Sumitomo has improved
Dunlop with $200 million worth of new plants and
equipment, coupled with an infusion of Japanese
production technology. An open-style management model
has replaced the industrial conflict approach and has
contributed to Dunlop's success. Increased labor
cooperation was achieved through investments in new
machinery, changes in working conditions and practices,
and training programs.

500. Winter, L. "The Men with a Yen for Europe." Vision.
40 (March 15, 1974): 73-75.

This article follows the progress of Japanese
investments in Europe, reviewing the value of Japanese
companies in the Common Market. Europe has been
attempting to attract Japanese investment and some of
the results are discussed. Additional topics include
re-exporting from Europe and problems the Japanese are
having with finance, marketing, and management.

United Kingdom and Ireland

501. Beresford, M. D.   "Joining Battle with Japan."
Management Today. (Oct. 1981): 60-67.

This piece shows the U.K. perspective on the Japanese

industrial challenge in Europe. Protectionism is
viewed as having a dangerous effect on the world
market; the establishment of joint ventures between
European and Japanese investors is discussed and
encouraged, as are the benefits of Japanese investments
in general. The four main categories marked for more
concentrated development in the E.E.C. are: 1. energy,
2. standard of living, 3. knowledge-intensive and
innovative technologies and, 4. next generation
technologies. There is also a discussion asserting
that productivity and work attitudes have improved in
the U.K. under Japanese management.

502. Bownas, G. "Japan Is Attractive Partner for U.K. in
Trade and Investment." Japan Economic Journal:
International Weekly. 20.1025 (Sept. 28, 1982): 11-
12.

This item takes an in-depth view of the current trade
relationship between Japan and the U.K. It analyzes
new commercial gains and setbacks, discussing some of
the inevitable trade frictions that have presented
themselves between the two countries. There is an
overview of other international investment by the
Japanese as well as some examples of its production
ventures worldwide. Hope of a mutually successful
financial relationship between Japan and the U.K. lies
in the two countries' ability to work cooperatively.

503. Brody, Michael. "British Unions Go Japanese."
Fortune. 112.13 (Dec. 9, 1985): 60-66.

Taking advantage of the U.K.'s high unemployment rate
and declining union membership, many U.S. and Japanese
companies have signed liberal contracts with the once-
militant U.K. unions, including the Electrical,
Electronic Telecommunications, and Plumbing Union,
called the Electricians. Among the unions' concessions
are accepting one job classification for all workers,
replacing strikes with arbitration and, dropping
restrictive work rules. Due to a single-union contract
with the Electricians, Toshiba was able to reopen its
U.K. plant. The Electricians signed a contract with
Hitachi which gave them sole negotiating rights for all
unions at the Hitachi plant. A single-union contract
between the Amalgamated Union of Engineering Workers
and Nissan incorporates labor flexibility and Japanese
work practices but stops short of compulsory
arbitration.

504. Cudlipp, R. "Japan in the Big League of Overseas
Investors." Japan. 78 (Autumn 1983): 2-8.

This article presents the development of Japanese
investments in Europe by country and industry. Special
attention is given to investments in the United
Kingdom. The effects of European import restriction on
Japanese investments are explored. Statistics are
provided for 1980-1983.

505. Doyle, Peter, John Saunders, and Veronica Wong.
     "Japanese Marketing Strategies in the U.K.: A
     Comparative Study." Journal of International Business
     Studies. 17.1 (Spring 1986): 27-46.

     This study compares the marketing strategies and
     organization features of Japanese subsidiaries with
     local competitors in the U.K. market. It examines the
     differences pertaining to: 1. market share versus
     short-term profits, 2. environmental opportunities, 3.
     rate of innovation, and 4. aggressive marketing
     tactics. Personal interviews were conducted with the
     top marketing decision makers in 15 leading Japanese
     companies in the U.K. and their 15 major British
     competitors. Results showed that the Japanese sub-
     sidiaries are much more market-oriented, concentrate
     more on market share, and are more alert to strategic
     opportunities than their British competitors. British
     firms and Japanese subsidiaries, however, have similar
     organizations. The differences in performance are due
     to marketing skills rather than national cultures.

506. Doyle, Peter, John Saunders, and Veronica Wong. "Why
     Japan Out-Markets Britain." Management Today. (May
     1985): 62-69.

     Japan's world economic growth may result from the
     quality of Japanese marketing. Marketing decisions
     tend to be decentralized, and Japanese companies more
     readily exploit marketing opportunities. Interviews
     were conducted with top marketers in 15 Japanese firms
     operating in the U.K. and their counterparts in 15
     British companies. While 87% of the Japanese listed
     aggressive growth or market domination as their goal,
     only 20% of the British did so. The Japanese employ a
     strategic marketing mix, focusing on quality and range
     extensions. The Japanese concentrate their marketing
     efforts on high-potential segments, while the British
     spread theirs across the entire field. Two-thirds of
     the Japanese senior managers were concerned with
     promoting group responsibility and teamwork, as
     compared with 27% of the British. The most successful
     U.K. companies were closer to Japanese strategy and
     organization.

507. Dunning, John H. "Japanese Investment in U.K.
     Industry: Trojan Horse or New Catalyst for Growth?"
     Multinational Business. 4 (1984): 1-6.

     Japanese direct investment in the U.K. shows a great
     potential, especially when viewed in a European
     context. The Japanese involvement in the motor
     industry and in video recorders may now lead to the
     arrival of Japanese electronic component makers. At
     the least, their arrival ensures that the final
     product is produced in Britain, although the U.K.
     government would prefer indigenous British firms to
     supply these components. In 1984, the Japanese rubber
     giant Sumitomo's purchase of part of the U.K.'s Dunlop
     operations was an attempt to compete in world markets.

More acquisitions are likely to follow. Japanese
operations in the U.K. has increased standards of
performance and quality as well as favorably affected
the efficiency of their competitors. Changes in the
structure of U.K. industry has been mostly to their
advantage. However, there are signs that the U.K.
might become an assembly platform for Japanese
companies that out-compete indigenous firms.

508. Dunning, John H. Japanese Participation in British
Industry. The Croom Helm Series in International
Business. London: Croom Helm, 1986.

This offers the results of a field survey on Japanese
manufacturing affiliates in the U.K. taken between 1983
and 1984. The results detail the extent and form of
Japanese participation in British industry and the
reasons for it. Some organizational relationships
between the Japanese affiliates and their parent
companies are outlined, with some data about the
performance of the affiliates relative to the others
connected with the parent companies as well as compared
to other local competitors. The ways this Japanese
presence has impinged on the local economy are
explored. Transfer of management style and technologies is examined. Some thoughts about future
prospects are offered.

509. "First Independent Japanese Auto Plant in E.C. Starts
Production." Business Japan. 31.10 (Oct. 1986): 42-
43.

On Sept. 8, 1986, Nissan Motor Manufacturing U.K. Ltd.
celebrated the shipment of the first car off the
assembly line. Five years of preparation went into
making this the first independent Japanese auto plant.
Nissan's local production is important in view of the
voluntary curb on Japanese car exports to the European
Economic Community (E.E.C.). Nissan's U.K. plant will
assemble 24,000 Auster models, with full production of
over 100,000 units scheduled for the 1990's. The cars
will be treated as imports from Japan at first, but
when full output is attained, they will have a
local-content of 60% and will be able to be exported to
the E.E.C. countries as British-made products. Honda
Motor is the only other Japanese car manufacturer
engaged in production in the E.E.C. With the
increasing criticism of Japanese car exports, these 2
companies' successes in the U.K. with local support is
a major accomplishment.

510. Gabel, H. Landis, and Anthony E. Hall. "The Nissan
Corporation." Journal of Management Case Studies.
1.2 (Summer 1985): 97-101.

This study traces the history of the policy of
internationalization conducted by the Nissan Corp.
in the 1980s. The aim was to sell 40% of the
production domestically, to sell 30% in exports, and to
manufacture and sell another 30% overseas. A large

assembly plant was planned for location in the U.K.,
but development was slowed by numerous factors. Losses
by Nissan of 2% of the Japanese domestic market also
contributed to the difficulty of carrying out the
strategy.

511. Gow, Ian. "Japanese Business in Britain: Raiders
      Invaders or Simply Good Traders?" Accountancy.
      97.1111 (March 1986): 66-73.

      A discussion of Japan's role as a technological and
      economic giant is offered. The status of Japanese
      overseas investment is assessed, and the role of Japan
      in the U.K. is pinpointed. The way in which Japan has
      penetrated the U.K. economy is described, with
      attention to the direct production and joint
      arrangements in which Japanese products are made in the
      U.K. Many factors which have led to the Japanese
      presence are identified: the constant pursuit of
      comparative advantage, cheap labor, new markets, and
      the promotion of trade trough exports to third country
      markets. Opinions about the effect on the British
      remain divided.

512. "Japan Starts Exporting Jobs." Economist. 265.7007
      (Dec. 17, 1977): 96-97.

      An account of the direct overseas investments of Japan
      is offered. There is a cataloging of these investments
      according to country of destination, as well as by
      industrial sector, for the year 1977. The pattern of
      investment in Western Europe is outlined for the period
      1965-75. Other details are offered to cover the
      investments in Britain and Ireland by sector for the
      year 1975. In addition to this data, information is
      offered on the top 20 Japanese investors with a large
      overseas presence.

513. "Japanese Overseas Investments: Great Britain."
      Oriental Economist. 47.830 (Dec. 1979): 47-54.

      This treatment offers a discussion of the Japanese
      direct investment in the United Kingdom. Statistics
      are presented for the period 1972-1978. Various
      profiles are given of the characteristics of the firms
      acting as investors in the U.K.

514. Minard, Lawrence. "Look Who's Building Plants in
      Britain!" Forbes. 127.6 (March 16, 1981): 60-63.

      Japan has begun to establish manufacturing operations
      overseas, primarily as a way of avoiding protectionist
      measures by various countries. $2 billion has been
      invested so far in the U.K. As many as 13,000 people
      are employed in these installations. Various firms
      make TV's in Britain, and ball bearings are produced
      there. The E.E.C. has import restrictions which are
      escaped by these operations. Britain is a favored
      location because of its industrial base, its good
      market, and its access to components. There is also a

better political establishment than is found in France
or Italy, and less reliance on immigrant labor than is
found in Germany. The success Japan has encountered in
dealing with the unions perhaps relates to the creation
of stable jobs. The Japanese single-status employee
approach has been introduced.

515. O'Brien, Peter. "The Yamazaki Effect: MT Concentration
Foreshadowed." Multinational Business. 3 (Autumn
1987): 43-44.

Japanese firms are being forced into direct foreign
investments as a result of import restrictions.
Yamazaki has established in the U.K. a L35 million non-
unionized factory to manufacture computer numerically
controlled lathes and machining centers, receiving
direct grants from the U.K. government. This consti-
tutes about one-half of all U.K. production. German
firms have expressed strong opposition to these
Japanese investments. An additional problem is local
content, which is defined as wages and factory
operating costs that qualify for tariff-free sales
within the region. Yamazaki claims it will rapidly
reach 60%. Many U.K. firms do not qualify, suggesting
that many small and medium sized firms will give way to
greater concentration.

516. Pitman, Joanna. "Japanese Securities Companies: Jaded
Palates in Yen Sector." Euromoney: Japanese
Securities Companies Supplement. (Sept. 1987): 30-
32, 37.

Conditions in the stock market, including the Euro-yen
market, have resulted in a slowdown in the sale of
Japanese equities to overseas investors. These sales
have been the mainstay for the majority of the 29
Japanese securities houses located in London. Lately,
these houses have been selling U.K. stock to Japanese
clients, and many would like to expand their operations
into the gilts market. As members of the International
Stock Exchange, the "Big 4"Japanese houses -- Nomura,
Daiwa, Yamaichi, and Nikko -- can make markets in U.K.
equities. A confrontation with U.K. brokers has not
yet occurred. However, Nomura intends to start market-
making in U.K. equities by the fall of 1987.

517. Reitsperger, Wolf D. "Japanese Management: Coping with
British Industrial Relations." Journal of Management
Studies. 23.1 (Jan. 1986): 72-87.

Theoretical discussions of the Japanese investments in
the U.K. often question the role of culture in behavior
and control issues. Industrial relations processes
must be examined in detail, in sample Japanese
companies' operations. Four firms are studied, and the
Japanese rationale appears to be that industrial
relations is a part of the overall manufacturing
strategy. It removes obstacles to smooth production.
On the other hand, the U.K. view is that personnel and
industrial relations play a mediating function.

Japanese managers use a combination of practices.

518. Sawers, David. "The Experience of German and Japanese
     Subsidiaries in Britain." Journal of General
     Management. 12.1 (Autumn 1986): 5-21.

     In this comparison of productivity in parent companies
     vs. subsidiaries, firms in Germany and Japan were
     studied, with respect to their U.K. subsidiaries.
     Fifteen firms were described in all. The result was
     that the U.K. productivity levels were lower than
     levels at the parent company locations. While Japan's
     performance gap exceeded that of Germany's, the U.K.
     equivalents which did best seemed to profit from
     imitating the activities of their foreign counterparts.
     Some of the factors identified as contributing to high
     productivity were product design, well-planned
     production equipment, staff efforts, labor flexibility,
     functioning at full staff levels, good labor relations,
     preventative maintenance, individual responsibility,
     careful worker and manager selection.

519. Shack, Jonathan. "The Japanese Bank On London."
     Euromoney. (April 1985): 179,181.

     Japanese banks now constitute 22% of total U.K. banking
     assets with 35 banks in the City, the second largest
     foreign group in London after U.S. banks. This
     expansion results from the desire for closer contact
     between Japanese multinationals and their customers,
     Japan's increasing role as an exporter of capital, and
     internal pressures to change the banks' traditional
     lending activities. The liberalization of Japan's
     banking environment will further affect their expansion
     in London. Japanese banks in London have made
     significant advances in the Eurobond and floating rate
     note (FRN) markets, interest rate and currency swap
     business, and until late 1982, the syndicated loan
     market. For the medium term, money market activities
     will likely remain profitable for the Japanese banks in
     London, and the internationalization of the yen will
     contribute to the diversification process.

520. White, Michael. "Japanese Management and British
     Workers." International Journal of Manpower. 3.4
     (1982): 9-14.

     Japanese manufacturing operations in the U.K. present
     an opportunity to assess the transferability of
     Japanese management methods and its practicality for
     U.K. industry. This article reviews the findings of
     the Policy Studies Institute (PSI), which conducted a
     survey of workers in a development area in which a
     major Japanese employer is found. The study indicates
     that the Japanese management system can be effective in
     gaining workers' support and cooperation. Workers are
     particularly satisfied with job security; and there is
     a renewed awareness of increased qualifications. The
     Japanese system places high priority on rules and
     procedures, with mistakes by workers treated with

strictness.

521. "Why Japanese Find Ireland So Attractive." Business
Europe. 19.46 (Nov. 16, 1979): 365.

This article traces the development of Japanese
investments in Ireland. Reasons are given for making
these investments, and the role the Japan External
Trade Organization (JETRO) played in Japan-Ireland
relations.

522. Wilson, Dick. "They Are Optimistic About British
Industry." Director. 38.4 (Nov. 1984): 60-62.

Japanese managers in the U.K. are quite optimistic
about the U.K.'s industrial future. Andy Imura,
National Panasonic (U.K.,) believes there is a
promising future for information related products,
including satellites and broadcasting. Y. Noguchi,
Mitsubishi Electric (U.K.,) believes the trade unions
are becoming realistic, particularly those in new
industries such as electronics. The Thatcher
government is given credit for this optimistic outlook.
Although the extensive complacency of the past is
disappearing, Japanese executives complain that British
executives are slow at responding to developments in
the world market.

AFRICA

523. "Africa-Japan." Africa. (Nov. 1986): 71-76.

Japan-Africa trade relations are discussed, along with
Japanese economic assistance to African countries.

524. Arthur, F. "Japan and Africa; Financing Holds Key to
Progress on Big Projects." Africa Economic Digest,
AED; Weekly Business News, Analysis and Forecast.
6.47 (Nov./Dec. 30-6, 1985): 29-31.

The Japanese government has an overseas development
assistance budget of 4,310 million dollars in 1984. It
is primarily interested in infrastructure projects, but
is reluctant to finance capital-intensive contracts
involving advanced technology. Japan's contracts with
Africa are outlined. Trade with Africa has been
declining for some years. In 1984 imports dropped to
1,165.6 million dollars from 1,610 million dollars in
1982. During the same period, exports fell from
4,167.5 to 2,998.4 million dollars. This development
has been reflected in Africa's share of Japan's total
direct overseas investment, which dropped from 6.3% in
1982 to 3.2% in 1984. Statistics are provided on
Japan's 10 largest trading partners in sub-Saharan
Africa for 1983-85.

525. "Japan Looks Ahead." Financial Mail. (Nov. 12, 1976):
1-64.

A general outline of Japanese-South Africa trade and
economic relations is offered. Details of the Japanese
economy from 1969-74 are pinpointed, and the potential
for a natural alliance between the two economies is
noted. The Japanese wholesale trading companies and
multinationals structure is analyzed. The profitability requirements and capacity of banks are
examined, and the potential for an emphasis on Japanese
direct foreign investment is traced. Computers, steel,
and shipbuilding industries are given special focus.

526. "Japan Strengthening Her Links with Africa." Japan;
      Quarterly Review. 51 (Aug. 1974): 23-26.

      Investments in Africa account for only 6% of the total
      overseas trade of Japan, and direct investment there
      amounts to only 2.5% of Japan's world totals.
      Nonetheless, Africa is a major potential source of raw
      materials and resources. Japan's use of foreign aid to
      Africa and its sponsorship of resource development
      projects is outlined.

527. "Japanese Overseas Investments: Middle East and
      Africa." Oriental Economist. 48.840 (Oct. 1980):
      37-43.

      Japanese investments in various countries are
      considered, with facts about Saudi Arabia, United Arab
      Emirates, Ethiopia, Kenya, Liberia, and Zaire. The
      data includes statistics about investors, capital,
      employees, business lines, annual sales, production
      figures for 1978, partner firms, investment
      objectives, results, and geographic location of
      operations.

528. Kotani, Toru. "Africa and Japan: Rising Sun over
      Africa?" Africa Report. 30.6 (Nov./Dec. 1985): 68-
      71.

      With Foreign Minister Shintaro Abe's recent African
      initiative, there may be expanding private sector
      involvement in the continent. Recent media coverage of
      the drought and famine have resulted in more publicity
      for Japanese food aid to the region. The
      administration of the procurements of food, however,
      has come under criticism. There now exist new
      possibilities for a new Japanese-African relationship.

529. Morrison, G., and D. Morris. "Japan and Africa."
      Africa Development. 10.6 (June 1976): 585-96.

      As Japan comes out of its economic recession, it is
      deepening its trade relations with African countries.
      Japan's foreign investments are starting to expand, but
      so far there is little activity in Africa. Japan's
      imports and exports from and to Africa are given for
      1975. There is also a discussion of Japan's nuclear
      energy program in Africa.

530. Moss, Joanna and John Ravenhill. The Emerging

<u>Japanese Economic Influence in Africa; Implications for</u>
<u>the United States</u>. Policy Papers in International
Affairs. Berkeley: Institute of International Studies,
University of California, 1985.

The primary goal of this book is to compare the
performance of the U.S. private sector with that of
Japan in a Third World region. Africa was chosen
because it is a relatively "neutral" market for
competition between U.S. and Japanese exporters. A
study is made of the U.S. and Japan's trade relations
with Africa consisting of market-share analysis,
changes in balance of trade, and changes in the
composition of trade. Japanese direct foreign
investments in Africa are examined, including the role
of trading companies in the investment process. In
addition Japanese overseas development assistance is
discussed, followed by a description of Japanese and
U.S. government programs in support of overseas
commercial activities.

531. Owoeye, Jide and Franklin Vivekananda. "Japan's Aid
Diplomacy in Africa." <u>Scandinavian Journal of</u>
<u>Development Alternatives</u>. 5 (Dec. 1986): 145-155.

Japanese financial and technical assistance programs in
Africa are described with a discussion of the potential
for future Japan-Africa trade.

532. Shreeve, G. "Africa's Long-Term Promise Woos Japan."
<u>Africa Economic Digest, AED; Weekly Business News,</u>
<u>Analysis and Forecast</u>. 2.42 (Oct. 23, 1981): 2-4.

This article provides a overview of the role of
Japanese investments in Africa. Japan's African
investments have been concentrated in oil production,
motor firms, exploration projects, and mineral
supplies. Commodity trade between the countries is
reviewed with statistics given for 1978-1980, as well
as a look at Japanese trading practices.

533. Yanaihara, Katsu. "Japanese Overseas Enterprises in
Developing Countries under Indigenization Policy - The
African Case." <u>Japanese Economic Studies</u>. 4.1 (Fall
1975): 23-51.

The indigenization policies in developing countries
present Japan's foreign firms operating there with a
new set of problems. A general overview is given of
Africa as a case study. Details include enterprise
characteristics, investment incentives, and direct
investment. Consequences of the Africanization of
capital and personnel are explored.

IV

ASIA AND THE
PACIFIC OCEAN REGION

This chapter on Asia is subdivided into Asia in
general, the Middle East, Southeast Asia, Pacific Rim
Countries, and the Pacific Ocean Region and Australia. The
Subject Index should be consulted for individual country
listings.

THE ASIAN REGION IN GENERAL

534. Akira, Kubota. "Transferring Technology to Asia."
     Japan Quarterly. 33.1 (Jan./March 1986): 37-44.

     Japanese economic development aid to developing nations
     is discussed. Many nations in the Asian region are
     asking for the introduction of sophisticated
     technology. They think this is the only way for them
     to catch up with their developed trading partners. The
     nations are requesting that developed nations open
     their markets, and take a cooperative stance toward
     transfer of technology. They oppose protectionist
     acts. An example is made of the case of the South
     Korean Pohang Iron and Steel Co. There is a discussion
     of high-tech monopoly, turnkey projects, and the role
     for smaller firms.

535. Altschul, James. "Japanese Banks Keep Faith in China."
     Euromoney. (July 1984): 138-141.

     Japanese banks remain committed to The Peoples'
     Republic of China even though most foreign bankers have
     been disappointed. Eighteen Japanese banks have
     offices in Beijing. Nomura and Daiwa Securities are
     the first securities firms to open operations in
     Beijing. Although immediate profits are not present,
     the Japanese foresee a long-term potential in the
     Chinese market. Since the Chinese government prefers
     government-to-government loans, they have not taken out
     commercial loans. The Bank of Japan, IBJ, and Sanwa

Bank are the only banks currently making a small profit. The South China Sea oil exploration is of keen interest to the Japanese banks.

536. Asian Regional Conferences on Industrial Relations. Industrial Policies, Foreign Investment and Labor in Asian Countries. Tokyo: Japan Institute of Labour, 1978.

This volume contains the proceedings of the 7th Conference entitled Asian Regional Conference on Industrial Relations, held in Tokyo in 1977. Its general areas of concern include the recent developments in the foreign investment sphere, as well as the labor situation in various Asian countries.

537. Awanohara, Susumu. "Writing Off the Past; Tokyo Pays Exporters for North Korea's Old Unpaid Bills." Far Eastern Economic Review. 43 (Oct. 23, 1986): 151.

Japan's MITI has finally compensated domestic exporters owed money by North Korea since the mid-1970's. Traders felt that Japan-North Korea trade could grow considerably if the default problem could be solved. In 1984, North Korea introduced its joint-venture law encouraging foreign capital into the country. Since then only a few major investments have been made by the Japanese despite urgings by North Korea. An overview is given of North Korea's trade with Asia, Western Europe, Australia, U.S.S.R. and China for 1984-85.

538. Campbell, Nigel. "Japanese Business Strategy in China." Long Range Planning. 20 (Oct. 1987): 69-73.

This article describes Japan's business strategy for investments, technology transfer, and building local relationships in China. The role of trading companies is discussed. Also included is a survey of 115 foreign companies in Beijing which shows how the Japanese approach differs for their European and American competitors.

539. Ikeda, Masahito. "Trends of Japan's Direct Investment for Asia: With Emphasis on Investment in Manufacturing Industries." EXIM Review. 6.2 (1985): 56-96.

Japanese direct foreign investment in Asia appears to be concentrated in the areas of textile, electric appliances, and automobiles.

540. "Japan. A Shift in Regional Investment Pattern." Asia Research Bulletin; Monthly Economic Reports with Political Supplement. 11.3 (Aug. 31, 1981): 3:832-835.

This article discusses Japan's prime investment targets overseas. Asia is the center of attention, constituting an important investment region. Investments in the 1980's are covered with a listing of Japanese

affiliated firms in Asia. Figures are provided for
1951- 1979.

541. "Japan Aids China's Development-And Reaps Benefits for
     Itself." World Business Weekly. 3.24 (June 23,
     1980): 5-6.

     Japanese investment in China is discussed. The
     methodology for Japanese penetration in Chinese
     development is traced, beginning with the use of
     development loans at low interest rates with deferred,
     payments which in turn are tied to understandings about
     the purchase of Japanese equipment. Areas of invest-
     ment include ports, hydroelectrics, mining and
     forestry. U.S. competition will be increasing, but at
     present some limitations of the U.S. Export-Import Bank
     have tended to lower investment levels. U.S. super-
     iority in the production of hydroelectric and open-pit
     mining machinery may offer the U.S. a competitive edge
     in these fields.

542. "Japan Emerging as Asia's Top Foreign Investor."
     Business Asia. 6.47 (Nov. 21, 1975): 369-371.

     In this treatment of the emergence of Japan as
     economic leader in its region, an analysis of the
     geographic distribution of Japanese foreign investments
     from 1951 to 1974 is offered. From this data, trends
     in Japanese investment can be ascertained. The
     characteristics of investment patterns in various
     regions are traced.

543. "Japan-ROK (Republic of Korea) Economic Relations under
     Fire." Oriental Economist. 41.758 (Dec. 1973): 14-
     16.

     In Korea, direct Japanese investment gives rise to some
     perceptions that Japan is attempting to dominate the
     economy. Anti-Japanese sentiment is described. There
     has been a large amount of Japanese investment
     recently. About 60% of the investments from foreign
     country in Korea comes from Japan.

544. "Japanese Overseas Investments: The Republic of Korea."
     Oriental Economist. 47.823 (May 5, 1979): 33-43.

     An account is given of Japanese foreign investments in
     the Republic of Korea for 1978. Direct investments
     from U.S. and other industrial countries are also
     covered. Currently 340 Japanese-affiliated enterprises
     operate in South Korea. Large-scale investments in
     Korea are described.

545. Khan, Z. R. "Japanese Relations with India, Pakistan
     and Bangladesh." Pacific Affairs. 48.4 (Winter
     1975/76): 541-557.

     There are statistics presented covering various periods
     in the relation of Japan and India, Pakistan and
     Bangladesh. The role of Japan as a creditor in India

is shown (1952-72). Investments are also detailed.
The relationship of Japan and Pakistan is covered,
(1966-70) and the steel plant development projects and
major loans are recounted. The export-import pattern
for India and Pakistan with Japan are examined (1970-
72.) The bridge and road construction projects of the
Japanese in Bangladesh are described.

546. Kojima, Kiyoshi. "The Allocation of Japanese Direct
     Foreign Investment and Its Evolution in Asia."
     Hitotsubashi Journal of Economics. 26.2 (Dec. 1985):
     99-116.

     The pattern of Japanese direct foreign investment is
     shown to differ between Asian host countries. This is
     demonstrated by the use of a three country model of
     comparative investment advantage to show that Japanese
     direct foreign investment is efficiently allocated
     between regions. An analysis is offered of how the
     pattern of Japanese direct investment is upgraded over
     time by examining the relationship between host country
     industrialization and the pattern of Japanese
     investments, as well as a comparative investment
     advantage index. A discussion follows of the
     relationship between Japanese direct investments and
     structural changes in the host country. Statistics are
     included.

547. Kojima, Kiyoshi. "Direct Foreign Investment to
     Developing Countries: The Issue of Over-Presence."
     Hitotsybasi Journal of Economics. 19.1/2 (Dec.
     1978): 1-15.

     A model of over-presence of direct foreign investment
     in developing countries is developed. Japanese direct
     foreign investment in Asia and other developing
     countries is placed in the context of its relation to
     the total economic activities of the host countries.
     Comparisons are then made with U.S. Recommendations
     are made for the reorganization of North-South trade.

548. Kotkin, Joel. "The New Yankee Traders." Inc.. 8.3
     (March 1986): 25-28.

     The Japanese investing in China have many obstacles to
     face interacting with the People's Republic of China.
     On the other hand, the many U.S. capitalists of Chinese
     descent have some advantages simply through family
     contacts in China. The problems of Japanese investors
     stem sometimes from their business attitudes and
     unwillingness to share technological advances. There
     is also a heritage of dislike dating from the days of
     the Japanese invasion of China during the Second World
     War.

549. Lee, Chung H. "International Production of the United
     States and Japan in Korean Manufacturing Industries; A
     Comparative Study." Weltwirtschaftliches Archiv,
     Tubingen. 119.4 (1983): 744-753.

In this comparison of the U.S. and Japanese direct
investments in Korea, various manufacturing industries
are considered. There are special characteristics of
U.S. and Japanese firms operating there. An account of
the different sectors and their distributions is
offered, with a comparison of the size, market style,
and localities. There is information of a statistical
nature from the years 1974-1978.

550. Lee, Chung H. "Transfer of Technology from Japan and
the United States to Korean Manufacturing Industries; A
Comparative Study." Hitotsubashi Journal of
Economics. 25.2 (Dec. 1984): 125-136.

This is a study of the transfer of technology through
both direct investment and licensing operations. A
comparison is offered, using U.S. and Japanese
activities in Korea as a basis. Technologies are
compared in terms of their various sectors, the
specific techniques, and the method of the
transference. Categories of labor-intensive high
tech, capital-intensive high tech, labor-intensive low
tech, and capital-intensive low tech industries.
During the period 1962-1978, there were no consistent
differences found on this basis in the technologies
transferred.

551. Lee, Chung H. "United States and Japanese Direct
Investment in Korea: A Comparative Study."
Hitotsubashi Journal of Economics. 20.2 (Feb. 1980):
26-41.

This comparison of U.S. and Japanese direct investment
in Korea covers the period 1962-1975. The Kojima
hypothesis that Japanese direct foreign investment
results in harmonious trade patterns while U.S.
investment results in the destruction of trade with the
host country is examined. The difference in market
orientation between U.S. and Japanese firms engaging in
direct foreign investments is examined. Korea's economic
growth and the effect of foreign investments are
considered.

552. Lee, Eddy, ed. Export-led Industrialization and
Development. Geneva: International Labour
Organization, 1981.

In this book which explores limits on employment and
economic growth in Asian countries, there is a chapter
on Japan's general trading companies. The question of
the role of general trading companies as an
organizational form is raised, and the prospects for
their use in other Asian countries is discussed. The
nature of general trading companies is explored,
especially as to their contribution to exports and
manufactures from developing countries. The issue of
whether and how they fit into export-led industrialization in various Asian countries is discussed.

553. Lincoln, Edward J. Japan's Economic Role in Northeast

Asia. Asian Agenda Report. Lanham, Maryland:
University Press of America, 1986.

In light of the political conditions in the Northeast
Asian region, Japan's foreign investments will play a
significant role in future economic relations.
Critical issues in U.S.-Japanese relations are also
explored. Data was gathered from political leaders in
Northeast Asia and Japan, by American investigative
teams. Topics include the nature of the economic ties
and the U.S.-Japan relationship, the status of Japan's
relations with the newly industrializing countries, and
the role of China and the Soviet bloc.

554. Matsuda, Mat T. "China's Electronics Growth May Get
     Stimulus from Japan." Advertising Age. 50.35 (Aug.
     20, 1979): S1,S14.

     A new joint venture is underway between the governments
     of Japan and China, which will provide highly
     sophisticated electronic goods. The capital investment
     is moderate, but potentially it could grow to a $10
     billion project. The plan was announced by Konosuke
     Matsushita, Matsushita Electrical Industrial Co.,
     during a 10-day visit to China after meeting with
     Chinese leaders. Dozens of Japanese firms in the
     electronics industry will work under the new Sino-
     Japanese corporation. The Chinese feel that the joint
     venture is vital for their rapid industrial
     modernization to develop their infant electronics
     industry.

555. Nakatani, Keiji. "The Present Situation and Problems
     of Direct Investment in China." EXIM Review. 7
     (Oct. 1986): 99-143.

     This article surveys the current status of Japanese
     investments in China and the direction investments will
     assume in the future. Emphasis will be placed on joint
     ventures. Included are the results of a survey on
     Japanese companies' interest in investment in China,
     conducted by the Export-Import Bank of Japan.

556. Pearce, Jean. "Friendly Ties Reinforced by Buddhist
     Bond: Interview with Arthur Basnayake, Ambassador of
     Sri Lanka." Business Japan. 32.6 (June 1987): 30-31.

     Arthur Bsnayake, the Ambassador of Sri Lanka to Japan,
     discussed relations between the two countries. Japan
     and Sri Lanka have a common religion and culture. Sri
     Lanka is trying to overcome the trade imbalance in
     Japan's favor and Japan has helped by lowering tariffs.
     Sri Lanka exports about $80 million worth of goods to
     Japan, while Japan exports about $260 million to Sri
     Lanka. About 20 joint ventures between Japan and Sri
     Lanka were established in the 1960's, but those are
     primarily for the domestic market. Sri Lanka wants
     ventures targeted at exports. The country offers cheap
     labor and few restrictions on ownership. Basnayake
     thinks Japan should invest more in Sri Lanka.

557. Rasin, R. S. "Japanese Capital for Asian Economic
     Growth." Tokyo Financial Review. 10.10 (Oct. 1985):
     2-5.

     The potential for growth of Japanese investment in Asia
     is assessed. By the year 2000, the regional growth
     rates are likely to reach 7%-9%. For the long run,
     Japan's economic health will be tied to the stability
     of Asia and its potential. It is therefore important
     for Japan to take the lead in supplying capital and
     stimulate the necessary growth for the region.
     Forecasts and statistics are offered 1960-2000.

558. Sherk, Donald R. Foreign Investment in Asia;
     Cooperation and Conflict between the United States and
     Japan. San Francisco: Federal Reserve Bank of San
     Francisco, 1973.

     This work deals with developing Asian countries and the
     instrument of that development: direct foreign
     investment by the U.S. and Japan. The changing
     military, political, and economic relationships that
     form the basis for this development are clarified. The
     realignment of exchange rates, the advent of the
     People's Republic of China, the extrication of the U.S.
     from the Vietnam conflict, the new relations between
     Japan and the U.S., and the protectionism growing in
     the U.S. all contribute to the complex international
     environment. Topics introduced include a survey of
     U.S. direct investment, foreign direct investment
     models, the role of Japan, Japanese and American
     investment in Asia, host countries' attitudes, and a
     vision of the future.

559. Stutely, Richard, and Henry Azzam. "Arab Banking: Gulf
     Reforms Aim at Economic Stimulation; Trade Shrinks, but
     Investment Potential Up." Asian Finance. 13.5 (May
     15, 1987): 78-82.

     Falling oil prices and reduced government spending are
     creating difficult times for banks in the Arab Gulf
     states. In general these states are responding by
     improving their control over the banking system and
     easing monetary policy to stimulate their economies.
     Even though commodity trade has been declining in
     recent years, the flow of capital from the Arab
     countries to Japan has risen steeply to insure a strong
     relationship with Japanese exporters and a place in the
     growing Japanese financial and capital markets. It is
     highly probable that Japanese producers will increase
     their joint-venture activities in the Gulf.

560. Wilson, Dick. "Shrinking Asian Handout from Japan."
     Far Eastern Economic Review. 86.49 (Dec. 13, 1974):
     58-59.

     The decline of growth in Japan's GNP is expected to
     produce a sharp drop in the amount of foreign
     investments for 1975. Asia will be the region most
     adversely affected. Statistics are given for aid and

investments in 1973, along with investments in East
Asia as of March 1974.

561. Wilson, Dick. "Two Giants on the Move." Banker.
128.634 (Dec. 1978): 43-47.

The China-Japan friendship treaty represents China's
need for technology and capital to accelerate its
development, and the Japan's search for lucrative
direct foreign investments for the appreciating yen.
Both powers view U.S. Asian policy with suspicion,
believing that the U.S. is withdrawing, allowing the
U.S.S.R. to enter. China fears that Vietnam is being
used to help encircle and subvert its government, while
the U.S.S.R. fears being locked out of the Pacific.
Japan is also pressuring Korea, which is beginning a
major industrial development, into trade collaborations
out of fear of Taiwan and the Association of South East
Asian Nations (ASEAN). China's liberalization policies
may permit a rapprochement with Taiwan. Hong Kong
will benefit from increased trade with China, which is
appealing to Hong Kong's industrialists to implement
their industrial equipment in China.

THE MIDDLE EAST

562. "Japanese Overseas Investments: India, Sri Lanka and
Iran." Oriental Economist. 48.839 (Sept. 1980): 53-
57.

This offers a survey of Japanese investments in India,
Sri Lanka and Iran, giving data by investors.

563. Ozawa, Terutomo. "Japan's Mid-East Economic
Diplomacy." Columbia Journal of World Business. 9.3
(Fall 1974): 38-46.

Japan's oil diplomacy is examined in light of the
pressure of the recent crisis. Preliminary moves by
Japan toward the Mideast market and further gains made
are discussed, along with the role of trading
companies. In addition major Japanese projects in the
Middle East are described.

564. Sultan, A., D. Shirreff, J. Whelan, et al. "Japan and
the Middle East 1977." Middle East Economic Digest.
(Oct. 28, 1977): supplement 1-20.

A review is presented of Japanese exports and
investments with the Middle East in light of the
competition with the West. An example is given of a
strong Japanese company operating in the Middle East.
In addition, joint ventures, credit, and aid is
covered, providing statistics on investments for 1972-
1976. Contracts for 1976 between Japan and the region
are given.

565. Turner, Louis, and James Bedore. "The Trade Politics
of Middle Eastern Industrialization." Foreign Affairs.

57.2 (Winter 1978/79): 306-322.

Less developed countries from the Middle East and North
Africa are attempting to penetrate the industrialization
cycle by producing and exporting refined petroleum
products. Four problems, however, face these nations
as they start industrialization: 1) overcapacity in the
world's petrochemical industries, 2) high construction
cost, 3) high managerial labor cost, and 4) high
transportation costs. The scarcity of energy is drawing
industry closer to the sources. The U.S. stands to
gain from Saudi industrialization. The Japanese are
looking at direct investments in the region to assure
themselves a continued source of energy. Western
Europe will not be receptive to the Middle East entry
into industrial markets. Oil producing countries
should think in terms of regional markets as a path to
successful industrial integration.

566. Whelan, J., M. Roth, R. Bailey, et al. "Japan and the
      Middle East." Middle East Economic Digest; Weekly
      News, Analysis and Forecast. Special Japan Review.
      (Dec. 1981): 1-43.

An overview of Japanese trade relations with the Middle
East is represented with a discussion of Japan's policy
of compromise and its dependence on Middle East oil.
Japanese direct foreign investments are also examined
along with the activities of sogo shosha, bankers,
electronics, car sales, and telecommunication projects.
Focus is concentrated on the major Japanese contractors
in the region: Mitsubishi Heavy Industries: JGC
Projects, Penta-Ocean, Suez Dredging, and Sumito
Electronics Industries. Technology transfer and joint
ventures are included. Market surveys are given for
Algeria, Egypt, Gulf states, Iraq, and Libya.
Statistics are provided for Japanese imports from and
exports to the MIddle East.

567. "Whither Japan's Business Ventures in Iran?"
      Oriental Economist. 48.834 (April 1980): 10-14.

During the 1979-80 period, the U.S. government ordered
a curtailment of trade with Iran, which resulted in
serious cutbacks of activity for Japanese interests
there. The resumption of activity after the progress
in solving Iran-U.S. hostage crises led to new growth
in Iran's export contracts. The commitments of firms
for supply of parts and other materials, and the manufacturing activities have resumed their former levels.
The present situation is outlined. The activities of
Honda and other smaller firms are described. A listing
of the Japanese firms active in Iran is given.

SOUTHEAST ASIA

568. Barang, M., Tan Boon Kean, G. Peck, et al. "Challenge
      on Japan's Hi-Tech Frontier." South; The Third World
      Magazine. 80 (June 1987): 101-103.

The impact of the high yen on export performance has
caused Japanese companies to invest in several
Southeast Asian countries. Japan's total investments
in Southeast Asia in 1986 are estimated at some 13.5
billion U.S. dollars. These developments give hope to
the host countries for some badly needed technology
transfer. So far, the results are not encouraging. An
assessment is made of the experiences of host countries
with Japanese technology transfer and know-how and with
the attitudes in Tokyo.

569. Constantino, Renato. The Second Invasion; Japan in
the Philippines. Manila: 1979.

The author is concerned about the growing presence of
Japanese global corporations in the Philippines. He
seeks to explain contemporary Japanese policies as an
expression of its self-interest and imperialism, hiding
behind a mask of altruism. Reviewed is Japan's
economic and military expansion in World War II and its
post-war economic development and boom. Next Japan is
viewed in its relation to rival capital countries and
its increasing involvement in Southeast Asia. Lastly,
Japanese direct investment in the Philippines is
examined and its effects on the economy.

570. Debes, Cheryl, James Treece, and William Holstein.
"Japan's Investment Binge in Southeast Asia."
Business Week (Industrial/Technology Edition). 2971
(Nov. 3, 1986): 42-43.

Japanese investments in Southeast Asia are rapidly
rising with the higher value of the yen. For over 20
years, the U.S. has been involved in building the
economy in the region, but now economic problems are
causing a fall in investment activities. The crash of
the region's major exports - oil, rubber, tin, and
other raw materials - is forcing their governments to
place greater emphasis on manufactured goods for
export. Southeast Asian governments are therefore
creating investment incentives to move in this new
direction. The Japanese yen has risen 50% against the
currencies of the area, making it easy for them to buy
assets at bargain prices. Manufactured goods of these
Japanese companies are exported to the U.S., expanding
the U.S. market for Japan.

571. Draper, Charles. Private Foreign Investment in
ASEAN. The Economic Cooperation Centre for the Asian
and Pacific Region Study no. 7. Bangkok: The Economic
Cooperation Centre for the Asian and Pacific Region,
1974.

This brings together information which is available on
the countries of ASEAN and their attitudes, policies,
and government regulations regarding foreign investors.
This includes fiscal and non-tax investment and export
incentive measures, obligations and restrictions
affecting foreign investors, and the recent trends
which investment has been following. The goal of the

work is to further the climate of understanding for
investors and host countries alike. In some cases
there is a dearth of clear data available, and
statistics presented can at times not be found adequate
to the goal of the study.

572. Gross, Martin. "Foreign Direct Investment in ASEAN:
Its Sources and Structure." Asian Economies. (June
1987): 18-35.

An analysis is provided of the volume, regional and
industry structure of investment by Japan, the United
States, the United Kingdom, and West Germany in ASEAN
countries.

573. Hiemenz, U. "Foreign Direct Investment and
Industrialization in ASEAN Countries."
Weltwirtschaftliches Archiv. 123.1 (1987): 121-139.

An analysis is provided of German, Japanese, and U.S.
investment in ASEAN countries. A brief overview of the
sectoral distribution of foreign direct investment
across ASEAN countries and across manufacturing
industries is presented. In addition, comparison is
made of the pattern of foreign direct investment from
different home countries to a number of industry
characteristics in the host countries. Evidence is
given on the trade orientation of affiliated companies
and the importance of intra-firm trade vis-a-vis total
trade flows. Statistics provided for 1974-1983.

574. Hirono, R., G. Sicat, K. Ariff, et al. "Southeast
Asia's Economy and Japan." The Developing Economies.
11.4 (Dec. 1973): 325-497.

Economic development in Japan, Malaysia, and Singapore
is discussed in the context of changing patterns of
economic interdependence in Asia. The growth and
structural change in the manufacturing sector in
Thailand is reviewed for the 1960-1969 period. The
formation and development of the Association of
Southeast Asian Nations (ASEAN) is reviewed and seen as
the desire for economic independence of the Southeast
Asia region. The trials and achievements of Japanese
economic assistance to the region is analyzed.

575. Holloway, N., B. Roscoe, J. Galang, et al. "Building
an Empire; Japan's Thrust for Overseas Assets Builds
Up." Far Eastern Economic Review. 133.36 (Sept. 4,
1986): 59-66.

The strong yen should reduce Japan's massive current-
account surplus and speed up the outflow of capital.
Nomura Research Institute in Tokyo suggests that
Japan's net overseas assets will increase from 120
billion dollars at end of 1985 to 556 billion dollars
in 1995. Much of the new investment will be spent in
East Asia, and probably by preference in Taiwan and
South Korea. However, these two countries have
numerous restrictions on direct investment and as a

result many Japanese firms may instead set up
operations in Hong Kong and in ASEAN. Analysis of
Japanese investments in five Asean countries -
Indonesia, Singapore, the Philippines, Malaysia and
Thailand - is presented. Statistics are given for
1967-1985.

576. Imoto, Tomofumi. "Developing Countries: Expansion of
Trade in Manufactured Products and the Development of
the International Division of Labor." EXIM Review.
2.1 (1981): 20-41.

Case studies are presented of Singapore and Malaysia
with emphasis placed on Japanese investments and its
effects on the international division of labor.

577. Jang, Wong Nang. "ASEAN Wants to Move Closer to the
Yen." Euromoney. (Oct. 1980): 171,173.

Japan is rapidly becoming a major source of capital and
equipment for the Association of Southeast Asia Nations
(ASEAN.) ASEAN is a vital supplier of raw materials
and the Japanese investments mean the payment of
dividends and interest in yens. The expanding Japanese
investment in these newly industrializing countries is
a concern since their products incorporate Japanese
technology and research and may be banned by
protectionist nations. Japan's dependence on the ASEAN
nations may persuade Japan to grant ASEAN special
treatment, specifically an agreement providing for
long-term investments in yen both in good times and
bad. By denominating ASEAN exports and investment
capital funds in yen, the ASEAN group could eliminate
the currency risk when paying for Japanese-made
imports.

578. Janssen, Peter. "Economic Report: Thailand." Asian
Business. 23.8 (Aug. 1987): 33-40.

This is a treatment of the Thai economy, which
highlights the reasons for the recent growth. The 1985
recession was overcome because the U.S. dollar was
pushed down and this in turn lowered the Thai currency.
There was a fall in oil prices in 1986, and domestic
and foreign interest rates were reduced. Even more
significant was the increase in exports of certain
types of products to Japan. Investors from Japan also
took a leading role in the development. $124 million
in investment from Japan went to Thailand, and some
Japanese corporations have relocated there.

579. "Japan-Thailand Economic Relations." Business in
Thailand. 17.10 (Oct. 1986): 47-116.

The Thai-Japanese relationship is examined in this
study. The increase in cultural exchange has bolstered
the ties between the two countries. Japan's
development of Thai methods in marketing and technical
processes are having significant impact. Japanese
training and assistance are also described. Projects

in which the Japanese are involved are outlined, and
companies participating are profiled. The activities
of the Japan External Trade Relations Organization are
considered.

580. "Japanese Investment in Thailand." Bangkok Bank.
Monthly Review. 22.5 (May 1981): 182-192.

This article contains a discussion of Japanese
investments abroad, and its costs and benefits. It
includes reasons for investments abroad and what
Thailand has to offer to Japan. Also analyzed is the
impact of the Japanese investments on the transfer of
technology, ownership and management, and capital
inflows and outflows. Statistics are given for 1960-
1980.

581. "Japanese Investment in Thailand." Business in
Thailand. 5.3 (March 1974): 64-68.

The effects of the opposition to Japanese direct
investment in Thailand are considered. The impact of
opposition by student groups, for example, is not yet
clear. Such political conditions are examined.

582. "Japanese Overseas Investments: Indonesia 1."
Oriental Economist. 48.837 (July 1980): 49-54.

This article offers information for a study of the
Japanese investments in Indonesia. The period covered
is from 1970 to 1979. A cataloging of companies,
capital ratios, business lines and geographic locations
is offered. There is discussion of sales and
production objectives and results, as well.

583. "Japanese Overseas Investments: Indonesia 2."
Oriental Economist. 48.838 (Aug. 1980): 44-49.

A continuation of the data presented in last month's
issue, this summation of data about Japanese
investments in Indonesia focuses on the year 1978.
There is a presentation of information about capital
ratios, business lines, partnerships among firms, and
data about sales, production, capital ratios, and
employees. Geographic location of operations is also
given.

584. "Japanese Survey Reveals Cooled Interest in Southeast
Asian Investment." Business Asia. 8.36 (Sept. 3,
1976): 281-284.

This is a study of the investment by Japan in
Indonesia, Malaysia, the Philippines, Singapore, and
Thailand. Other regions are also mentioned. The year
considered is up to the end of March, 1976. The
largest share of the investment goes to Indonesia.
Probabilities for future investment concentration are
discussed.

585. "Japan's Overseas Investments: Malaysia." Oriental

Economist. 47.820 (Feb. 1979): 30-38.

Japanese overseas investments in Malaysia are described
with coverage of joint ventures and policies regarding
them. The effects of economic recession and their
impact on investments are assessed. Malaysia's policy
toward foreign direct investment is discussed. A list
of investors in Malaysia is provided.

586. "Japan's Overseas Investments: Philippines." Oriental
     Economist. 46.818 (Dec. 1978): 24-32.

     This article provides a general overview of Japanese
     investments in overseas countries for 1960-1978 with
     focus on the Philippines. Investments made in the
     Philippines by countries are also outlined with primary
     concentration given to statistics on Japanese
     investments in the Philippines.

587. "Japan's Overseas Investments: Thailand." Oriental
     Economist. 47.819 (Jan. 1979): 49-60.

     An historical account is given of Thailand's
     industrialization in the 1962-1977 period. In
     addition, statistics on Japanese investments in
     Thailand until 1977 are presented.

588. "Japan's Trading Satellites." Economist. 254.6859
     (Feb. 8, 1975): 62-63.

     In this general treatment of the Japanese foreign trade
     situation, there is a treatment of direct investment
     as well. Details are offered for direct investment by
     industry and by country in Southeast Asia and
     Australiasia, as of March 31, 1974.

589. Katano, Hikoji. Japanese Enterprises in ASEAN
     Countries; Statistical Outlook. Kobe Economic and
     Business Research Series 8. Kobe: Research Institute
     for Economics & Business Administration, Kobe
     University, 1981.

     This book intends to examine the meanings of Japanese
     direct investment in the ASEAN countries. Part I
     analyzes general rules of industrialization and
     influences of foreign direct investment in the ASEAN
     nations. Part II uses the results of Part I and
     examines the merits and demerits of Japanese private
     direct investments in these countries. In addition, it
     looks at the role of general trading companies in the
     region and the importance of textile enterprises. Part
     III is a statistical supplement including direct
     investment by industries and local enterprises and
     direct investment by Japanese enterprises.

590. Katano, Hikoji, Atsushi Murakami, and Kiyoshi Ikemoto.
     Japan's Direct Investment to ASEAN Countries. Kobe
     Economic & Business Research Series. Kobe: Research
     Institute for Economics & Business Administration, Kobe
     University, 1978.

Case studies on Japan's direct investment to ASEAN are
studied to bridge the gap between purely theoretical
analysis and its practical evolution. This is seen as
particularly important in light of the increasing trend
of Japanese direct investment and the growing
importance of ASEAN for the Japanese economy. Areas
covered include: problems of Japanese economic
cooperation, foreign capital inducement policies,
Japanese textile investments in Thailand, the role of
Japan's trading companies, the evolution of Japan's
trading policies, and industrial projects and
preferential trading arrangements.

591. Keck, Jorn. "Japan's Direct Investment in South East
     Asia." Intereconomics. 9 (Sept. 1976): 255-259.

     Japan's investments in the Southeast Asia region are
     explored. Their development and significance are
     assessed, for the period 1951-75. The structure of the
     investments varies by region, and by industrial
     branches. In the various countries, Japanese
     investment makes a specific impact on the balance of
     trade. Attitudes toward the activity of foreign
     capital are changing in the region.

592. Kesavan, K. V. Japan's Relations with Southeast Asia;
     1952-60: With Particular Reference to the Philippines
     and Indonesia. Bombay: Somaiya Publications Pvt.
     Ltd., 1972.

     This study recounts the political and economic ties
     between Japan and two countries, the Philippines and
     Indonesia. A history of their relations before the
     Second World War is offered. The attitudes of the two
     countries toward Japan after the war are described.
     There is then a treatment of the reparations problem
     and Japan's attempt to win the confidence of the former
     enemy nations. Some documentation is offered to show
     the extent to which Japan succeeded in its reparations
     agreements. The role of Japan's trade with each nation
     is also recounted.

593. Kinoshita, Toshihiko. "Investment Environs in
     Indonesia as Viewed by Japanese Investors."
     Management Japan. 19.1 (Spring 1986): 17-27.

     The Indonesian economic and social situation has not
     recently been conducive to Japanese investors.
     Japanese affiliates here have shown declining sales in
     the automotive industry, electric home appliances, and
     iron-related industries. Deteriorating market
     conditions and rising costs are undermining profits.
     Losses are reported and at least 6 affiliates were
     liquidated in the past two years. Indonesia is
     interested in export-oriented foreign investment rather
     than import-substitution. For Indonesia, the transfer
     of technology is imperative for faster economic
     development. This technology transfer has a 5 step
     approach moving from learning operation skills to the
     development of full-scale technology on a local basis.

594. Kinoshita, Toshihiko. "Japanese Investment in
     Indonesia; Problems and Prospects." Bulletin of
     Indonesian Economic Studies. 22.1 (April 1986): 34-
     56.

     The majority of Japanese investment in Indonesia is
     import-substitution orientated and located primarily in
     manufacturing. Declining Japanese investment in recent
     years is attributable to economic factors and
     to Indonesian government policy. Ways are suggested in
     which the Indonesian government could establish
     conditions more favorable to foreign investment.
     Statistics include Indonesian trade with selected
     countries 1980-84; trend of Japan's loans and
     investments to Indonesia 1980-90; new foreign
     investment projects approved by the Indonesian
     government 1969-84; and growth in production of
     Japanese affiliates in the Indonesian manufacturing
     sector 1982- 84. An overview is presented of the
     current position of Japan's loans outstanding and
     equity participation in Indonesia. The logic behind
     the shrinkage of Japan's direct investment to Indonesia
     is revealed.

595. Kojima, Kiyoshi. "Japanese and American Direct
     Investment in Asia; A Comparative Analysis."
     Hitotsubashi Journal of Economics. 26.1 (June 1985):
     1-35.

     Comparisons are made between Japanese and American
     direct foreign investments in Asia, focusing on four
     newly industrializing countries (Korea, Hong Kong,
     Singapore, and Taiwan) and four ASEAN countries
     (Indonesia, Philippines, Malaysia and Thailand.) The
     study shows that the patterns of Japanese and U.S.
     direct foreign investment are quite different. This is
     explained by differences in the behavior of U.S. and
     Japanese firms. It further showed that Japanese
     investments have contributed to the development of host
     countries with more efficiency than U.S. investments.
     The analysis is however limited to impacts on trade and
     GNP.

596. Krongkaew, Medhi, ed. Current Development in Thai-
     Japanese Economic Relations; Trade and Investment:
     Papers and Proceedings of the Conference on Current
     Development in Thai-Japanese Economic Relation: Trade
     and Investment, August 10-12, 1979, Pattaya, Thailand.
     Bangkok: Thammasat University Press for Faculty of
     Economics, Thammasat University, 1980.

     The large impact of Japanese investment in Thailand is
     documented, as overall Thai-Japanese economic relations
     are reviewed. The role of Japanese trade policy toward
     Thailand is examined, and the significance of Thai
     exports to Japan is treated. The general trading
     companies' role in Thailand is considered, and the
     joint venture investments are described. A significant
     portion of the study goes beyond the descriptive level,
     and projects policy recommendations to meet problems of

trade imbalance, environmental pollution, tactics of
bilateral trade negotiations, and the like. The import
of technologically advanced processes and quality
management development is also mentioned.

597. Laumer, H. "Japanese Private Direct Investment in East
and Southeast Asia." IFO Digest; A Quarterly Journal
on Economic Trends in the Federal Republic of Germany.
7.1 (March 1984): 30-36.

Japan's investment patterns in the East and Southeast
Asian countries are improving, though there is some
criticism in the host countries. Many changes have
been taking place since the 1970's. The dollar amount
of the investments by Japan in the region is $53.1
billion. Indonesia is the major center of activity.
Various kinds of investment structures are found, with
differences depending on the resources and basic
conditions found in the area. Trading companies play a
strong role. The data offered come from the period
1951-82.

598. Lim, Chee Peng, and Lee Poh Ping. The Role of
Japanese Direct Investment in Malaysia. Occasional
Paper. Singapore: Institute of Southeast Asian
Studies, 1979.

This study focuses on Japanese direct investment in
Malaysia, covering first its main features. These
include the time pattern, reasons for Japanese direct
investments, size of investments, type of activity,
equity and control, marketing, management, and
profitability. The impact of Japanese direct
investment on the Malaysian economy is then studied,
concentrating on the effects it has produced on
employment, training, and subcontracting. The transfer
of technology is given special consideration for its
importance in the foreign direct investment process.
Case studies are offered to illustrate points made.

599. Masao, Fujioka. "Japan's Direct Investment in
Indonesia. Emphasis Is on Loans and Development of
Resources." Japan Economic Journal. 17.870 (Sept.
18, 1979): 24-25.

A look is taken at the investment climate in Indonesia
and the Third Five-year Plan. Indonesia is promoting
the inflow of foreign capital and Japan is an important
source of direct investments. The Japanese are
concentrating on the development of natural resources
and the extension of loans. The article further
discusses foreign trade, income disparities, LNG
project, and joint ventures.

600. Matsumoto, Katsuo. "External Elements of China's
Economic Policy and Japan's Financial Assistance to
China." China Newsletter. 42 (Jan./Feb. 1983): 9-14.

An examination is presented of the external economic
policy of China that resulted in China's asking for

Japanese financial assistance. Japan's decision on
financial aid for China is discussed with a description
of Japan's loan commitments to China and ASEAN-
countries, as well as its aid policy. Statistics are
provided for 1977-1982.

601. Naya, Seiji and Narongchai Akrasanee. Thailand's
      International Economic Relations with Japan and the
      U.S.; A Study of Trade and Investment Interactions.
      Thammasat University, Faculty of Economics, Discussion
      Paper Series. Bangkok: Thammasat University, Faculty
      of Economics, 1975.

      With the focus on trade and investment-trade
      interactions, this paper is a consideration of the Thai
      economy. The role of the U.S. and Japan is assessed.
      While the U.S. position has begun to decline, Japan's
      dominance is becoming more pronounced in influence.
      Topics treated include import patterns for American and
      Japanese commodities, Thai export performance in the
      U.S. and Japan, and the size and types of Japanese and
      U.S. direct investment. An evaluation is then
      provided, to outline the major differentials in
      American and Japanese trade arrangements with Thailand.
      There are conclusions and recommendations for policy
      development.

602. Nemetz, Peter N. The Pacific Rim; Investment,
      Development and Trade. Vancouver: University of
      British Columbia Press, 1987.

      Also copywrited by the Journal of Business Administ-
      ration in 1986, this publication is a collection of
      articles about the role of Japan in the Pacific Rim
      region. The relationship between trade and investment
      by Japan is defined, and the nature of investment in
      various countries is delineated: Thailand, China, and
      Canada. Fields of investment include a diverse range,
      from ocean minerals, to agriculture and coal. The
      roles of labor-intensive industry investment and energy
      industry investment are examined. The conclusions
      reached imply that a greater concern for long range
      planning is needed to insure the future health and
      stability of the entire region.

603. Oguro, Keuchi. "Japan's Direct Investments Toward Asia
      Facing Turning Point." Digest of Japanese Industry
      and Technology. 217 (1986): 11-16.

      Japanese firms have invested heavily in Asian newly
      industrializing countries (South Korea, Taiwan, Hong
      Kong and Singapore) and in ASEAN-4 (Indonesia,
      Malaysia, Thailand and the Philippines.) Japanese
      investments, including direct investments toward Asia,
      can be divided into three types: 1. investments
      covering a broad range from developing mineral
      resources to forest resources and shrimp; 2.
      investments conforming with industrialization policies
      of host nations on import replacement industry; and 3.
      investments aimed at export production in developing

countries using cheap labor cost, various investment
incentives and preferential tariff scheme given by the
advanced countries. Further discussions include the
changes in investment opportunities, the recent
investment trend by Japanese firms, and the requested
objective assessment of business activities.
Statistics are provided for 1971-1985.

604. Onishi, Akira. The Role of Japan in the Development
of Southeast Asia. Kuala Lumpur: Malaysian Economic
Association, 1974.

As a background to the study, the author maintains that
it is necessary for the world economy to even out the
disparities between the developed nations and those
that are now developing, and to move toward an eventual
levelling off of growth, worldwide. Since Japan is in
the position to exert heavy influence on the Asian
region, it is imperative that the Japanese policies
toward investment be mindful of that impact. A reform
of development strategy is advocated.

605. Ozawa, Terutomo. "Japan's New Resource Diplomacy:
Government-Backed Group Investment." Journal of World
Trade Law. 14.1 (Jan./Feb. 1980): 3-13.

The Japanese economy is highly vulnerable to changes in
supply conditions because it is dependent on overseas
resources. The sharp increase in crude oil prices
announced by the OPEC in June 1979 has sharply raised
Japan's wholesale prices. Japan's recent resource
diplomacy shows a sense of urgency with new elements in
its efforts to secure overseas resources. An example
of this diplomacy is the Asahan project, involving the
building of a hydroelectric power dam on the Asahan
River in Sumatra, Indonesia. An aluminum refinery will
be constructed to use the power along with
infrastructural facilities. The following investment
pattern emerges: 1. a search for a key investment
opportunity with a nation whose natural resources are
critical to the Japanese economy; 2. once the project
is accepted, the host government seeks financing in the
form of economic aid from Japan; and 3. the Japanese
government may put off its final commitment, but will
eventually come to the aid of Japanese industry.

606. Panglaykin, Yusuf. "Business Relations between
Indonesia and Japan." The Developing Economies. 12.3
(Sept. 1974): 281-303.

Japanese-Indonesian trade relations are explored,
delineating the volume and composition of trade.
Japanese-based multinationals are primarily responsible
for handling the business relationships. Behavioral
characteristics of Japanese investments are discussed.
Indonesian government policies toward foreign companies
are reported along with their effects on Japan-
Indonesia relations.

607. Panglaykim, Yusuf. Business Relations between

Indonesia and Japan. Jakarta: Yayasan Proklamasi, Center for Strategic and International Studies, 1974.

In this short essay, the author discusses the Japanese "big ten" and indicates how they have served as initiators of direct foreign investment. The point of view of Indonesians with their rather limited bargaining position serves to inform the narrative. The choice of the joint venture as a mode of operation is examined, alongside the "package deal" mechanism. The implications of this type of procedure are drawn out. Limitations in the approach of Indonesian entrepreneurs and institutional limitations are cited among the factors contributing to the current status quo.

608. Panglaykim, Yusuf., with the assistance of Mari Pangestu. Japanese Direct Investment in ASEAN; The Indonesian Experience. Singapore: Maruzen Asia, 1983.

This book treats the determinants which lead to direct foreign investment. The multinational corporations and sogo shosha are investigated, along with the Japanese integrated national system. Various theories are considered. The amount of Japanese foreign direct investment found to be directed at the ASEAN region is analyzed in terms of the determinants that are observed. There is an assessment of the character of the joint ventures between Indonesia and Japan. The role of the package deal ventures is described, with the view that such tied agreements will be rare in the future, since the Indonesians have now attained new sophistication.

609. Pearce, Jean. "Cause for Celebration: An Interview with Dr. Wichian Watanakun, Ambassador of Thailand." Business Japan. 32.7 (July 1987): 55-56.

From an interview with Thailand's ambassador to Japan, Wichian Watanakun, there is an explanation of the history of the two countries' relations. Since 1887, there has been open commerce. The Japanese have been Thailand's primary source of imports and the 2nd largest export market. The types of cooperation and infrastructure development aid by Japan are recounted. The use of soft loans and the tourist industry are discussed.

610. "Poor ASEAN Meets Rich Japan." Economist. 306.7543 (March 26, 1988): 65-66.

Members of the ASEAN have been saying that Japan is not keeping the region's overall health in mind as it moves in to make investments in member nations. As the largest investor in Indonesia, Thailand and Malaysia and number two in Singapore and the Philippines, Japan has a major role. Some of the complaints are that Japan will not permit enough imports from ASEAN, and that Japan cannot counteract the negative effects of World War II on the region. Its image remains

tarnished. Some positive trends are beginning to
emerge, as Japan eases quotas and ASEAN develops its
ability to handle the Japanese investment well.

611. Purkayastha, Prabir, and J. Burgess. "The Japanese."
     Business in Thailand. 10.9 (Sept. 1979): 59-74.

     This article considers the opinions of the Japanese on
     the investment climate in Thailand. Japanese
     investments are reviewed for the 1973-1978 period along
     with joint ventures in progress. A look is taken of
     the balance of trade between Japan and Thailand for the
     years 1973-1978. In addition, Japanese financial
     institutions located in Thailand are discussed.

612. Rastapana, Srirat. "Thailand-Japan Trade Ties: Tough
     Talks." Business Review. 12.22 (Sept. 1984): 168-
     170.

     In a brief look at the trade relations between Thailand
     and Japan, there are observations of the large deficit
     that the Thais have incurred in its trade with Japan.
     The trade deficit in fact climbed by 146% in 1983 over
     1982. At the same time, Japan has the largest share in
     foreign investment in Thailand. While the Thai
     government intends to work towards a reduced trade
     deficit, pressures for its continuation will be strong
     for the immediate future. There are data offered from
     1977-83.

613. "A Rising Trend in Japanese Investment." Asia
     Research Bulletin; Monthly Economic Reports) with
     Political Supplement. 11.6 (Nov. 30, 1981): 862-865.

     This is a treatment of Japanese investments in
     Thailand. While it seems that Japan's investments
     there are low, relative to investments in other
     countries in the Asian region, there are some reasons
     for this trend to be observed. An outline of the
     movement of capital by Japan's investors is offered.
     Some details are given by various industrial sector,
     and covering the years 1960-1980. Based on the data
     for this twenty year period, some projections for the
     future are given.

614. Sandhu, Kernial Singh, and Eileen P. T. Tang, eds.
     Japan as an Economic Power and Its Implications for
     Southeast Asia; Papers Presented at a Conference
     Organized by the Institute for Southeast Asian
     Studies. Singapore: Singapore University Press for
     the Institute of Southeast Asian Studies, 1974.

     A number of papers in this collection consider the
     impact of the Japanese economy on the other countries
     in Asia, making some reflections on the history and
     likely future of Sino-Asian economic relations. There
     are treatments of specific topics, as well: economic
     aid by Japan, perceptions of Japan by others, the
     significance of Japan's economic power, and reviews of
     the relations between Indonesia and Japan, and Thailand

and Japan. Political and historical considerations
play a significant role in the papers.

615. Sazanami, Yoko. "Japanese Trade in the Pacific Rim:
     The Relationship Between Trade and Investment."
     Journal of Business Administration. 16.1/2 (1986):
     53-73.

     The trade and investment activities between Japan and
     other Pacific nations is described for the period of
     1972-1982. Trade patterns appear to develop
     independently of investment patterns. Japan's key role
     in export-import trade with the Association of
     Southeast Asian Nations is indicated, with details of
     its heavy industry export and its raw materials import
     pattern. The policy of Japan before the oil crisis was
     motivated by the desire to develop raw materials
     supplies. After the oil shock, the trend was to move
     high-energy consuming factories to other nations
     through direct investment.

616. Sekiguchi, Sueo, ed. ASEAN-Japan Relations;
     Investment; Proceedings of a Workshop and a Conference
     Organized by the Japan Center for International
     Exchange and the ASEAN Economic Research Unit of the
     Institute of Southeast Asian Studies Held on 5-6
     December 1981 and 20-23 May 1982 at Singapore and Oiso,
     Japan Respectively. Variant Title: A.S.E.A.N.-Japan
     Relations. Singapore: Institute of Southeast Asian
     Studies, 1983.

     Beginning with a synthesis offered by the editor, this
     collection treats Japanese direct investment in
     Indonesia, Malaysia, the Philippines, Singapore, and
     Thailand. Some common themes in the papers include a
     concern with the role direct foreign investment
     occupies in the host country, the factors which affect
     the investment, the political economic and social
     impact of the investment, and the future possibilities
     for the direct foreign investment. Policy recom-
     mendations are also developed for the possible
     improvement of the Japanese direct foreign investment
     relationships with the countries studied.

617. Sekiguchi, Sueo. Japanese Direct Foreign Investment
     and ASEAN Economies; A Japanese Perspective.
     Discussion Paper. Osaka, Japan: The Institute of
     Social and Economic Research, Osaka University, 1982.

     This discussion paper was released for limited
     circulation. It is observed that direct foreign
     investment has the potential to expand host countries'
     income through increased employment, mobilization of
     local capital, and greater industrialization. But the
     foreign investor often controls local markets and can
     interfere with autonomous development of the host
     countries. Social and political frictions also present
     themselves. In light of these conditions, this paper
     discusses policy issues. Background description is
     given, then a treatment of the various interest groups

172   Japanese Direct Foreign Investments

in Japan which are concerned with direct foreign
investment. Factors that will influence future
developments are analyzed, especially in light of the
role of China. Recommendations for policy are offered.

618. Sherk, Donald R. "Foreign Investment in Asia -- Japan
Vs the U.S." Columbia Journal of World Business.
9.3 (Fall 1974): 95-104.

Japan's investments in East and Southeast Asia are
increasing at a rapid rate, reaching and even
surpassing the level of U.S. investments. As a result
these countries are reviewing their policies towards
these two countries. U.S. investment has been
propelled by the growth in foreign sourcing, along with
heavy investments in oil exploration and related
activities. Although Japanese total investment does
not equal that of the U.S., it is concentrated in
consumer products in urban centers with higher
visibility. In the 1970's, the U.S. and Japan will
find a qualified "open-door" in Asia. Greater
competition with the U.S. will ensue as Japan advances
in the high-tech fields.

619. Siahaan, Luckman, et. al. Japanese Direct Investment
in Indonesia; Findings of an Experimental Survey.
Institute of Development Economies Joint Research
Program Series 9. Tokyo: Institute of Developing
Economies, 1978.

This work addresses the costs and benefits that foreign
investment has made in Indonesia. Net economic gain,
to be defined in a narrow sense as the gain if social
returns exceed private returns, is a concept that
raises some questions. Comparisons are offered for
patterns and characteristics in the investment
activities of other major investors in Indonesia in
addition to Japan, as well. Possible areas of economic
gain to Indonesia include higher real incomes for
Indonesian workers, or higher revenues from taxes, or
lower product prices to local consumers. Indirect
benefits include the external economies generated by
Japanese investment. Topics include the foreign
investment policy in Indonesia, a profile of
investment by source nation, and estimates of the
economic contribution of Japanese direct investment.
Conclusions are offered.

620. Sinha, R. "Japan and ASEAN; A Special Relationship?"
World Today. 38.12 (Dec. 1982): 483-492.

The development of Japan's economic relationship with
Southeast Asian countries is reviewed with attention on
Japanese attitudes towards developing countries.
Foreign trade, Japanese direct foreign investments and
aid to Southeast Asia are presented with statistics for
1980. Prospects for future cooperation between the
region and Japan are outlined.

621. Stewart, Charles T., Jr. "Comparing Japanese and U.S.

Technology Transfer to Less-Developed Countries."
Journal of Northeast Asian Studies. 4 (Spring 1985):
3-19.

This comparison of technology transfer between the U.S.
and Japan concentrates primarily on Thailand and
Indonesia. It examines the two countries' investment
patterns, promotional efforts, ownership, and licensing
arrangements. In addition it looks at the potential
of the workforce in these less-developed countries and
compares U.S. and Japanese assistance in human resource
development and training.

622. "Stronger Japan-ASEAN Economic Relations." Fuji Bank
Bulletin. 34.5 (Sept./Oct. 1983): 4-11.

The development of political, economic, and cultural
ties between Japan and the ASEAN countries is reviewed
in this article. ASEAN countries' economic growth and
industrialization is examined in connection with trade
with Japan and Japanese direct investments. Statistics
are given with projects for 1970-1990.

623. Sullivan, Kevin. "Japanese Banks Adopt a More
International Role." Asian Business. 23.1 (Jan. 1987):
64-65.

Japanese banks are taking advantage of domestic surplus
funds to invest overseas. The development of a new
Japanese financial pattern will affect the Asian
region, particularly countries like the Peoples'
Republic of China, Indonesia, Thailand, and Malaysia.
They may suffer a decline in new foreign loans and
investments. Since the 1970's, the expansion of
banking services for Japanese corporations overseas has
been a clear trend, limited however by domestic
restrictions on foreign banks to establish local branch
networks. In the 1980's, Hong Kong and Singapore are
financial centers of interest to Japanese banks. A
spokesperson for the Japanese banks denies they have
failed to appreciate the potential of the Asian
investment and that they have a "herd" mentality.

624. Taira, Koji. "Colonialism in Foreign Subsidiaries:
Lessons from Japanese Investment in Thailand." Asian
Survey. 20.4 (April 1980): 373-396.

The concepts of direct foreign investment and
colonialism are compared and contrasted. The problems
involved in offering significant local control over the
ventures are compared with decolonialization. It
remains a problem that Japanese managers retain key
positions of Japanese subsidiaries and affiliates in
Thailand. Thai critics advocate full indigenization
of all ranks of management. Japanese responses are
offered. Statistics on the managerial staffing of
Japanese ventures in Thailand are given.

625. "Thai-Japan Relations." Business Review. 10.9
(Oct. 1982): 55-82.

The role of JETRO is examined in promoting Thailand-
Japan trade. The economic situation in Japan is
considered along with foreign trade and development
aid. Japanese investments in Thailand are discussed,
focussing on joint ventures in plastics. Company
profiles are given for Thai Hino Motor Sales, Marubeni
Corp., Sanyo Universal Electric Co., and Siam GS
Battery.

626. "Thai-Japan Trade Relations." Business in Thailand.
     5.6 (June 1974): 41-52.

     The changing patterns of Thai-Japan trade are discussed
     covering Thailand's imports from Japan (1969-73) and
     Thailand's exports to Japan (1970-73.) In addition,
     Japanese direct investments in Thailand are reviewed
     with attention given to industrial joint ventures. A
     Japanese perspective is given on Thai-Japanese trading
     relations as well as policies for economic and
     technical cooperation.

627. "Thai-Japanese Relations." Business Review
     12 (June 1984): 83-100.

     This articles details Thai-Japanese economic relations.
     Trade between the two countries is covered, along with
     Japanese direct foreign investment, joint ventures, and
     economic assistance. Perspectives are presented on the
     future direction of their trade relations.

628. "Thailand. A Rising Trend in Japanese Investment."
     Asia Research Bulletin; Monthly Economic Reports with
     Political Supplement. 11.5 (Nov. 30, 1981): 862-865.

     Japanese trade with Thailand is outlined for the years
     since 1950. In Thailand there is a preference for
     consumer import substitution industries. Prospects for
     trade between the two countries is presented. Japanese
     investments is broken down by sectors. Statistics are
     given for the 1960-1980 period.

629. Thornton, John. "The Nature of Japan's Trading
     Relationship with ASEAN countries, Hong Kong, and South
     Korea." ASEAN Economic Bulletin. 3 (March 1987):
     368-378.

     The impact of Japan's geographic proximity, market
     familiarity, and direct foreign investment on the
     economies of the ASEAN countries, South Korea, and Hong
     Kong is explored.

630. Tinbergen, J., R. Stojanovic, B. Madeuf, et al.
     "Exploring Global Interdependence." International
     Social Science Journal. 30.2 (1978): 219-376.

     This issue contains a collection of essays on
     international relations. It includes J. Tinbergen,
     "International cooperation;" R. Stojanovic,
     "International relations;" B. Madeuf and C.-A.
     Michalet, "A new approach to international economics,"

stressing the role of multinationals; G. Poquet,
"Global modelling;" R. Triffin, "International
monetary system;" R. Vayrijnen; International
patenting; Jayantanuja Bandyopadhyaya, "Climate and
development;" O.T. Bogomolov, "Comecon;" and Kunio
Yoshihara, "Japanese investment in Southeast Asia."

631. Uetani, Hisamitsu. "Cooperative Regional Entity for
Japan, ASEAN Nations." Financier (The Pacific
Basin). 10.6 (June 1986): 24-27.

The ASEAN-Japan Cooperation Committee has been created
to form a cooperative regional organization. It aims
to stimulate new growth by using technological
innovation and private sector entrepreneurship. ASEAN
countries need to open their markets to the world,
becoming consumers as well as exporters. The last few
years has seen a decrease of Japanese investments in
the region owing to the unstable economic conditions
and limitations placed on foreign capital. Nonetheless
regional cooperation is progressing with parts swapping
occurring between countries. Also, the Japanese
government has worked with ASEAN through the Pacific
Basin Human Resources Network Project. In 1987, at the
ASEAN-Japan Businessmen's meeting, regional cooperation
will be discussed.

632. Vorasirisunthorn, A. "Japanese investment in
Thailand." Bangkok Bank. Monthly Review. 28.6 (June
1987): 221-227.

An outline is given of Japanese investment policies in
the Asian region, particularly Thailand, resulting from
the rising yen. Examples of Japanese direct foreign
investments are provided with names of firms, host
country, invested amounts, and product fields.
Comparisons are made of the economic growth of
countries in the region for 1984-1986. Also discussed
are the industrial sectors emphasized by Japanese
investors. Statistical data on foreign investments is
presented by Thailand's Board of Investment, showing the
share of Japanese investments. A list of Japanese
firms in Thailand receiving promotional privileges is
given for 1986 and early 1987.

633. Watanabe, Masahide. "Malaysia." Japan Economic
Journal. 16.819 (Sept. 19, 1978): 11-13.

A brief look is taken at Malaysia's foreign policy, in
particular Malaysian-Japanese trade for 1977. The role
of tourism in the economy is discussed, along with
Japanese investments in Malaysia.

634. Weinstein, Franklin B. "Multinational Corporations and
the Third World: The Case of Japan and Southeast Asia."
International Organization. 30 (Summer 1976): 373-
404.

The hopes that multinational corporations will act as
an engine of development to the benefit of the devel-

oping countries are shown to be premature. The
"softness" of the third world and its inability to
control multinationals must be acknowledged. In fact
the regulations tendered by developing states are often
ineffectual. The growth of multinationals can be seen
to inhibit the development of indigenous institutions,
and it may do more to impede than to stimulate development in the developing countries.

635. Yoshihara, Kunio. "Determinants of Japanese
      Investments in South-East Asia." International Social
      Science Journal. 30.2 (1978): 363-376.

      There is a specific decision framework for the Japanese
      firms investing abroad. They are faced with several
      alternatives, licensing or exporting, as well as still
      other possibilities, including home production vs.
      overseas production. These alternatives form a basis
      for tracing the path of decision-making for a part-
      icular firm. Barriers to foreign investment are also
      examined, and recent changes are outlined which show
      how political and economic shifts have reduced the
      barriers. Profitability of foreign investment can be
      seen as the result of comparative advantages of various
      industries, particularly the labor-intensive ones. The
      import-substitution policies of some Southeast Asian
      countries also contributed to the incentives.
      Revaluation of the yen also plays a subsidiary role.

636. Yoshihara, Kunio. Japanese Direct Investment in
      Southeast Asia. Occasional Paper. Singapore:
      Institute of Southeast Asian Studies, 1973.

      Japanese direct investment which is tied also to trade
      is the major focus of this paper. Three types of
      investment are identified: import substitution,
      resource exploitation and export-oriented activities.
      Each of these investment methods is examined, and
      further definition is offered. The type of industries
      established, the average size of investment, the
      typical pattern of equity shares, and changes in the
      investment flow over time are then elucidated.
      Conclusions are offered. It is noted that structural
      change is continuing, and future prospects for
      increased overseas investment in the Southeast Asia
      region are particularly bright. The implications for
      the region are sketched.

637. Yoshihara, Kunio. Japanese Investment in Southeast
      Asia. Monographs of the Center for Southeast Asian
      Studies, Kyoto University. Honolulu: University Press
      of Hawaii, 1978.

      This study of Japanese foreign investment in
      manufacturing provides empirical evidence of the
      activities in Southeast Asia. The region is sub-
      divided to provide a convenient means of presenting the
      research. Of the total foreign investment of Japan,
      manufacturing in Asia represents a significant part of
      the picture. The data sources are from the Bank of

Japan approval records. For the first time these figures are examined in some specific detail. Background information about economic changes is given. Comparisons of the data for sub-regions is offered, and particular manufacturing industries are then highlighted. Some analysis of the motivation for the firms to move abroad is offered, with general conclusions.

THE PACIFIC RIM COUNTRIES

638. "The Automobile Industries of Asia NICs and Globalization of Japanese Auto and Auto Parts Manufacturers." LTCB (Long-Term Credit Bank of Japan) Research. (May 1987): 1-10.

This article provides an assessment of the South Korean and Taiwanese automobile industries. It explores their emergence as auto exporting countries and the implications this will have for Japan. This analysis is placed in the context of the globalization of Japanese automobile manufacturers and auto components makers.

639. Baillie, Adam, Dave Dodwell, and Anthony Rowley. "Hong Kong Faces Up to the Future; An Economy on Cloud Nine; Japan Takes a Major Role; 'Those Who Have Stayed Have Never Regretted Their Choice, and I Trust They Never Will'." Director. 40.10 (May 1987): 90- 104.

A review is given of Hong Kong's economy in light of the 1997 transfer to the Peoples' Republic of China. The economy is booming; fears of a collapse of the local banking system have subsided; and the linked exchange rates works to protect the economy. Japanese manufacturing firms are increasing their activities in the Hong Kong economy, taking over from the U.S. the impetus for export growth. The government approves of Japan's enlarged role. An interview with David Ford, Chief Secretary of the Hong Kong government, indicates he is confident of Hong Kong's future role as an international trading center after 1997.

640. Bird, J. P., E. Wieman, G. Clark, et al. "Japan: Exporter of capital." Insight for Decision-Makers in Asia. (Dec. 1974): 58-67.

In addition to making major investments in the U.S. and Europe recently, Japan has been involved in a massive initiative in other parts of the Asian world. This article examines Japanese interests in Singapore, its continuing flow of investments in Taiwan, and discusses other Asian companies that have been involved with Japan'-s industrial sector, focusing on the years between 1969-1973.

641. "Changing Patterns of Japanese Investment in Major Asian Industries." Business Asia; Weekly Report to Managers of Asia/Pacific Operations. 13.4 (Jan. 23, 1981): 31.

There has been a major restructuring in the way
Japanese companies are investing in Asian countries.
Gearing away from former trading practices, there is
now a trend toward technological transfer instead.
Steel is becoming an important product for
consideration, as is the automobile industry.
Cooperation with Taiwan in automobile production for
export shows a new direction for trade between the two
countries. The articles gives an analysis of the
impact of Japan's electronic industry on Asian
countries and provides figures for the years 1979
through 1981.

642. Drysdale, Peter, ed. Direct Foreign Investment in
Asia and the Pacific. Pacific Trade and Development
Conference, 3d, Sydney, 1970. Canberra: University of
Toronto Press, 1972.

There are four broad subjects included in the present
volume: general issues raised by direct foreign
investment, foreign investment among advanced countries
in the Pacific, case studies in foreign investment in
developing countries, and balance of payments and
policy issues in the region. A summary of the
proceedings is also presented. Originating at the
Third Pacific Trade and Development Conference, the
collection represents a variety of perspectives. The
overriding theme of the study is the economic effects
of direct foreign investment, with political
interactions as a second focus. There are contrasting
views of the significance of direct foreign investment
from the different parts of the world represented.

643. Goldstein, Carl. "Hong Kong '88 -- Japanese Cash
Threatens U.S. Dominance." Far Eastern Economic
Review. 140.14 (April 7, 1988): 74.

The Japanese investors in Hong Kong are becoming more
dominant, and may be able to overtake the U.S. position
there. As a free port, Hong Kong is very attractive.
With the strong yen and the high costs of operating in
Japan for manufacturing, there is an acceleration of
the interest in Hong Kong by Japan. Hong Kong also has
a well developed infrastructure, and serves as the
gateway to the Peoples' Republic of China. A profile
of the nature of the Japanese investments in Hong Kong
is offered. Some predictions about the rate of growth
in Japanese projects in Hong Kong is also given.

644. Gregory, Gene. "Asian 'Newcomers' Carve Up Japan's Key
Markets." Far Eastern Economic Review. 99.8 (Feb.
24, 1978): 40-44.

This article discusses the impact of South Korea,
Taiwan, Hong Kong and Singapore on Japanese industry.
The imports from these countries exceeded Japanese
corresponding exports. Japanese investments in and
exports to these countries is described, along with
Japanese mergers in the textile-industry.

645. "The Japanese in Singapore: A Growing Economic
     Presence." Insight for Decision-Makers in Asia.
     (Nov. 1976): 28-43.

     In Singapore the fourth largest foreign investor is the
     Japanese. This treatment covers overall trade with
     Japan, and details of the Sumitomo petrochemical
     project are offered. The costs of operating in
     Singapore are outlined. A description of Mitsubishi
     and joint ventures shipyards is also given.

646. "Japanese Overseas Investments: Taiwan." Oriental
     Economist. 48.836 (June 1980): 42-45.

     This article covers the facts about Japanese
     investments taking place in Taiwan. The Japanese
     investor is profiled. Information is offered about the
     capital invested and capital ratios. The start-up
     process for various operations is discussed. Some
     considerations of the employees and business ties, as
     well as sales and production activities are offered.
     Partnership activities and objectives of investors are
     outlined, and results of the businesses are discussed.

647. "Japan's Overseas Investments: Hong Kong." Oriental
     Economist. 47.822 (April 1979): 28-42.

     The extent and nature of Japanese investments taking
     place in Hong Kong during the period of 1960-1978 are
     discussed. The investors are profiled. An analysis of
     the capital ratios of the investments is provided.
     There is a consideration of the companies, amount of
     capital utilized, and nature of employment. The
     products and annual sales are outlined. An account is
     offered of annual sales and partnerships among firms.

648. "Japan's Overseas Investments: The Republic of
     Singapore." Oriental Economist. 47.821 (March
     1979): 51-61.

     This offers an overview of the Japanese direct
     investments located in Singapore. A discussion of the
     period up to 1977 is provided. The industrial sectors
     and distribution, as well as other factors are
     considered.

649. Kojima, Kiyoshi. Japan and a Pacific Free Trade
     Area. Berkeley: University of California Press, 1971.

     This collection focuses on the origin of the Pacific
     Free Trade Area idea as a new way for expanding trade
     and for accelerating economic development. The
     benefits are expected to be shared between the advanced
     Pacific and developing Asian countries. Japan is
     expected to play a leading part. Topics include Japan
     and world trade liberalization; an approach to
     integration through agreed specialization; the Pacific
     Free Trade Area proposal; trade preferences for
     developing countries; the PAFTA and Asian developing
     countries; a Pacific Currency Area; and the role of

PAFTA as a new design for world trade expansion.

650. Pearce, Jean. "Free Port, No Trade Restriction, Mark
     Singapore Development." Business Japan. 33.1 (Jan.
     1988): 31-32.

     This recalls an interview with Singapore's Ambassador
     to Japan. The topic is the economic relationship of
     Singapore with Japan. A key factor is the large trade
     deficit of Singapore, which totals almost $3 billion.
     It is recommended that Japan could buy more goods from
     Singapore, including buying more of the manufactures
     produced by the Japanese firms in Singapore. As a free
     port, foreign interests can wholly own their plants.
     Political stability and other assets make Singapore an
     attractive place to invest.

651. Robins, Brian. "Pacific Basin Financing -- Japan:
     Straddling the World; Both Borrower and Lender."
     Euromoney; Pacific Basin Financing Supplement.
     (May 1987): 24,31-38.

     The significance of Japan's role in the Pacific Basin
     is assessed. For the countries there, such as
     Singapore and Hong Kong, Japan's activities lead to
     increased capacity and investment flows. Diversif-
     ication of currency risk by Japan has brought greater
     interest into the area. Many foreign banks are
     establishing affiliates in Japan, and becoming active
     in foreign mergers and buy-outs. Japan's role has been
     a leading one because of the large surplus of invest-
     ment money. Nonetheless, the existence of restrictions
     from Japan will also tend to require them to borrow and
     blend their operations with capital from overseas
     markets.

652. Smith, Charles. "The High-Yen Syndrome -- Japanese
     Companies Eagerly Eye Investment Opportunities in
     China." Far Eastern Economic Review. 139.10 (March
     10, 1988): 63.

     There is a growth in interest among Japanese firms in
     the introduction of investments in China. Up to now
     there have been very few such ventures. But there is a
     new attitude, that stems from a number of sources: the
     yen is strong, there are growing costs associated with
     producing in Taiwan, and there could be much higher
     wages in Korea soon. Mabuch Motor, a firm in the
     electric motors field, plans to build small electric
     motors and employ 4,000 workers in its Chinese
     location. If China decides to open special export-
     processing zones in coastal cities, the outlook for
     Japanese investment there will be even better.

653. Smith, Charles. "The Regional Economy and the Japanese
     Giant." Banker. 122.558 (Aug. 1972): 1057-1062.

     This articles focuses on Japan's rapid economic growth
     in the Pacific rim countries and the implications of
     this growth for the region. GNP and growth rates are

provided for East Asian countries as well as statistics on imports. Japan in particular is highlighted with an account of its growth in the region and its future investment activities. A guide to financial institutions in the Pacific Basin is included in light of future joint ventures and foreign investments in the region.

654. Watanabe, K. "Japanese Overseas Investments: Taiwan." Oriental Economist. 48.835 (May & June 1980): 38-45 & 42-45.

A tabular survey is given of Japanese investments in Taiwan. Presented is the name of company, capital ratio, date of operation, employees, product lines, sales, partner firms, and objectives.

655. Yoshihara, Kunio. Foreign Investment and Domestic Response. Singapore: Eastern Universities Press SDN.BHD., 1976.

The case of Singapore as a host country with large foreign investment is an interesting one, and can serve to illustrate many of the features of direct foreign investment in any small and medium sized nation. While Singapore is exclusively urban, it nonetheless provides an example in which the motives for foreign investment can be examined. The role of investment in the rapid industrialization of Singapore, and the problems that are linked with it can be seen. The following topics are offered: a background treatment, a macro view of the industry, a discussion of method, and specific study of Japan's and other nations' investment in Singapore. The relative positions of foreign controlled industries are examined. Non-economic factors in economic decision-making are also kept in mind.

656. Yu, Tzong-Shian. "The Development of Relations between the Republic of China and Japan since 1972." Asian Survey; A Monthly Review of Contemporary Asian Affairs. 21.6 (June 1981): 632-644.

This articles describes the economic relation between Taiwan and Japan since 1972. The structure and relative importance of Taiwan's trade with Japan is reviewed. In addition, Japanese foreign investments and technical cooperation is discussed on an industry by industry basis. Non-economic relations are covered, as well as policy recommendations. Statistics provided for 1966-1979.

PACIFIC OCEAN REGION AND AUSTRALIA

657. Edo, Junko. Japanese Aid to the Pacific Islands Region. Honolulu: Pacific Islands Development Program, East-West Center, 1986.

Japanese aid to the Pacific Islands region recently

changed with the establishment of 200-mile exclusive
economic zones. This book examines overall Japanese
official aid to the region, explores the surrounding
problems, and suggests some options. Japanese official
development aid is first discussed in general, followed
by it specific application to the Pacific Islands
region. Case studies are then offered covering aid for
fisheries and manpower development and technical
transfer. The concluding chapter reviews and discusses
overall Japanese aid principles and policy.

658. Fujioka, Masao. Japan's International Finance; Today
     and Tomorrow. Tokyo: The Japan Times, Ltd., 1979.

     A collection of the author's articles and speeches over
     20 years, this work spans the early days of Japan's
     financial internationalization and the Tokyo Summit.
     Liberalization is described, in terms of trade and
     payments, with Japan's plan to double income. The
     introduction of Japan to the roster of advanced
     countries and the new policy resulting from this new
     status are outlined. The time of the Nixon shock and
     international monetary reform is recalled, and the
     period of the oil crisis is reviewed. The nature of
     Japan's economic power is analyzed, with attention to
     the balance of payments, financial markets, world
     polarization, and issues for the current phase,
     following upon the Tokyo Summit. Specific topics for
     future concern which involve direct investment are
     found in the concluding sections.

659. Hasegawa, Sukehiro. Japanese Foreign Aid; Policy and
     Practice. Praeger Special Studies in International
     Politics and Government. New York: Praeger Publishers,
     1975.

     An attempt is made to explain the role of Japanese
     foreign aid in achieving Japan's own evolving national
     goals. It examines aid policy and practice in the
     context of Japanese understanding of social nexus and
     their perception of national and international
     developments. The 1953-1973 period is examined in two
     ten-year segments. During the first ten years,
     Japanese aid was extended for immediate commercial
     objectives and domestic material prosperity. The
     following ten years saw aid increasingly directed at
     the improvement of Japan's societal welfare and the
     pursuit of Japan's leadership role in the Asian region
     and its "proper" place in the international community.

660. "Japanese Investment in Asia/Pacific Region Will
     Continue to Surge." Business Asia. 12.7 (Feb. 15,
     1980): 49-52.

     This study concentrates on Japan's investments in the
     Asian Pacific region. The fluctuations in the exchange
     rate for the yen will have a significant impact. Some
     consideration is offered for various industries and
     various regions. Statistics are given for 1978.

661. "Japanese Overseas Investments: Australia." Oriental
     Economist. 48.834 (April 1980): 34-45.

     This is a consideration of the Japanese investments
     taking place in Australia. The nature of the
     corporations, and their capital commitments are
     discussed. There is also data about the geographic
     location of Japanese investment activities within
     Australia.

662. "Japanese Overseas Investments: Others." Oriental
     Economist. 48.841 (Nov. 1980): 39-41.

     There are statistics offered to account for the
     activities of Japanese investments in various
     countries, including New Zealand. The names of the
     companies and their size and type of operation are
     given. Some of the actual sites are listed.
     Information about number of employees and nature of
     production are also given.

663. "Japan's Overseas Investments: New Zealand and Guam."
     Oriental Economist. 48 (Nov. 1980): 39-41.

     Japanese direct foreign investments in New Zealand and
     Guam are discussed. Information is given on investors,
     companies, products, amount of capital involved,
     effects on employment, and annual sales. Prospects for
     continued investment are mentioned.

664. Kojima, Kiyoshi. Japan and a New World Economic
     Order. Boulder, Co.: Westview Press, 1977.

     This book is an attempt to suggest a new direction for
     world and regional economic ordering, from a Japanese
     point of view. The problems to be explored are
     examined with the oil crisis as a starting point. The
     establishment of tariff barriers is explored and reform
     of the international monetary system is discussed. Two
     models of direct foreign investment are delineated, the
     trade-oriented approach of Japan and the anti-trade
     oriented approach of the U.S. A theoretical examin-
     ation of these two models is offered. The long term
     growth path of the Japanese economy is outlined. Ways
     to reorganize north-south relations in the Asian
     Pacific region are also described. The author's
     proposals for economic integration in the Asian-Pacific
     region provide the concluding topics.

665. Kojima, Kiyoshi and Miguel S. Wionczek, eds.
     Technology Transfer in Pacific Economic Development;
     Papers and Proceedings of the Sixth Pacific Trade and
     Development Conference Held by National Science and
     Technology Council in Mexico City, July 1974.. Center
     Paper. Tokyo: Japan Economic Research Center, 1975.

     The papers of this conference on the transfer of
     technology in the Pacific region are divided into 4
     parts: 1. the context of international relations in the
     Pacific region as it affects development, trade and

technology; 2. the international trade of technology;
3. the intra-national diffusion of technology; and 4.
technology and comparative advantages in trade. One
paper in particular concentrates on Japan: "Transfer of
Technology and Japanese Experience" by Saburo Okita and
Shuji Tamura.

666. Loutfi, Martha F. The Net Cost of Japanese Foreign
     Aid. Praeger Special Studies in International
     Economics and Development. New York: Praeger
     Publishers, 1973.

The author begins with a survey of the Japanese economy
to gain an understanding of its rapidly evolving nature
and to be able to put its foreign aid and trade into
perspective. The pattern and structure of Japan's
foreign trade is analyzed, so that the background is
provided to see how Japanese foreign aid fits into the
pattern of Japanese international economic relations.
After this a closer examination of Japan's foreign aid
is offered. Japan's motives are discussed, along with
the cost of providing development aid. The net costs
to Japan is viewed in terms of the opportunity cost and
of the real resource transfer involved. It is
concluded that Japan does incur significant net costs
in offering foreign aid and that political motivation
plays an important role in undertaking the cost of aid.

667. McClelland, A. E. "Solomon Islands Offers Chances for
     Trade Expansion." Overseas Trading, Melbourne. 29.9
     (May 13, 1977): 246-247.

This outlines the industry and agriculture in the
Solomon Islands. Japan's establishment of joint
ventures is discussed. Activities in copra, rice, palm
oil, and other product areas are mentioned. The
fishing industry is profiled, and the role of Australia
is documented briefly. The status of foreign trade is
assessed.

668. "Nihon Keizai Survey Discloses: Enterprise Investments
     Overseas Are on the Rise." Japan Economic Journal;
     International Weekly. 19.949 (April 7, 1981): 1-2.

Japanese foreign investments are on the rise despite
past difficulties Japanese enterprises have had. For
the most part, investments are located in countries
where the risk factor is the least. This includes
Asia, U.S., and Oceania. Of particular importance are
investments for securing natural resources, and a look
is taken at the import requirements of raw materials.

669. Ozawa, Terutomo. International Transfer of Technology
     by Japan's Small and Medium Enterprises in Developing
     Countries; Study Prepared at the Request of the UNCTAD
     Secretariat. New York: United Nations Conference on
     Trade and Development, 1985.

This typescript is a report consisting of five
chapters. There is a treatment of small and medium

sized enterprises as they seek overseas investment
opportunities. The investment patterns of the different sectors are traced. The five different types of
technology that are transferred are then distinguished,
with a review of the "outer" channels of technology
transfer. Then there is a discussion of the "inner"
mechanism involved in transfer of technology -- that of
the training and management of local employees. Finally
there are case studies offered.

670. Ozawa, Terutano. <u>Transfer of Technology from Japan to</u>
      <u>Developing Countries</u>. New York: U.N. Institute for
      Training and Research (UNITAR), 1971.

This work investigates the transfer of technology from
Japan to developing countries. Its scope includes the
actual experience of developing countries in the
process, and the aim is to foster principles and
criteria which will permit more effective application
of foreign technology to promote the development of
local skills. The methodology incorporates the study
of the transfer arrangements, the nature of the
transfer, the channels used, the forms of contract
used, the suppliers' positions, and the evaluation of
the transfer process. This study focuses on Japan's
role as technology transfer agent.

671. Rix, Alan. <u>Japan's Economic Aid; Policy-Making and</u>
      <u>Politics</u>. New York: St. Martin's Press, 1980.

This study investigates ideas about economic aid in
Japan and the development of aid organization. The
growth of the Japanese aid administration and its place
within the priorities of national policy is discussed.
The creation of the Japan International Cooperation
Agency is examined. The interaction between
administrative behavior and traditions in Japan is
noted, as well as the procedures and imperatives of
annual budgets. A description of the aid system is
offered, and a reflection on the overall impact of
Japan's aid system is given. Diplomacy and information
are also considered as they affect the aid system in
Japan.

672. Shorrock, Tim. "The Pacific Basin: Japanese
      Multinationals Have Been the Main Beneficiaries of the
      Area's Economic Growth." <u>Multinational Monitor</u>.
      4.10 (October 1983): 9, 10, 22.

The Japanese multinationals have benefitted from the
growth of the Pacific Basin, and the American
manufacturing in the region has been weakened. It is
argued that the growth of the economy of the region has
paralleled the stages of Japanese economic expansion,
to Japan's advantage. The relocation of manufacturing
sectors which once were the mainstay of U.S. industry
has cost Americans their leadership in manufacturing.
Japanese expansion is traced through the 1970s, as part
of an account of the political conditions which
permitted the shift toward Japanese dominance.

673. "Walkman Factories Don't Walk." Economist.   306.7541
     (March 12, 1988): 66-67.

     This article notes that the high-technology activities
     of Japanese firms are remaining in Japan, while lower-
     tech products are moved to locations abroad. Most of
     the electronics research functions take place in Japan,
     and the most interesting new development takes place
     there. Matsushita, the largest consumer electronics
     firm, has 30 laboratories and 9,300 engineers working
     in Japan. Some of the new products include high-
     definition video, portable video cameras, and compact-
     disc players. When these are older, it is expected
     that their manufacture will be moved abroad so that
     still newer products can be developed domestically.

AUTHOR & EDITOR
INDEX

TITLE INDEX

SUBJECT INDEX

About the Compiler

KARL BOGER received his Ph.D. in Economics from the New School for Social Research and his Masters in Library Science from SUNY, Buffalo. He has compiled *U.S. Industrial Policy: An Annotated Bibliography of Books and Government Documents* and *Postwar Industrial Policy in Japan: An Annotated Bibliography.*